Microeconomic Policy

Microeconomic Policy gives the student a wider view of microeconomics than is often the case, linking principles to settings and showing how theory complements policy and vice versa. Cohen sees a satisfactory balance between private interest, public concern and social norms as the challenge to present society; where microeconomic policy making and design create harmony between the market economy, state intervention and institutional governance.

By linking theory to policies and application, *Microeconomic Policy* will enable students to acquire proficiency and recognize balance in policy analysis and preparation. It contains comprehensive coverage of a broad range of policy areas including:

- Competition and technology policy

- Information and governance policy

- Industrial and environmental policy

- Social and income policy

- Public Sector failure and reform.

In each chapter, theory is complemented with an assessment of the empirical literature on the economic effects of policy measures, illustrative Policy Examples that highlight different problems and complementary analytical methods, Background Boxes, Discussion Questions and suggestions for further reading.

This textbook provides an important and fresh approach to the understanding of microeconomic policy that will be much appreciated by professionals in this field, and invaluable to students.

S.I. Cohen is Professor of Economics at Erasmus University Rotterdam and the Founding Director of the Foundation for Economic Research Rotterdam.

Microeconomic Policy

S.I. Cohen

London and New York

First published 2001
by Routledge
11 New Fetter Lane, London EC4P 4EE

Simultaneously published in the USA and Canada
by Routledge
29 West 35th Street, New York, NY 10001

*Routledge is an imprint of the Taylor & Francis
Group*

© 2001 S.I. Cohen

Typeset in Times New Roman by Wearset,
Boldon, Tyne and Wear
Printed and bound in Great Britain by
TJ International Ltd, Padstow, Cornwall

British Library Cataloguing in Publication Data
A catalogue record for this book is available from
the British Library

Library of Congress Cataloging in Publication Data
Cohen, S.I.
  Microeconomic policy/S.I. Cohen.
  p. cm.
  Includes bibliographical references and index.
  1. Microeconomics. 2. Economic policy.
I. Title.
  HB172 C554 2000
  388.5–dc21   00-030607

ISBN 0-415-23600-2 (hbk)
ISBN 0-415-23601-0 (pbk)

To Els, Bram and Bas

Contents

Figures

··

Tables

Policy examples

Preface

··

The challenge to society is to sustain a satisfactory balance between the three angles of private interests, public concern and social norms. In principle, microeconomic policy making can be seen as the intersection between the three angles of the market economy, state intervention and social institutions.

Acquiring some proficiency in microeconomic policy analysis and preparation by the fresh graduate requires an intermediate textbook which places the policy issues in the intersection between these three angles and which includes more real world economic problems, discussions and interpretations than usually conveyed in standard microeconomic textbooks.

The textbook compiled here goes a few steps towards meeting this demand by linking principles to settings, policies and applications. It is intended to serve as a background for the graduating student who hopes to engage in microeconomic policy preparations and provides her/him with a reasonable coverage of policy areas, how to approach them and with which methods to handle them. The policy areas covered are comprehensive and include, among others, those relating to competition, technology, industry, environment, public goods, income transfers, market governance and state reforms. Each chapter contains a brief assessment of the empirical literature on the economic effects of the policy measures discussed in the chapter. Each chapter also contains illustrative applications which are adapted from various sources. The illustrations – called policy examples – highlight different policy problems and complementary analytical methods.

The level of reading is meant to be an intermediate one, and lies halfway between the introductory book of P.O. Johansson, *An Introduction to Modern Welfare Economics*, CUP, 1991 and the advanced book of C. Henry, *Microeconomics for Public Policy*, Clarendon, Oxford, 1991.

Parts of the textbook served as lecture material for master degree students at the economics faculty of Erasmus University Rotterdam, The Netherlands. The textbook composition and presentation style have benefited from interactions between lecturer, colleagues and students. Several applications and examples come from governmental advisory work by the author. I hope that I have been successful in making the gained insight in this advisory work accessible to a wider scope of readers.

Discussions on how to approach the student in teaching microeconomic policy, with former and current colleagues Jaap van Dijk, Maarten Janssen, Frank van Tongeren, Hans Tuyl and Frank van de Weerdhof have been fruitful and the influence of these discussions are hopefully recognizable in the outcome.

Several persons who were students at the time, and are now allied with business, government or research institutions, have been helpful in checking formulations and delivering feedbacks. I am thankful for their effort. They are Machiel van Dijk, Jeroen Geldof, Evert Jan Jansen, Sjoerd van der Meerendonk and Martine Rutten.

A few readers of the preliminary text have been helpful in detecting errors and omissions, I am grateful for this help. In this connection I would particularly like to thank Maarten de Zeeuw and Bas Smits. Preliminary versions of the text were typed by Annet van Loon and Jayne van der Padt. It was a great pleasure working with both.

S.I. Cohen

Chapter 1

Background

··

1.1 Introduction

Welfare economics is concerned with the evaluation of economic alternatives from the perspective of the well-being of the whole society. It aims at providing a coherent framework for appraising the desirability of economic alternatives. Because decisions on virtually every important public policy issue involve trade-offs between aims, and the reallocation of resources, appraising these divisions within an analytical framework of welfare economic is invaluable.

The basic elements of such an analytical framework were developed with reference to the general economic system in the first half of this century. In this period welfare economists were preoccupied with establishing and applying criteria of social welfare to the general economic system, analysing efficiency conditions and studying their implications for the shaping of real economic systems. This framework formed the basis for evaluating the competitive market economy and variations of the state controlled economy.

Application of welfare economics to the evaluation of the general economic system, mainly in the first part of this century, has been guided by a methodology which can be stylized in four steps:

(a) specify the welfare criteria contained in maximum welfare W^*,

(b) specify the required conditions and underlying assumptions for obtaining maximum welfare W^* in an ideal economic system,

(c) take the two alternative options of economic systems, competitive markets and state control; study and evaluate the mechanisms of such systems in the real world in realizing W, and

(d) study and evaluate the performance of the

1

two systems and the resulting differences between W and W^* for each system in the real world.

As more insight was gained in this area and certain conclusions were drawn, attention shifted in the second half of the century to the evaluation of more specific economic policies, projects or actions within the competitive market economy and more recently in state-controlled economies. Applied welfare economics today considers the foundations of the economic system as given, that the total present state of welfare can be described by W and that for the given consumer preferences, production technologies and factor endowments from an economic alternative, the potential welfare could be at a maximum, for example W^*. The tasks of welfare economics today are:

(e) to show for the given state of welfare that $W < W^*$,
(f) track the causes behind the gap,
(g) formulate alternative proposals of raising W to W^*, and
(h) facilitate a choice by appraising benefits, costs and compromise redesigns of the alternative proposals.

This chapter will first deal with the previously stated four steps (a)–(d) in the study of the general economic system and its further elaboration into the mechanisms of competitive markets and state control. These contain the building blocks of the analytical framework which characterize contemporary microeconomic policy making and appraisal. The next chapter outlines the treatment context of the competitive market economy supplemented with state intervention, and gives an overview of the context of each of the following chapters, each of which deals with a specific microeconomic policy problem, along the lines of

steps (e)–(h), mainly within the competitive market economy. Brief attention will be given to microeconomic policy making in state-controlled economies.

1.2 Welfare criteria

It is usual to distinguish between *welfare criteria*, such as economic efficiency, social equity, stability and viability, and *performance indicators*, such as economic growth rate, indexes of income distribution and poverty incidence, inflation rate and material resources depletion rate.

Our primary attention will go to the two main welfare criteria: (economic) efficiency and (social) equity. Alternative forms of economic organization or economic policies are usually found to have different implications in terms of efficiency and equity. In appraising such alternatives, the economist should be prepared to initially separate but ultimately combine the use of both criteria of efficiency and equity.

Working with both criteria simultaneously is very difficult for it can happen that while alternative A is preferable on efficiency grounds, alternative B is superior on equity grounds, and there is no objective way of weighing the two criteria. Besides, judgements on efficiency grounds can be objective, but those on equity grounds contain subjective elements, and are thus not conclusive. While the economist can set up generally accepted standards of efficiency, neither the economist, nor other scientists, can set up universally accepted standards of equity. Understandably, the economist is inclined in these circumstances to separate economic analysis based on efficiency grounds from that on equity grounds.

But that policy-making economic analysis has to be conducted along both lines of efficiency and equity is obvious and necessary. A functional separation between these two criteria should not be misunderstood for posing one criterion above the other. In particular, there are many problems in real life whose solution is more effective when economic efficiency and social equity are considered simultaneously, and sometimes the combination of both perspectives offers the only possible solution. One society may choose to have firms pay a basic salary to underemployed labour. Another may choose to lay the labour off, tax the firms, and set up a bureaucratic machinery to distribute transfer payments to the laid-off, some of whom may enjoy untaxed earnings in the hidden economy. There can be evidence that the first society, by solving simultaneously for efficiency and equity, is better off than the second society which solves for the two criteria separately.

How do economists deal with the concept of economic efficiency? The objective measure of economic efficiency is conventionally taken to be Pareto-optimality. In view of unresolved difficulties in cardinally measuring, comparing and aggregating individual welfare, economists tend to settle at an ordinal measurement of improvement in welfare. This is found in the Pareto criterion which states that any change that makes at least one individual better off and no one worse-off is an improvement in social welfare. Conversely, a change that makes no one better off and at least one worse off is a decrease in social welfare. Stated otherwise: a situation in which it is impossible to make anyone better off without making someone worse-off is said to be Pareto-optimal or Pareto-efficient.

It should be emphasized that the Pareto criterion is a value judgement as it might not be shared by everybody. For example, someone might want to know something about who will benefit and by how much, but the underlying philosophy of methodological individualism does not permit utility comparisons. Despite its status of a value judgement, the Pareto criterion represents for most economists a workable concept of efficiency based on mutual respect of individual utility.

Next to the Pareto criterion there are other more specific notions of economic efficiency which are relevant in other contexts. For example, the concept of X-efficiency focuses on an organization's ability to mobilize the use of its inputs and distribute them optimally on the organization's activities so as to obtain normal output. Furthermore, while static efficiency commonly refers to the optimal allocation of resources over activities for the economy as a whole at a given time, dynamic efficiency refers to such an optimal allocation over time. Dynamic efficiency can be proxied by changes in total factor productivity over time, which in turn is the result of changes in technology, i.e. process and product innovation, demographic composition, income distribution and in the mixture of activities.

How do economists deal with the concept of social equity? In spite of many proposed measurements of social equity there is no consensus on an overall measurement. The minimum what economic analysis can do in these circumstances is to measure what the relevant parties will win and will lose as a result of a policy change. Problems and progress in the measurement of an overall (social) equity effect will be taken up in Chapter 7.

Background
Pareto's optimality principle ... and more

Modern economics owes a great deal to Vilfredo Pareto. In his *Manuel d'Economie Plitique* (1906) and *Economie Mathematique* (1911) Pareto lays out the conditions for a general equilibrium model which gives the highest satisfaction to consumers and producers. Pareto-optimality is the equilibrium point from which no move can be made that would increase the welfare of a consumer or a producer and make no one worse off. In Paretian economics, an economic equilibrium, where agents are price-taking maximizers of ordinal utility or profit, is Pareto-optimal. Furthermore, Pareto-optimality is in principle obtainable under the same conditions in both a competitive markets-based economy or a socialist state-controlled economy with a more equitable income distribution. Here are the forerunners of the first and second fundamental theorems of welfare economics as were later developed by Arrow and Debreu.

In this chapter we reflect briefly on the value orientations of Pareto-optimality, these being liberalism, methodological individualism and the equality of all individuals. This chapter reflects also on the greater or lesser likelihood of obtaining Pareto-optimality in the real world under the two opposite regimes of competitive markets and state control. Behavioural distortions enter into both regimes to different extents and drive them away from Pareto-optimality.

Understandably, in his writings on an abstract model of the economic system, Pareto could not possibly treat people's behaviour. As is well known, next to his abstract work, Pareto made major contributions to sociology, politics and statistics with important bearings for the nature and design of economic policy. We mention two of these below.

First, in his *Trattato di Sociologia Generale* (1916) Pareto sees human behaviour as being determined exclusively by instinctive actions and in-born feelings. People have brains but they use them in giving a false rationalization of an otherwise non-rational and non-controllable behaviour. Practice determines theory, and there are no possibilities for fundamental changes in society. Politics is monopolized by cunning elite groups who replace each other from time to time; most other people are passive. He concludes elsewhere that there cannot be an objective role for the scientist (economist) as a policy advisor. The thoughts are pessimistic regarding human nature and social progress, and hence, negative on policy.

Second, Pareto's belief in the dominance of instinct, innate capabilities and predeterminate human behaviour is consistent with his interpretation of income distribution statistics, among others. For instance, Pareto's Law states that there exists an inevitable tendency for income to be distributed in the same way across countries and time, regardless of country institutions. The implication is clear: there is no sense in pursuing an equity policy. The function he estimated is $N(x) = A/x^{\alpha}$, where $N(x)$ is the number of people having an income greater than or equal to x. The equation fitted quite a number of countries, particularly at the upper tail of the distribution, giving values of α around 1.6. More recent empirical evidence establishes significant variations in income distributions across countries reflecting different choices as regards institutions and policies. It is generally recognized now that any income distribution is the combined result of inborn capabilities and acquired opportunities as being conditioned by institutions and policies. We shall treat this topic at some length in Chapter 7.

Vilfredo Pareto was born in Paris on 15 July 1848. The family migrated to Italy in 1852. Vilfredo enrolled at the Polytechnical Institute in Turin where he graduated in mathematical and physical sciences in 1867. He worked for a couple of years as a railway engineer after which he combined academic writings with company jobs and policy advice. He fought against state intervention, protection, duties and subsidies. His liberal writings and governmental attacks made him increasingly isolated in Italian politics. The company jobs did not prosper either due to speculative losses. He was a full-time academic from 1890 onwards. In 1893 Pareto followed Walras at University of Luzanne.

Very different from most other thinkers, it was only in 1896, at the age of 48, that he produced his first economic writings on income distribution and economic policy, which were followed by other major works as reviewed above. He was active in writing up to his death in 1923.

1.3   Requirements for obtaining maximum welfare in a general economic system

The circular flow of production, income and expenditures in a general economic system is shown in Figure 1.1. The economy allocates factors among producers, commodities among consumers, and factors among commodities. Assume this economy to be general in the sense that there is as yet no detailed specification of how the economy is particularly organized, and via which mechanisms, such as markets or commands, co-ordination and allocation takes place.

The economy in Figure 1.1 is represented by two consumers, two producers, two commodities and two factors of production. Furthermore, marginal rates of substitution for consumers are denoted by MRS and these apply to commodities they consume and factors of production they own. Marginal rates of transformation for producers are denoted by MRT and these apply to commodities produced and factors deployed. Marginal productivity of labour is denoted by MP.

An economically efficient allocation in the sense of Pareto-efficiency will come into being in such a general economy if ten marginal conditions of maximum welfare will hold. These ten conditions are grouped together into what is called efficiency of consumers, of producers and of consumers with producers. Consumers

efficiency relates to the efficient distribution of commodities among consumers. Producers efficiency relates to the efficient distribution of factors among producers. Then there is the conformance of the efficiency of consumers with producers, statically and over time, with time t as index.

Consumers efficiency:

(1.1) $MRS_{ij}^a = MRS_{ij}^b$

(1.2) $MRS_{il}^a = MRS_{il}^b$

(1.3) $MRS_{kl}^a = MRS_{kl}^b$

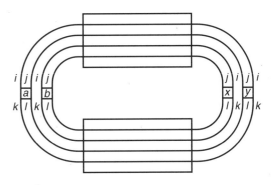

a, b = consumer;
x, y = producer;
i, j = commodity;
k, l = factors of capital and labour;
MRS = marginal rate of substitution for consumer;
MRT = marginal rate of transformation for producer;
MP = marginal productivity of labour.

Figure 1.1

5

Producers efficiency:

(1.4) $MRT_{ij}^{x} = MRT_{ij}^{y}$

(1.5) $MP_{il}^{x} = MP_{il}^{y}$

(1.6) $MRT_{kl}^{x} = MRT_{kl}^{y}$

Conformance of the efficiency of consumers with producers (also called commodity-mix efficiency) in Equations 1.7, 1.8, 1.9 refer to the static conformance, while Equation 1.10 guarantees intertemporal efficiency by connecting the efficiency conditions of 'today' with those for 'tomorrow'.

(1.7) $MRS_{ij}^{a,b,\ldots} = MRT_{ij}^{x,y,\ldots}$

(1.8) $MRS_{il}^{a,b,\ldots} = MP_{il}^{x,y,\ldots}$

(1.9) $MRS_{kl}^{a,b,\ldots} = MRT_{kl}^{x,y,\ldots}$

(1.10) $MRS_{t,t+1}^{a} = MRS_{t,t+1}^{b} = MRT_{t,t+1}^{x}$
$$= MRT_{t,t+1}^{y}$$

The fulfilment of these ten marginal conditions results in an allocation of commodities and factors on consumers and producers which is optimal in the sense of Pareto-efficiency. When such an allocation is reached under these ten marginal conditions, there is no economic reason for a reshuffling of allocation since any reshuffling, although it may bring an improvement for someone, will be at the cost of another.

1.4 Discussion of underlying assumptions

The above ten conditions for efficient allocations are necessary but not sufficient. The attainment of maximum economic efficiency is contingent upon the satisfaction of four underlying presumptions. These are generally described as the absence of indivisibility, uncertainties, externalities and collectivities.

The first set of presumptions states that the goal of the consumers is utility maximization, with consumer preference ordering satisfying nonsatiation, continuity and strict convexity. The goal of producers is profit maximization with producer technology sets satisfying boundedness, regularity and strict convexity. Furthermore, factors of productive labour and capital are homogeneous and divisible and commodities produced are homogeneous and divisible. The assumption of strict convexity requires diminishing utility in consumption, and diminishing or constant returns to scale in production. This convexity requirement assumes away all types of indivisibilities and increasing returns to scale in the production function. Non-satisfaction of the convexity assumption for any consumer or any producer will obstruct reaching a welfare-maximizing position.

The second set of presumptions states that consumers and producers use the same present and future information on rates of substitution, productivity and transformation. The satisfaction of this requirement is contingent on the existence and application of the same information and the absence of future uncertainty.

Third, if welfare is to be a maximum it must be impossible to increase welfare by producing more of the produced commodity or reduce the quantity of an otherwise produced commodity, or by using more of an unemployed factor, or reducing the quantity of an otherwise employed factor. The satisfaction of this requirement is contingent on the absence of external economies and diseconomies in consumption and production. It will be remembered that the neutral model assumed such an absence. A maximum welfare is obtained if the utility functions of consumers are independent from each other, and the production functions of producers are disconnected from each other.

Fourth, if welfare is to be a maximum it must be impossible to increase welfare by producing a potential good not otherwise produced, or by using a potential factor not otherwise used. The satisfaction of this requirement is contingent on the inclusion in the production functions of producers of all commodities that show up in the utility functions of consumers so that the efficient mix of commodities would include them. It will be seen later that such commodities which show up in utility functions but not in production functions are the so-called public goods. This requirement can also be rephrased as the absence of collectivities.

If all the four above presumptions are fulfilled, which is not likely, economic welfare will attain its maximum efficiency. But this maximum is not unique; for it presupposes a given distribution of income. Alternative distributions generate alternative allocations of commodities and factors. Equally efficient states can associate with different distributions. The above implies that if, in the hypothesized general economic system, the fulfilment of the efficiency conditions coincide with a consensus on the desirable distribution of income, then this system is truly socially efficient.

A conclusion of the discussion is that in all economic systems, irrespective of whether they are organized through market exchanges or centralized command, attainment of Pareto-efficiency is obstructed by the four limiting presumptions of indivisibility, uncertainties, externalities and collectivities. Besides, whatever degree of Pareto-efficiency is attained, this is subjectively related to the underlying distribution of income.

1.5   Mechanisms of alternative economic systems

In the real world, society can organize itself in alternative but internally consistent institutional patterns to fulfil its political, social, cultural, and economic needs, etc. Two different clusters of allied and internally consistent institutional patterns are prominent in modern societies. The two clusters are commonly known as market exchanges and centralized command. The circular flow of the economy in Figure 1.1 can be driven by either of the two mechanisms. *Market exchanges* characterize the market economy where economic decisions are exercised by utility maximizing consumers and producers facing common prices for common goods. This economic system is supported by such institutions as more or less competitive markets where indirect interactions between buyers and sellers take place, self-regulated but highly contestable internal markets, private ownership and free choice in a conventional democracy. *Centralized command* is typical of the state-controlled economy where major economic decisions by the population at large are entrusted to the state that practices more or less strict command on allocation of resources. The economic system is further supported by institutions of state property, direct instructions, and a one party political system.

1.6   Performance of alternative economic systems

Theoretical appraisal of the social efficiency of the two opposite economic systems has been controversial and sometimes of limited value. It is generally recognized, but not without qualifications, that the market economy, ME, is stronger on economic efficiency than the centralized command economy, CE. But there can be situations in which indivisibility, uncertainty, externality and collectivity are more common in competitive markets. The expectation is that it can be easier for a benevolent state with programmed equilibrium to control the conditions of convexity, uncertainty, externalities and collectivities than in the case of a competitive market equilibrium. This assumes that the CE has access to the right information and is able to handle this information better than the ME. This is proven to be unattainable at higher levels of economic development so that the expectation reverses with development.

Some argue that ME can be weak on equity, while CE can be strong on equity. Again here, there is the qualification that in matters of equality there is likely to be more favouritism by the entrusted state officials in CE than in ME.

Of course, both the exchange and command mechanisms are complementary ingredients of all economic organizations. Exchange and command co-exist in both ME and CE. Besides, in response to arising needs, and as a result of locked-in predetermined historical contexts, market and state react to each other and reinforce themselves in different ways in place and time. Furthermore, for any specific country identifiable with one or the other economic system, these interactions are conditioned by behavioural conventions which differ nationally.

Discussion Questions

1 Review your understanding of the following terms: welfare criteria, performance indicators, static efficiency, dynamic efficiency, consumer efficiency, producer efficiency, commodity-mix efficiency.

2 Conformance of the efficiency of consumers with producers requires that the marginal rate of substitution MRS between commodities i and j for consumers a and b be equal to the marginal rate of substitution MRT between i and j for producers x and y. Thus, $MRS_{i,j}^{a,b} = MRT_{i,j}^{x,y}$. Give three distinct arguments in terms of the above variables why the conformance does hold in practice. Illustrate with examples from consumption and production.

3 Distinguish between four types of constraints which cause failures of economic systems to achieve optimal economic welfare. Distinguish within each constraint between technical and behavioural dimensions. Construct a table which shows how often each failure occurs in the two economic systems of free markets and state control. Discuss the content of the table.

4 Applied welfare economics should ideally come to its policy recommendations using both efficiency and equity criteria, eventually with others. In practice, efficiency and equity are separated. Motivate this practice. Discuss the policy bias which this separation leads to, specially regarding shifting compensation and transfer responsibilities from the private sphere to the public sector. Support with examples.

Further reading

For original works in welfare economics see Pigou, A.C. (1924): *The Economics of Welfare*, Macmillan, London; Graaf, J. de V. (1957): *Theoretical Welfare Economics*, CUP, London. Updated reviews are found in Rowley, C.K. and Peacock, A.T. (1975): *Welfare Economics*, Martin Rebertson, London. See also Broadway, R. and Bruce N. (1984): *Welfare Economics*, Basil Blackwell, Oxford.

Important original works debating the efficiency of resource allocation in decentralized market versus centrally-planned economies include the following references. See Lange, O. (1935): Marxian economics and modern economic theory, in *Review of Economic Studies*, Vol. 2; Schumpeter, J. (1950): *Capitalism, Socialism and Democracy*, Harper, New York; Hayek, F.A. (1963): *Collectivist Economic Planning*, Routledge and Kegan Paul, London.

Chapter 2

Market economy: review of mechanisms, limitations and responses

2.1 Introduction

In this chapter we shall specify the conditions and presumptions which must be satisfied in a model of the perfect market economy in order to achieve Pareto-optimality. We shall then evaluate in which ways the corresponding real market economy deviates from the model, and what is the response of the market and government to these deviations, and what are the consequences of these responses. Such an assessment is helpful in determining the effective combination between market and government responses. We shall pursue efficiency and equity separately. We shall end the chapter with a listing of appropriate methods commonly used for assessing, designing and selection of microeconomic policy.

2.2 Efficiency

Conditions for satisfying Pareto-optimality

The market economy can be seen to consist of millions of economic agents who are motivated by self-interest. Each agent pursues his/her own goals of maximization and strives for his/her own equilibrium independently from others. The consumer maximizes utility subject to a budget constraint. The producer maximizes profits subject to technological constraints.

The market economy relies on the competitive price mechanism which is characterized by indirect exchanges between many independent buyers and many independent sellers. All agents take note of the *relative prices* for competing commodities at which the market settles and agents react by buying or selling, without getting involved in a direct exchange. There are no exchange costs in place or time.

If all agents behave competitively there will be free entry and exit, there will be no barriers whatsoever to exchange, all agents will be price-takers at the same price for the same commodity, and a simultaneous equilibrium will be obtained by all agents in all markets – hence the term general equilibrium.

It will become clear now via several figures and equations how relative prices of competing goods in a perfect market economy determine the conditions for fulfilling efficiency and equilibrium.

Figure 2.1 displays the preferences of the maximizing consumer a in the form of indifference curves with respect to commodities i and j and a budget line which constrains total expenditure. The slope of the budget line is determined by the market-settled relative prices of competing commodities P_i and P_j. The consumer equalizes his/her marginal rate of substitution for competing commodities MRS_{ij}^a to the relative prices of competing commodities P_j/P_i and so all consumers. As a result Equation 2.1 is obtained.

(2.1) $MRS_{ij}^a = MRS_{ij}^b = P_j/P_i$

Figure 2.2 displays the choice for maximizing consumer a between commodities bought and labour offered. The consumer equalizes his/her MRS_l between consumption and leisure to the settled relative market prices of these two competing alternatives P_l/P_i and so all consumers, given Equation 2.2.

(2.2) $MRS_{il}^a = MRS_{il}^b = P_l/P_i$

Figure 2.3 examines how the maximizing producer x decides on use of labour l in the production of commodity i (or j). The producer employs labour to the point where marginal value equals the wage rate he faces. Equation 2.3 obtains when all producers do that.

(2.3) $MP_{il}^x = MP_{il}^y = P_l/P_i$

Figure 2.4, which is similar to Figure 2.1 for the consumer, deals with the choice of producer

x between production of commodities i and j. Producer x faces profit lines x_1, x_2, x_3 in an increasing order. The slope of these lines is given by the relative market prices for the two commodities. Producer x will choose an allocation between commodity i and j where the highest point is attained. The producer will equalize the MRT_j to the relative prices of competing commodities he faces, giving Equation 2.4.

(2.4) $MRT_{ij}^x = MRT_{ij}^y = P_j/P_i$

From Equations 2.1 and 2.4 it follows that $MRS_{ij}^a = MRS_{ij}^b = \ldots = MRT_{ij}^x = MRT_{ij}^y \ldots$

Since the same applies to the equality between the remaining relevant pairs of substitution and transformation rates, all conditions in Chapter 1, Equations 1.1 to 1.9, for satisfying Pareto-optimality will be fulfilled.

Given the static premise of a perfect market economy, condition 1.10 relating to Pareto-optimality over time is also fulfilled as such.

It is worthwhile mentioning that an Edgeworth box diagram is helpful in demonstrating consumer efficiency, i.e. the efficient allocation of commodities among consumers, as well as producer efficiency. For instance, consumer efficiency can be plotted as a set of points of tangency between the indifference curves of two consumers, a and b, for products i and j, whereby a's indifference curves are drawn in relation to a's 0 point of origin, and b's are drawn with respect to b's opposite 0 point of origin. The contract curve is found by joining these points of tangency. Each point on the contract curve is a Pareto-efficient consumption allocation since any movement from it will increase the utility of one consumer at the cost of the other.

Summarizing, in the perfect market economy, market prices carry significant information. Each commodity price would reflect consumers' marginal valuation relative to other commodities. Moreover, the price of a

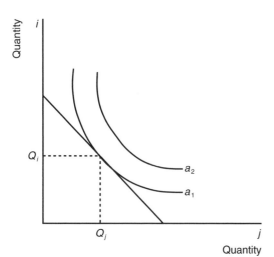

Figure 2.1

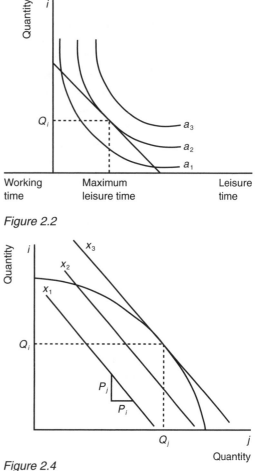

Figure 2.2

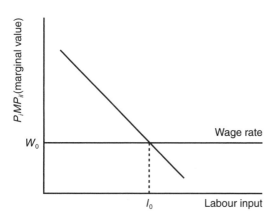

Figure 2.3

Figure 2.4

commodity must be equal to its marginal costs. Each price, therefore, expresses the lowest possible cost that society is ready to sacrifice for the commodity or factor concerned. Furthermore, the market prices are equilibrium prices which go with an equilibrium position from which it is impossible to make a change without making someone worse off, hence competitive markets are Pareto-optimal.

The First Theorem of Welfare Economics thus states that if the above-mentioned ten marginal conditions will hold then the resulting competitive market equilibrium is Pareto-optimal. Guided by equilibrium prices the self-interested decision of the economic agents lead to a social optimum in the Paretian sense. This is another way of viewing Adam Smith's notion of the invisible hand mechanism.

Underlying presumptions: technical and behavioural

The optimal performance of the neutral economy in the previous chapter depended on

11

the fulfilment of four technical assumptions; that is absence of indivisibilities, uncertainties, externalities and collectivities. The optimal performance of the market economy would require fulfilment of the same four technical presumptions as well as absence of behavioural bias in the same four directions. Inter-active and intra-active behavioural responses of consumers and producers are supposed not to aggravate the presence of indivisibilities, uncertainties, externalities and collectivities.

The *technical presumptions* can be restated as follows:

1 Consumers' preference ordering, satisfying nonsatiation, continuity and strict convexity. Producers technology sets satisfying boundedness, regularity and strict convexity. Factors of production, labour and capital are homogeneous and divisible. Commodities produced are homogeneous and divisible. Hence, no indivisibilities.
2 Same information given to all consumers and producers. No uncertainties.
3 The economy does not encounter external economies or diseconomies in consumption or production. No externalities.
4 All potential production of commodities and use of factors have been considered in the optimal allocation. No collectivities.

Behavioural presumptions can be stated as follows:

1 Consumers and producers, who maximize their utility and profit, respectively, pursue a perfect competitive behaviour: many producers and many consumers, posing no barriers for entry and exit, and all agents following price-taking behaviour. Although the assumption of the perfect competitive behaviour applies for a static world it is extendible to a dynamic world. For example,

all factor income from production of commodities goes to consumers who spend this fully on consumption of the commodities in the one and same period. Investment by firms in innovative technology to assure sustained growth at the micro level is not obstructed by entry or exit of future competitors. This assumption is crucial as it guarantees that perfect competition among many buyers and many sellers on each market in the short- and long-runs is sufficiently large to make it impossible for any single agent to influence market prices. As a rule, exchange takes place on the basis of price-taking behaviour only.

2 Perfect informational behaviour. Uncertainty and risk are eliminated by assuming that all agents abide with perfect informational behaviour. Furthermore, all transactions in all markets clear simultaneously. There are no obstacles facing smooth and instantaneous exchanges in place or time; no immobility of factors or commodities, no transaction costs, and no time lags. This assumption is very crucial as it assumes away uncertainty and risk by excluding asymmetric information and attempts by agents to create it. This assumption simplifies the model further by holding to static efficiency, assuming instantaneous market clearance with an infinite mobility of commodities and factors of production, no transport costs, no transaction costs, and no obstacles towards an instantaneous clearance between supply and demand in all markets at the same prices.
3 Externalities are absent, implying that preferences and utilities of agents are exogenously given, are independent of each other and are not affected by market transactions.
4 Collectivities are absent, implying that preferences and utilities of agents are genuinely revealed in market transactions.

A synthesis

Non-fulfilment of underlying presumptions in the real world results in efficiency problems which may be remedied by market solutions and/or state interventions. The model of the perfect market economy contains presumptions which are mostly difficult to maintain in the present-day market economies. As a result, situations arise where $W < W^*$. Such situations indicate market failures, which possibly call for corrective market responses and/or state interventions. Table 2.1 is a summary presentation which will be discussed at some depth in the following chapters, so the presentation can be short here.

It is recalled that presumptions on the absence of technically-caused indivisibilities, uncertainties, externalities and collectivities were found to fail in the neutral economic system, see Chapter 1. Since such restrictions on efficiency as observed in Chapter 1 are in a sense technical, and will be present in all economic systems, it is disputable to assign their failure in a market economy totally to the market mechanism. It will be mistaken to call the technical failure a market failure.

More important is that the market mechanism and imperfect behaviour may aggravate the technical restrictions. For example, not only does non-convexity create barriers and pave the way towards monopoly, but monopolistic behaviour of firms may also lead to intensifying indivisibilities in the production function. Similarly, while uncertainty exists on technical grounds in any economic system, asymmetric informational behaviour of firms in a market economy increases uncertainty faced by other firms; besides, the maximization hypothesis does not usually hold in a world of uncertainty. Again, while externalities exist on technical grounds in any economic system, it is likely that the emphasis on private benefits and costs

in the market economy aggravates the gap between social and private benefits and costs and, with the presence of interdependent behavioural patterns among agents, will moreover strengthen the recurrence of externalities. Finally, the problem of collectivities is aggravated by non-revealed and intentionally-distorted preferences in the context of free-riding behaviour.

The perfect market economy preassumes several behavioural requirements from its agents. The nonrealization of these behavioural presumptions, and only these, can be fully assigned to a failure of market mechanisms. Each behavioural presumption violated can be seen as a form of market failure to which certain market corrections and/or public policies will respond.

Market failures can be dissected along the following lines too. The underlying basic hypothesis of the model of the perfect market economy is the competitiveness of the markets. Granted there is a functioning market for related products, this may still not be sufficiently competitive due to the indivisibility factor. The other situation is that of incompleteness or, in the extreme, the absence of markets and this will be due to one or a combination of the uncertainty, externality and collectivity factors. The forthcoming chapters treat each factor separately.

2.3   Equity

Egality under liberal and discretionary regimes

Returning to the model of a perfect market economy, the second important property of the resulting competitive market equilibrium is that any such equilibrium is defined in terms of given initial endowments. The Second Theorem of Welfare Economics thus states that any Pareto-optimal state is an equilibrium for some initial distribution of endowments. The significance of the theorem is that, if the postulated assumptions are fulfilled in a real market economy, then economic efficiency will be guaranteed by market forces. Although the competitive market equilibrium is by no means optimal in a distributionary sense because the outcome depends entirely on the original distribution of endowments, yet the initial distribution of endowments can be reset beforehand at the socially-desired pattern, after which market forces will take care of efficient allocation. The role of the state would then be restricted to applying *a priori* lump-sum transfer payments which are consistent with the desired initial distribution of endowments.

The Pareto criterion is an efficiency criterion based on value judgements which favour methodological individualism. It is not meant to evaluate a policy change that makes some gain and some lose, as it excludes comparisons of utility and takes individual preferences as the sole basis for social welfare. Since most policies involve differential outcomes, the strict Pareto criterion stops, and this was also observed when we moved from the first theorem to the second theorem of welfare economics. To remedy the analysis, economists have gone some way in the possibility of linking efficiency effects with equity effects via transfer payments, which is known as the compensation principle.

Kaldor (1939) and Hicks (1939) suggested the following approach to adapt the Pareto criterion to differential outcomes. Assume that a change in the economy is being considered, which will benefit some 'gainers' and hurt others 'losers'. If the amount of money of the 'gainers' is greater than the amount of the 'losers', the change constitutes an improvement in social welfare, because the 'gainers' *could* compensate the 'losers' and still have some 'net gain'. Thus, the Kaldor–Hicks compensation

criterion states that a change constitutes an improvement in social welfare if those who benefit from it could compensate those who are hurt, and still be left with some 'net gain'.

The Kaldor–Hicks compensation criterion evaluates alternative situations on the basis of monetary valuations of different persons. In particular, it implicitly assumes that the marginal utility of money is the same for all the individuals in the society. Given that the initial income distribution is unequal, this assumption may not be plausible.

Note also the difficulty that the compensation principle does not require that actual payment of compensation be made. The compensation principle is stated in terms of *potential* compensation rather than *actual* compensation. The policy change is considered desirable if its revenue exceeds its cost so that it is possible to undertake a potential improvement in redistribution. Whether or not redistribution is actually carried out is considered to be an important but a separate issue. If, on the other hand, actual compensation were required there would be no fundamental difference between the compensation principle and the Pareto principle. For example, if gainers from a policy change still remain gainers after having (possibly more than) compensated losers, the considered policy change clearly represents a Pareto-improvement since no one is made worse off and at least one individual is made better off.

It is instructive at this point to place the Pareto-efficiency criterion and its pragmatic adaptation by Kaldor, Hicks and others to suit equity considerations in the real world in the broader theory of public choice. Arrow (1951) took a different approach to that adopted by Pareto, Hicks and Kaldor. He supplemented the Pareto principle by other widely-accepted axioms ending up with a complete social ordering satisfying the conditions of unrestricted domain and independence of irrelevant alternatives. The conclusion is that, short of a dictatorial choice, it is impossible to define a complete social ordering. Arrow's impossibility theorem states that it is impossible to satisfy reasonable axioms on the social choice process without making one person a dictator over all social choices.

Sen (1970) presented yet another impossibility theorem showing that the acceptance of certain personal liberties in combination with the Pareto principle are sufficient to produce cyclic social decision functions.

Ng (1971) and Mueller (1989) discussed ways which societies may pursue in resolving the paradoxes of Arrow and Sen. The general conclusion is that the solution rests ultimately on the use of cardinal, interpersonally-comparable utility information, and if this is not feasible to collect, then it is for the benevolent ruler who plugs in such information.

At the other end of the spectrum, Bergson (1938) drifted away from the liberal philosophy and maintained that when actions will benefit some and hurt others it is impossible to evaluate the action without making value judgements on distributional matters. Bergson suggested to make explicit value judgements on distributional matters in the form of a social welfare function. He, too, found no method of constructing it objectively, apart from assuming a discretionary regime and relying subjectively on the benevolent ruler who institutes the distribution policy – and who can be democratically elected, or not.

The practical relevance of the Second Theorem was further stripped by Diamond and Mirrlees (1971). The Second Theorem recommends that higher welfare is obtained – the situation is corrected – if the state applies ex-ante the desired income distribution via lump-sum transfers. The transfers should be financed by lump-sum taxes on inborn abilities so as to avoid distorting work incentives. However, Mirrlees pointed out that such a condition would require that the state should have complete information on individual abilities. This condition is not feasible on both technical and behavioural grounds as it is in the interest of the individuals not to reveal their true abilities to avoid the levy.

A synthesis

Recall from the Second Theorem that any Pareto-optimal state is an equilibrium for some initial distribution of endowments. First, it was thought that this distribution could be easily reset ex-ante without distorting work incentives until Mirrlees showed the contrary. Second, the Kaldor–Hicks compensation principle, extended to compensate the losers from a gain made by the gainers, is also ex-ante; as argued above, this principle is also not implementable. Third, Arrow and Sen have shown furthermore the impossibility of the Paretian liberal. Fourth, Bergson has shown, at the other extreme, the necessity of assuming the benevolent ruler in a discretionary regime as the way out. How should the real world be conceived by the economist so as to resolve the public choice dilemma?

An economist's rationalization of the real world can see the real world to consist of a benevolent ruler who reviews the income distribution situation at the end of the year and resets this ex-post, giving due consideration to the perception of a desirable initial distribution and unintended differential outcomes during the year. Transfers are then affected in consistency with the resetting. If the resetting is well-done and duly implemented, then the model of the perfect market economy can be described to stand firm with regard to the equity dimension, even though this happens with a lag in time. And should the ruler be non-benevolent, it can be argued that his replacement by a benevolent ruler who could correct the distribution ex-post, and perhaps also in real terms, is again a matter of time lags.

Reasoning along the above lines, real world practices of redistribution policies can be successfully integrated within a general framework of applied welfare economics. The presumption of a benevolent ruler, which may not materialize in the short-run but is more certain through democratic processes in the long-run, is a basic condition for resolving the dilemma of public choice.

Background
Arrow's Impossibility Theorem . . . and more

It can be correctly stated that what Pareto did in the way of stating required conditions for optimal welfare in a neutral economy, was rigorously formulated and extended by Arrow to the market economy. In papers by Arrow, Debreu, and jointly, in 1951–4, they developed the general equilibrium model of the perfect market economy, and established its efficiency and stability properties. They did this using the methodological premises of neoclassical economics: rationally-behaving utility maximizing agents and markets which clear via prices and quantities. Arrow and Debreu went further to prove the equivalence between competitive equilibrium and Pareto-optimality (first fundamental theorem of welfare economics), and the relativation of Pareto-optimality for varying distributions of initial endowments of resources (the second theorem). This breakthrough opened the way for major advances which have significantly shaped economics in the last five decades, to mention a few: incomplete markets, oligopoly games, overlapping generations, computable general equilibrium models for policy making, etc.

It is striking that the same year that Arrow treated the possibility of the market economy reaching optimal welfare, 1951, coincided with completion of his dissertation on the Impossibility Theorem. Here, Arrow takes private choice for what it is and shifts attention to social choice, which if it is to be optimal, should satisfy five conditions briefly described as comprehensiveness, monotonicity, independence of irrelevant alternatives, non-imposition, and non-dictatorship. The Impossibility Theorem asserts the non-existence of institutions satisfying all of the conditions (see entry *Arrow's Theorem* by K.J. Arrow in *The New Palgrave Dictionary of Economics*, Macmillan, 1996).

The contribution of Arrow was central for later developments in the economics of public choice, law, institutions, and information. (See references to Arrow's work on the learning curve, Chapter 3, and on non-price signalling information and contractual markets, Chapter 4, this book.)

Understandably, the findings of Arrow on the eminent conflict between private interest and social choice resulted in many adopting a pessimistic attitude towards policy making and the resolution of conflict between private interest and the social good. But not in the case of Arrow. He kept the opinion that people in the real world develop institutions and norms which see to it that individual actions converge in harmony towards the social good; in his opinion, this was mainly due to mechanisms of bounded rationality. A quotation from Arrow on the role of ethical codes in the medical profession in combating uncertainty and misconduct gives a flavour of his thoughts (see Chapter 4, this book). The belief in a harmonious resolution of the conflict between the private and the social, and the mobilization of economic policy towards this end is very well demonstrated from another quotation:

If I am not for myself, then who is for me?
And if I am not for others, then who am I?
And if not now, when?

Source: Rabbi Hillel in K.J. Arrow (1974),
The Limits of Organization, Norton.

Arrow is a strong advocate of state intervention in areas of infrastructure, education
and health.

.

*Kenneth J. Arrow was born in New York on
August 23, 1921. He obtained his M.A. in
Mathematics from Columbia University in
1941, then did further graduate work in the
Economics Department. He served during
World War II in US Army Air Corps as weather*

*officer exclusively in research assignments. In
1946, he joined the Cowles Commission, at
the University of Chicago. In 1949 he moved
to Stanford University and in 1968 moved on
to Harvard University. K.J. Arrow won the
Nobel Prize in Economics in 1972*

2.4   Areas of market failures and state interventions

A stylization of market failures showing unful-
filled assumptions, resulting manifestations and
problems as well as areas of self-regulated
market corrections and areas of public policy
are found in Table 2.1. Of course, these aspects
are not always symmetrically encountered in
real life, as Table 2.1 may suggest. For
example, competition policy is in reaction to
imperfect competition and imperfect information, but interacts and overlaps with policies in
the areas of monopoly, technology and industry. Different components of industry policy are
mostly responses to several types of market
failure, even though the main thrust lies in
externalities. Environmental policy is mostly
related to externalities, but contains collectivities as well. While health and education sector
policies are responses to imperfect competition,
imperfect information, externalities and collectivities, they are mostly related to collectivities.

It is also important to note that while, for
many instances of economic activities, market
solutions and state intervention stand opposite
to each other as competing alternatives, there
are likely as many instances in which they fulfil
complementary roles to each other.

A basic objective of this book is to develop
an understanding for those instances featuring

complementarity between markets and the
state. This is done by discussing the reactions
of markets and governments to various social
efficiency failures of the economic system, as is
already identified in Table 2.1, and will be the
subject matter of Chapters 3 to 7.

In Chapter 8 we examine in more general
terms interactions between market activities,
state intervention and the political economy,
and how they lead to varying combinations of
private and public shares in the total national
income (expenditure).

In Chapter 9 we call for treating the interactions within and between markets and the state
in the broader context of evolving and interactive behaviour between individual actors,
which will ultimately lead to the formation of
shared values and expectations. In the final
analysis, it is the kind of inclination of behavioural conventions and written laws in a specific society which would predominantly
determine the extent of social efficiency failures of the economic system, and responsively,
the specific mixture between market operations
and state intervention.

2.5   A stylized approach towards microeconomic policy preparation

It is worthwhile to put together in a stylized
form several major steps which can be followed

Table 2.1 Areas of market failure and state interventions

Violated technical and behaviourial assumptions	Manifestation in real world	Resulting problems	Self-regulated market corrections	Public policy	Treatment
Indivisibilities.	Nonconvexity is typical of increasing returns to scale and thus indivisibilities show up in production functions.	Natural monopoly: – restricted output and higher price, or – monopoly making, loss and closing down	Contestable markets	*Competition policy* in reaction to monopoly: nationalization, privatization, regulation and deregulation.	Chapter 3
Perfect competitive behaviour in a static context.	Non-competitive behaviour of producers. Market power taking forms of price-setting, barriers to entry, etc.	Imperfect competition: – deadweight loss – managerial slack – rent-seeking	Contestable markets	Competition policy in reaction to imperfect competition: dominant position and restrictive practices	Chapter 3
Perfect competitive behaviour in a dynamic context.	Producers direct technological investment towards rent-seeking, or weak incentives for firms to invest in technology when benefits are non-excludable.	Retarded growth.	Joint ventures.	*Technology policy* with focus on innovating firm. Technology policy with focus on perspective technology.	Chapter 3 Chapter 3
Uncertainties.	Uncertainty.	– Deadweight loss.	Advertisement.	*Governance policy:* information provision.	Chapter 4
Perfect informational behaviour.	Asymmetric information.	– Adverse selection – moral hazard. – obstruction of market formation.	Signalling.	Governance policy: transaction restructuring.	Chapter 4
Instantaneous market clearance implying infinite mobility, no transaction costs, no risk, no time lags.	Markets do not clear over time because of co-ordination failure, mobility costs, etc.	Co-ordination weak under uncertainty. Discouraged exchange.	Future markets.	State legislation and public interventions to *clear markets* and stimulate exchange. Immobile markets. Unstable markets.	Chapter 4 Chapter 4
Externalities. Independence of utilities of individuals.	Positive and negative externalities are abundant. Private interest behaviour accentuates externalities.	SMB > PMB leading to deadweight loss. SMC < PMC leading to deadweight loss. S = social; P = private; MB = marginal benefit; MC = marginal cost.	Externalities.	Positive externality: *industrial policy*. Negative externality: *environmental policy*.	Chapter 5 Chapter 5
Collectivities. Genuinely revealed preferences.	– Non-rivalry and non-excludability. – Free-riding.	– Unattended public goods and merit goods. – Collective provision not optimal.	Co-operative provisions.	Public goods and merit goods: – *social provisions* – *insurance schemes*.	 Chapter 6 Chapter 6
Consensus over socially desirable **initial distribution of endowments.**	No consensus. Compensation principle not operational, not neutral.	Trade-off efficiency and equity unresolved.	Altruism and charity.	Ex-post distributional policies. Continuous necessity to revise *distribution of income and wealth*. Long-term *re-endowment strategies*.	Chapter 7 Chapter 7

in microeconomic policy preparation, along lines similar to Friedman (1985) and Stiglitz (1988).

1 Identify the market failure: its origin, manifestations and consequences, this in discussions with representatives of affected agents;
2 Examine possibilities for self-regulating market corrections, eventually with minimal government support, which can resolve the failure;
3 In case a more active role for the state is required, identify alternative projects that might address the perceived problems, noting in particular the different load of the state effort in each alternative and the importance of particular design features for the determination of the benefits and costs of the project;
4 Identify and measure the efficiency consequences of alternative projects;
5 Identify and measure the distributional consequences of alternative projects;
6 Identify and measure the trade-offs between equity and efficiency considerations, this will require a normative evaluation of eventually compensatory measures;
7 Identify and measure the extent to which alternative projects affect other public policy objectives, and eventual redesigns to consider so as to neutralize negative effects; and
8 Make a balanced and contingent choice among the alternative projects, taking note of changes in the profiles of actors, technology, information and law that can alter the situation appreciably, requiring re-exploring consequences and appraising redesigns, as well as the long-term institutional constraints and the political process that could affect the final design, implementation and success of the alternative projects.

2.6 A brief listing of analytical methods

There are some six broad categories of analytical methods commonly used in microeconomic policy preparation, each of which is especially suitable for particular policy problems. The policy examples contained in each of the next chapters have been selected in such a way as to illustrate the use of these various methods in contexts which are most suited to the methods.

Government can be faced with problems in which it has to decide on taking over the actual production of an activity or the responsibility of running it, while leaving the actual production to the private sector. Such situations are those of natural monopoly and public goods. Generally speaking, the government faces in such circumstances two kinds of decisions: first, the investment–production, and second, the pricing–financing decisions.

First, an investment–production decision should answer whether undertaking the activity is worthwhile and if so what should be the capacity of production and quantity of output. Cost–benefit analysis is most suited to answer such questions, noting that such analysis can take varying degrees of robustness. In the case of natural monopoly there is no difficulty in estimating the extent of the market since the commodities concerned are very often private goods. Where the concern is with commodities which have public goods characters, it is important to trace the aggregate willingness to pay as a clue to the desired quantity of output. Such information suffers from free-riding behaviour of the demanding population and requires careful scrutinization.

Second, the pricing–financing decision requires knowledge on the preferences of agents under alternative prices and making judgements on fairness. Assessments of willingness and ability to pay via opinion surveys and budget analysis are highly relevant in this context.

Third, analysis of competitiveness requires assessing the total surplus, consisting of consumer surplus and producer surplus. The notions make it possible to measure the gain or loss in efficiency as a result of an increase or reduction in the quantity produced and consumed, and the price changes which accompany them. The notions are also helpful in showing redistribution effects of the shift as far as consumers and producers are concerned. Such assessments are especially relevant in guiding monopoly, competition and technology policies.

Fourth, analysts in the policy areas of competition, technology, industry and corporate governance usually make use of other assessment methods which rely on cross-country comparisons of indicators of competitive characteristics of firms and industries, their conduct, and performances. Conduction of structured interviews and sample surveys is also commonly undertaken. As one goes to technology policy and information policy even more pedestrian assessment methods are in use.

Fifth, government can be confronted with decision problems in which the major concern is to raise private costs to their social costs level, and private benefits to their social benefits level. The gaps between the private and the social are caused by negative and positive externalities. Cost–benefit analysis is less helpful here if there are significant externalities at economy-wide level. In such cases input–output, social accounting and general equilibrium models are better equipped to handle externalities. These models are able to accommodate both efficiency and equity aspects. They are especially suited to handling industrial, environmental and distributionary policies.

Sixth, governments may also have to decide on intertemporal problems of reallocations, especially in the context of social provisions and insurance schemes. Most commonly, decision making in these areas will be supported by in-depth studies of alternative schemes. General equilibrium models and microeconomic simulations of demographic processes and transfer payments fit well here.

Questions for discussion and further research

1 Review your understanding of the following terms and relate them to each other:
   (a) indivisibilities, uncertainties, externalities, collectivities; (b) First and Second Theorems of Welfare Economics.

2 What is the Kaldor–Hicks compensation criterion? Why was it introduced in welfare economics? And what are its shortcomings? How can you modify the criterion so as to rationalize ex-post redistributionary policies of the state?

3 State briefly the (a) First and (b) Second Theorems of Welfare Economics. Which technical and/or behavioural conditions should the market economy meet to be at its maximum welfare with respect to (a) and (b)?

4 Draw a matrix with the rows standing for areas of microeconomic policy, and the columns standing for the type of methods used in policy analysis. Indicate for each area of microeconomic policy which method(s) is (are) most suitable to handle the problem at hand. Motivate the answers.

Further reading

Next to original works in welfare economics such as by Pigou, A.C. (1924): *The Economics of Welfare*, Macmillan, London, later reviews of the field include Rowley, C.K. and Peacock, A.T. (1975): *Welfare Economics*, Martin Robertson, London. A balanced review of the theory of general equilibrium and economic welfare, at the intermediate level, is found in Russell, R.R. and Wilkinson, M. (1979): *Microeconomics, a synthesis of modern and neoclassical theory*, Wiley, Toronto. A recommendable recent review of the same is in Myles, G.D. (1995): *Public Economics*, CUP, Cambridge.

On the possibilities of a satisfactory combination of private and social choice, see Arrow, K.J. (1951): *Social Choice and Individual Values*, Wiley, New York.

Most textbooks dealing with applied welfare economics in market economies start with a review of market failures, a good example is that of Cullis, J. and Jones, P. (1998): *Public Finance and Public Choice*, OUP, Oxford.

Chapter 2 mentioned methods most commonly used in the analysis and planning of microeconomic policy. Among these are cost–benefit analysis which is most suitable for partial assessments, and computable general equilibrium models which are more suitable in case of economy-wide assessments. Later chapters treat policy examples which apply these methods. For working reviews of these methods, see Layard, R. and Glaister, S. (eds) (1994): *Cost–Benefit Analysis*, CUP, Cambridge; Shoven, J.B. and Whalley, J. (1987): *Applying General Equilibrium*, CUP, Cambridge.

Chapter 3

Indivisibilities: competition policy and technology policy

....

3.1   Competition policy

3.1.1   Introduction

Conditions of *perfect competition* require free entry and exit leading to a large number of companies producing the same good, each of which is confronted with rising marginal costs, each being a price-taker.

Through free entry and exit, a situation is created in the long run where price is reduced to the level of average total costs, and profits are eliminated. Such a long-run situation is shown in Figure 3.1. Here, long-run price coincides with average total costs (*ATC*), although occasionally the short-run price may drop to the level of average variable costs (*AVC*) without causing a shut-down of production. As equilibrium output is given by the volume where price P_o equals marginal costs (*MC*) equals marginal revenue (*MR*), rising marginal costs will limit firm size in the long- as well as the short term.

In the real world, there are monopolistic industries where the conditions for perfect competition are not fulfilled. In particular,

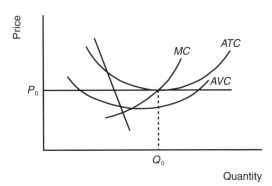

Figure 3.1

technological indivisibilities translate in increasing returns to scale (or decreasing costs) so that average total costs of the firm are decreasing over a large output interval. If demand is small in relation to the output volume produced by the firm, the industry ends up with one single firm offering the minimum costs for each desirable output volume. The problem of natural monopoly and policies to combat it are dealt with in sections 3.1.2, 3.1.3 and 3.1.4.

Even if a monopoly does not arise, the presence of indivisibilities gives an advantage to incumbent firms which could restrict entry; promote non-competitive practices and result in imperfect competition. The problem of imperfect competition and how governments make use of competition policies that counteract these market failures are dealt with in sections 3.1.5, 3.1.6 and 3.1.7.

In a dynamic world, in which firms are saving, undertaking investment in technological development, thriving to innovate and grow, and perhaps in the process capture market power in the future, a rationale can be put forward for adapting competition policy to a technology policy aimed at a remunerated growth for the investing firm. One of the arts of a successful government policy is to develop and apply a balanced mixture of competition policy and technology policy. Alternative

approaches to technology policy are treated in sections 3.2.1 to 3.2.5.

Is there a need for competition policy at all? Indivisibilities, i.e. economies of scale, have traditionally been considered the most important cause of market failure. Baumol et al. (1982) introduced the concept of contestable markets, i.e. the possibility that firms can enter and exit a market freely and without costs. Where contestable markets are present, it is argued, equilibria similar to those produced by competitive markets are possible even in a monopoly or oligopoly situation created by the existence of economies of scale. The free entry and exit tactics would induce incumbent firms to set a price equivalent to the average cost, thus eliminating any extra profit. The empirics show that while contestable markets can be approached in some branches of activity such as air transport and telecommunications, the condition of total absence of entry and exit costs is not observable in the real world, and often these costs are quite significant.

3.1.2   The problem of natural monopoly

The problem of natural monopoly appears when economies of scale are important. Economies of scale are characterized by lower average costs for larger production levels. Economies of scale can arise as a result of specialization (when an enterprise starts operating on a larger scale, the possibilities for specialization in the use of resource inputs increase as well), or when transport costs per unit fall as the market area becomes larger, or because of improved production equipment, and finally due to the dimensional factor; meaning that enterprises producing on a large scale often need proportionally less inputs per unit of output.

In extreme cases, industries with huge economies of scale will not be perfectly competitive and tend to have only one single producer. An industry consisting of only one firm with economies of scale is found in Figure 3.2. Note that the total demand curve which was applicable for many firms in Figure 3.1 is now concentrated in one firm, in Figure 3.2, resulting in a steep *MR* curve. Familiar examples of monopolistic industries with a significant degree of economies of scale are telephone, postal and railway services, and public utilities such as water, gas and electricity. This is also true in particular for certain services sold on a limited local market.

If the company, producing under decreasing cost conditions, exploits its monopoly position and maximizes profits, that is, produces where marginal cost (*MC*) equals marginal revenue (*MR*), the production volume would be less than the socially-efficient value, $Q_1 < Q_0$, and the price will be higher, $P_1 > P_0$. Figure 3.2 shows a deadweight loss equal to the shaded area and a distributionary shift from consumers to producers.

If one keeps to the marginal cost pricing principle whenever there are economies of scale, the consequence is that the company will thereby

operate at a loss. We have thus changed the company's output from Q_1, where a profit is obtained, to Q_0, which is better from a social point of view but which involves a financial deficit. A private firm that is made to operate at the desired level of production will make losses and will close. If it is thought that the activity is of a vital national interest and cannot be closed the logical consequence is that the nation should take over the responsibility for the existence of the activity and run it directly or indirectly.

Resolution of the problem requires action on two decision fronts. First it is necessary to find out in such circumstances whether it is worthwhile to invest, produce and sustain the activity. This is the *investment–production decision*. Second, if it is found that it is socially worthwhile to sustain the activity, then the problem arises of how to price the product and finance the activity, knowing that public financing via the tax system are mostly distortive. This is referred to as the *pricing–financing decision*.

The first important question facing public policy making is, therefore, whether any production at all in a situation of permanent financial loss is in the interest of society, and if the answer is affirmative, the second question on ways and means of pricing and financing by government or otherwise can then be tackled. Figure 3.3, adapted from Bohm (1987), is helpful in discussing these two questions.

The investment–production decision

The reason why social profitability is at all conceivable where there is a permanent financial deficit is that consumers value their intramarginal units (units between O and Q in Figure 3.3) more than the marginal unit, that is, higher than the price. The downward sloping demand curve is an expression, although imperfect, for this phenomenon. For our purpose here let us simply observe that, under certain circum-

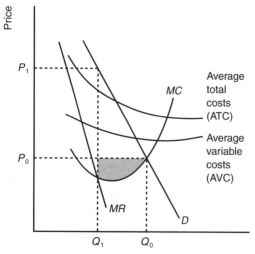

Figure 3.2

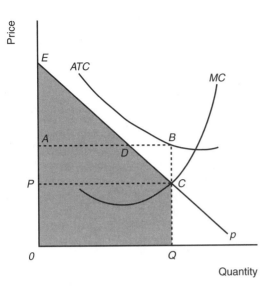

Figure 3.3

stances, the area under the demand curve provides an exact expression for the social 'benefit side' of the industry, that is, the consumers' total valuation of the *whole* volume of output Q (see Figure 3.3).

In certain other cases the area under the demand curve is a sufficiently close approximation of the size of total social benefits. With this general reservation, total social benefits can be indicated by the shaded area in Figure 3.3. Of this area, only the area $PCQO$ is financial revenue. The relevant level of total costs can be derived from the average total cost (ATC) curve; they are equal to the area $ABQO$. The criterion for deciding whether production is socially profitable or not is therefore that social benefits should be greater than total costs, that is to say, $ECQO > ABQO$ or $EDA > DBC$.

In the case illustrated in Figure 3.3, the investment criterion is obviously fulfilled, which means that production of this good can be said to be socially profitable. Observe that in this case (in contrast to the case in Figure 3.2) a financial surplus is not possible at any volume of production; in other words, the strict market economy

would not have resulted in any production of this good at all. Granted, it is difficult to estimate consumers' total valuation of Q_0 in Figure 3.2 in practice. However, some guidance can often be obtained if it is known that production gives a financial surplus at some volume of production (for example Q_1 in Figure 3.2). If this is so the volume Q_0 which has been shown to be superior to any positive level of output must also be socially profitable. For the investment decision a social cost–benefit analysis would be conducted, see technical annex on project appraisal.

The pricing–financing decision

Going ahead with investment and production is further complicated in practice since it may be difficult to raise the government revenue needed to cover the financial deficit at the efficient level of production without causing inefficiency in some other part of the economy in the process of taxation.

A remedy for this financing complication is available in some cases. By combining a price per unit of output with a fixed fee for the right to buy the commodity in question, socially efficient pricing may be obtained along with cost coverage, without reliance on public funds. Such *two-part tariffs* can be found in many decreasing cost industries, for example, telephone, public transport, water and electricity supply. Here, a unit or *user charge* is coupled with a *licence* or *subscription fee*, that is, a fee unrelated to the size of individual purchases. Sometimes this fixed fee is said to finance the fixed costs of the activity. More generally, it serves to withdraw an additional amount of the consumers' willingness to pay, large enough to let all costs be covered. In terms of Figure 3.3, the fixed fees should be set so that an amount not exceeding the area ECP and large enough to cover the *deficit ABCP*, produced by the user charge P, is withdrawn.

Natural monopolies offer a vexing problem for legislators and policy makers. Like any other monopolist, a natural monopolist will produce at the level where marginal revenue equals marginal cost, at Q_1 in Figure 3.2. It will charge a price of P_1. It will produce less and charge more than it would if price were equal to marginal cost, as would be the case with perfect competition (the output level Q_0 and the price P_0 in the figure).

In the case of a natural monopoly, the very nature of the decreasing cost of technology precludes perfect competition. Indeed, consider what would happen if price were set equal to marginal cost. With a natural monopoly, average costs are declining, and marginal costs are below average costs. Hence, if price were equal to marginal cost, it would be less than average costs, and the firm would be losing money. If the government wanted a natural monopoly to produce at the point where marginal cost equalled price, it would have to somehow support the industry to offset these losses up to the point of nationalizing the industry and fully regulating it. The opposite alternative is that the industry is privately owned and run but that the production and price of the product are regulated in some degrees.

Below, we give assessments of: (a) nationalization policies, raising at the same time the question of when a nationalized industry should cease to exist as such, and becomes privatized; and (b) the right combination between regulation and deregulation policies.

3.1.3 Nationalization versus privatization policies

The nationalized industries are basically the part of government production that covers the provision of private goods for sale through the market. Thus the nationalized industries in a typical country include railways and electricity, but not the army or the provision of education or housing, which are not sold commercially.

There are several reasons why governments have nationalized industries in the past. The first and foremost is the natural monopoly problem emanating from indivisibilities. The presence of large capital costs and economies of scale turn some industries into natural monopolies such as electricity and railways. As in these industries marginal cost lies below average cost, they cannot meet the social efficiency criterion that requires that prices be close to marginal cost, as otherwise they will incur losses. Furthermore, private investors are discouraged to enter these industries. An entrant would have to enter on a large scale and incur costs comparable with those of the existing firm, and this is unlikely. The entrant worries too that, should it enter, the existing firm will compete sufficiently keenly so that what promised to be high profits will disappear. Entry is even less inviting when there are large sunk costs: if the existing firm does compete and the entrant is forced to exit, the entrant will be unable to recoup much of its investment. In the extreme case of huge economies of scale, average costs may sharply increase when the market is divided between two firms, a firm with half the market may not be able to break even no matter what it does. Since private shareholders cannot be expected to initiate such enterprises, public ownership may then be inevitable, combined with public monitoring to ensure that the monopolist continues to minimize costs and produce efficiently. Public management may, therefore, be the simplest solution.

Other reasons than indivisibility such as externality and distribution may also be behind nationalization. The social gains from an efficient road or rail network exceed the private benefit for which direct users are prepared to pay. Furthermore, because a private profit maximizing railway would close most non-profitable rural railway lines, society might judge that this will severely reduce the welfare of citizens in remote areas or promote regional dissent, hence government takes over production directly to run the industry in the interests of the nation as a whole.

There are several problems which may accompany nationalized industries. It is hard to ensure that the industry does minimize costs. The regulatory public body has the difficult task of trying to ensure that the management of the natural monopoly is as efficient as possible. This is a problem of information access and mechanism design between agent (management) and principal (ministry) which will be addressed in Chapter 4. The managers of nationalized industries often lack adequate incentives to cut costs and modernize vigorously, particularly given the fact that government is frequently willing to subsidize the industry when it loses money. In addition, the nationalization of natural monopolies subjects them to a number of political pressures and employment interests from regional and central politicians. Firms may also be under pressure to provide some services at prices much below marginal cost, and make up the deficit from the revenues from other services, a practice referred to as cross-subsidization.

What is the alternative to state ownership of natural monopolies? Where production and technology distribution allows a contestable market, there is potential competition. The threat of entry will keep prices from rising above average costs. Potential competition will force the price to the same level that a regulator would. Thus, potential competition is all that is required, not actual competition. In this view, where technology allows it, government should encourage competition, privatization, and deregulate where possible.

Recent technological advances in telecommunications, energy supplies and transport demonstrate that the national markets for any of these services are linked world-wide, and as a result are big enough for three or more suppliers, and hence the drives in the last two decades towards privatization of nationalized industries in many industrialized and industrializing countries.

In the final analysis, it was thought at one time, empirical investigation should help in making a choice between nationalization and privatization by determining whether public or private sector firms are more likely to attain the lowest possible cost curve. An evaluation of the results of 30 studies conducted in different industries in different countries by Yarrow (1985) lead to the general conclusion that there is not much difference in cost between government enterprises and large private corporations, particularly when both are subjected to the same degrees of competition and regulation. For particular cases, it is difficult to determine empirically how much more or less efficient the government is as a producer than if the same infrastructural company is run by a private corporation. Many economists agree that the key issue is not the difference in ownership but rather how effective the monitoring of management and the forces of market competition. Privatization can lead to a better performance if it drives managers to act in more transparent and competitive ways.

In concluding, in situations where the private sector is not ready to enter into a socially desirable natural monopoly, nationalization with a well-monitored management is inevitable. In such situations government has to appraise the investment–production decision and the pricing–financing decision as described in section 2.1. For practical purposes the preparation of an investment–production decision boils down to a cost–benefit analysis of the proposed project. An investment project is profitable if the present value of net operating benefits – the stream of future operating profits discounted at the interest rate at which firms must borrow funds – exceeds the initial purchase price of the new capital good. Investment in the nationalized industry will proceed up to the point at which the rate of return just equals the interest rate at which firms can borrow. As regards the pricing–financing decision it suffices to refer here to the previously mentioned two-part tariffs.

In the opposite situation where the private sector is ready to enter in the natural monopolies and the government is launching a privatization programme of its nationalized industries, it is essential to develop a consistent and phased privatization strategy. This is necessary in view of the diverse objectives, conflicting interests and specific restrictions involved. To be successful, privatization has always to be accompanied by liberalization and greater competition within the national market and across the border, as well by establishing incentives and monitoring provided by regulatory public agencies. The results of various studies on the formulation of privatization programmes, which draw on the experience accumulated by staff and advisers of the World Bank, are reviewed in World Bank (1996, pp.44–65).

3.1.4 Regulation versus deregulation policies

In contrast to European countries which prefer to nationalize an industry, the USA tended to leave the industry in the private sector but regulate it. In the USA local utilities, for instance, remain private, but their rates are regulated by the individual states. At the national level, federal agencies regulate interstate telephone services and the prices that can be charged for the interstate transport of natural gas and oil.

In principle, regulators try to ensure that price is kept at the lowest possible level, commensurate with the monopolist's obtaining an adequate return on its investment. In other words, they try to keep price equal to average costs – where average costs include a 'normal return' on the firm's capital, on what the firms owners have invested in the firm. If the regulators are successful, the natural monopoly will earn no monopoly profits.

Two criticisms have been levelled against the regulatory system. The first criticism is that regulations often result in inefficient practices. For instance, prices are set so that firms obtain a 'fair' return on their capital; for the firms to make the highest possible level of profit under the circumstance, firms respond by increasing their amount of capital as much as possible, which can lead to too much or too costly investment. Or, the structure of prices is set so that some groups, often businesses, may be charged extra-high prices to make it possible to subsidize other groups. Furthermore, firms' incentives to innovate are greatly discouraged if every time they succeed in lowering costs, the regulators quickly force them to lower their prices as well, giving most or even all of the benefits to consumers. This problem is exacerbated when regulators require the shareholders to absorb all the costs of unsuccessful attempts at cost reduction. More recently, regulators have recognized that unless they provide some reward for innovation, it will not be forthcoming. Regulators tend now to allow the utilities to retain much of the increased profits they obtain from improved efficiency, at least for a period of a few years.

The second criticism relates to regulatory capture, which implies that the regulator gradually comes to identify with the interests of the company it regulates. Regulators tend to be pulled into the camps of those they regulate, so that they give way to bribery, corruption and lobbying. Regulators depend on executives of the regulated industry for the information necessary to regulate the industry, and tend to develop personal friendships with them. Regulatory agencies – the principal – comes to rely more and more on the experts, expertise and judgement of the regulated industries – the agent. Furthermore, there are instances in which regulators who show enthusiasm towards a particular industry are promised and get good jobs in that industry after leaving government service.

As stated before, the precise extent and nature of public involvement differs from country to country. Whereas European countries tended to acquire public ownership of the assets of natural monopolies, the USA preferred to handle the same problems through public regulation of industries whose assets were left in private ownership. Regulatory agencies set prices and specify quality and quantity of output. Hence, when countries concluded that the public sector was too involved in the economy, the initial policy priorities differed in Europe and the USA. Having few nationalized industries, the USA's emphasis was immediately on deregulation, which began with airlines in 1978. In Europe, privatization came first, but deregulation is now also under way.

In the last two decades, many governments became convinced that competition, however imperfect, might be better than regulation. There began a process of deregulation. Deregulation focused on industries such as airlines, railroads, and trucking, where there were thought to be, at most, limited increasing returns to scale. It sought to distinguish between parts of an industry where competition might work and parts where competition was unlikely to be effective. More recently the telecommunications industry has undergone the same fate and the railway sector is under discussion. Although deregulation of natural monopolies like electricity and water is lagging behind, there are serious initiatives to deregulate these as well.

Empirical investigations of the economic effects of regulation preceded those of deregulation reflecting the historical path of policy orientations in most countries. Joskow and Rose (1989) offer a most comprehensive review of the methods used and results obtained on the economic effects of regulation. As the term 'economic regulation' covers many different types of control with a variety of objectives, they found the nature and magnitude of regulatory effects to vary substantially depending on the structure of the regulatory process, the industry being examined and the economic environment. Several common themes emerge, nevertheless. The 'public interest' model is not borne by the regulation effects, but 'producer capture' models are seen to be too simplistic to account for the obtained picture. The structure of prices and revenue in public utilities reflect more political than economic efficiencies. And, regulation tends to increase costs and lower service quality.

The most up-to-date empirical evidence on the economic effects of deregulation is provided by Winston (1993). In tracing these effects it is necessary to isolate from the analysis the concurrent effects of the business cycle and technological change during the deregulation period and directly after, as well as the internal characteristics of the deregulated industry. Considering these, Winston predicts for nine sectors in the USA mainly during the 1980s, and in conformity with economic theory, lower prices and significant gains to consumer welfare as a result of deregulation. Other results are price variations that arise from cost and competitive considerations. Several important improvements in provided services also occurred, especially in airline, road, and motor travel, as well as in telecommunications.

3.1.5 The problem of imperfect competition

Imperfect competition may appear in many different forms. It may occur on the seller side or on the buyer side of the market; it may involve only a few units of equal size or fairly many, or it may involve more complex structures such as one big and several small units, etc. The origin of imperfect competition should lie in the first place in the possibility of reaping an advantage from production indivisibilities: i.e. the presence of some economies of scale. As most industries operate under less than full capacity they are able to set a market price which is higher than marginal costs. The advantage will not be as permanent as in the case of the monopolist but may be just sufficient to serve as a barrier for entry, which can be further substantiated by non-competitive behavioural practices such as predatory pricing, cartel formation, etc.

Three major problems result from monopolies and other imperfectly-competitive industries. These include a restricted output with a higher price, managerial slack and rent-seeking.

Restricted output

A perfect competitor will accept market price equal marginal cost and the result will be Q_0 of output in Figure 3.4. A monopoly which maximizes profits produces and sells a volume of output at which marginal costs and marginal revenue coincide, leading to a market price above marginal costs. This means that the output Q_1 will be less than optimal in a competitive market. The shaded area in Figure 3.4 will then express the *deadweight loss.*

The reduction in output and the consequent higher prices make the owners of the monopoly better off (than they would otherwise be) and makes consumers worse off. Consumer surplus is

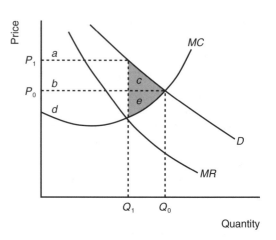

Figure 3.4

cut down and producer surplus is increased. There can be a large distributionary *transfer* of purchasing power from consumers to the producer.

Deadweight loss and transfer can be related to each other via areas a, b, c, d, e in Figure 3.4. Under competitive conditions of Q_0 and P_0 consumer surplus is the sum of areas $a + b + c$ while a producer surplus can be shown by areas $d + e$. Under imperfect competition with Q_1 and P_1 consumer surplus is reduced by $-b - c$ while producer surplus is increased by $+b - e$. This resulting in the net deadweight loss of areas $-c - e$.

It is difficult to quantify precisely how much worse off society as a whole is as a result of the deadweight loss and the distributionary transfer. Lower production levels mean less use of society's resources within an industry. Thus resources that the monopoly may have used might be deployed elsewhere and production of other goods might have been higher. From society's point of view the cost of the monopoly's reduced output is only the net difference in the value of how these resources are used. There may be as a consequence a production shift from one sector to another. The net value change as well as the net transfer effects cannot, however, be determined in a partial analysis.

Managerial slack

In practice, companies that are already making a lot of money without much competition usually lack the incentive to hold costs as low as possible. The lack of efficiency when firms are insulated from the pressures of competition is referred to as managerial slack. In the absence of the discipline provided by competition, resources are often not utilized efficiently. The discipline provided by competition limits the extent of managerial slack. High profits and other consequences of limited competition can be expected to give rise to a wasteful use of available resources and hence to an unnecessarily high level of production costs. The monopolist, in other words, may not regard feasible increases in profits as a sufficiently strong motive for unpopular reorganizations within the company. In this perspective, and with the implicit assumption that reorganization measures in themselves do not require large inputs of resources, the marginal costs curve MC_1 in Figure 3.5 turn out to be too high. In a hypothetical situation of active competition, say in a larger market, the marginal costs might be reduced to the level indicated by the MC_0 curve. The monopoly would thus lead to a second form of efficiency loss as shown by the shaded area in Figure 3.5 (reduced by the costs, if any, for reorganizing production). Figures 3.4 and 3.5 imply that the *total* efficiency loss from monopoly behaviour will equal the sum of the shaded areas in both figures.

The empirical evidence on the size of the efficiency losses from restricted output with higher price and managerial slack is both fragmentary and open to criticism. It is sometimes argued that the first effect – underproduction due to monopolistic pricing policy – is of no practical importance. The efficiency loss that stems from this effect, it is suggested, amounts to much less than one per cent of the

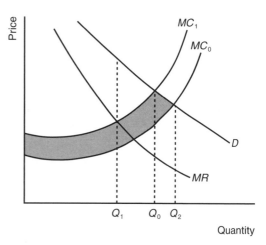

Figure 3.5

value of total production (GNP) in the economy. It should be observed, however, that even small percentages of the GNP in a long-run context may be important from a policy point of view. It is often assumed, however, that the loss from limited competition is due primarily to the second effect, that is the managerial slack.

Rent seeking

This is a situation where competing incumbents take various measures in order to improve their chances of winning the contest for the monopoly position. The cost of these measures might be quite large. For example, the individual company would obviously be willing to accept costs, if necessary, all the way up to the level of the expected value of future monopoly profits, if measures taken would guarantee victory over its competitors. In particular, society loses when monopolies devote resources to obtaining or maintaining their monopoly position or deterring entry. Furthermore, the profits earned by a company would ordinarily serve to encourage competitors to enter the business. However, rent-seeking firms use entry-deterring devices to discourage such entry, and make payments to lobbyists and politicians to maintain regulations that restrict competition so that they can keep their profits high. These lobbying and political activities are, for the most part, socially wasteful. As a result of all these losses, the waste from rent-seeking activities can be much larger than the loss from the restricted output.

Other effects

Finally, there is another controversial problem. Some believe that while competition motivates firms to develop new products and less expensive ways of producing goods, a monopoly, by contrast, may let the profits roll in, without aggressively encouraging technological progress. Others point to many cases where monopolists have pushed hard for technological progress. The issue is controversial in the sense that a large firm may be more able than a small one to invest in R&D, build up cost advantages of economies of scale and end up with a lower *MC* curve than otherwise in a competitive market.

While technological indivisibilities are a primary cause of failures of competition in the economy, other imperfections are the result of sharp business practices. As stated earlier, firms that are not natural monopolies may develop market power through strategies designed to deter the entry of competitors and to promote collusive behaviour among the firms in the industry. Just as with natural monopolies, this restricted competition results in higher prices and lower output than would prevail under competition. Dominant position legislation, also known as monopoly, merger and antitrust policies, are the policy responses to such monopolistic practices. These are reviewed below.

3.1.6 Dominant position legislation policies

Dominant position legislation has a history which has determined its evolution. Concern about business size and related manipulations has first led to the enacting of antitrust policies in the USA as far back as the Sherman Antitrust Act of 1890. This outlawed every contract or conspiracy in restraint of trade or commerce. The Sherman Act was supplemented by the Clayton Act in 1914, which forbade any firm to acquire shares of a competing firm when that purchase would substantially reduce competition. The act also outlawed interlocking directorates among competing firms, on the presumption that they would naturally lead to reduced competition. These antimerger provisions were further strengthened in 1950. Similar, but less restrictive legislations started in Europe after World War II.

Dominant position legislation becomes applicable when one firm or group of firms controls, say, one-third or one-quarter or more of a market. A monopolies and merger commission (MMC) is asked whether the monopoly or merger at hand is *not* acting against public interest, i.e. is not against (a) promoting effective competition, (b) interests of consumers and users, (c) reducing costs and (d) raising quality. If it *does* act against and is accepted as such by parties concerned, then negotiations are started which would lead to actions to curb the monopoly.

In general, dominant position laws are particularly concerned with horizontal mergers, that is, with competition within a market. These are distinguished from vertical mergers, in which a firm buys a supplier or a distributor, amalgamating the various stages in the production process within a firm.

In practice, the question of whether a firm is too big is usually put as, 'What is the size of the firm relative to the market?' and thus the debate centres on the question of defining the relevant market. One generally talks of the market for steel or the market for aluminium. But when the government sets out to enforce a policy of competition within a certain market, it must have a concrete way of defining that market. In general, the problem of defining markets and a firm's market power is related to two factors: the *concentration* of firms in the industry, and the *extent of product differentiation*.

Much policy analysis in the past was done in terms of concentration measures at the national level. More recently, international trade has increased in significance appreciably, and this has affected defining markets and measuring the extent of competition in product markets. Today, the degree of competition in a market must be assessed from a global viewpoint, rather than simply looking at how many firms produce a good in the country.

While all firms that produce the same good and sell in the same location are clearly in the same market, when the goods produced by different firms are close but imperfect substitutes, there may be problems of defining the boundaries of the market.

In practice, courts tend to look at two legal criteria for defining a market and market power. First, they consider the extent to which the change in prices for one product affects the demand for another. If an increase in the price of aluminium has a large positive effect on the demand for steel, then steel and aluminium may be considered to be in the same market, the market for metals. Second, if a firm can raise its price, say by ten per cent, and lose only a relatively small fraction of its sales, then it is 'large' – that is, it has market power. (In a perfectly competitive market, a firm that raised its price by ten per cent would lose all of its customers, so this is a natural approach to measuring the degree of competitiveness in the market.)

Furthermore, the law sees to it that before one large company can acquire a competitor or merge with another, it must convince the government that the acquisition would not seriously interfere with competition.

Evaluations of past policies in developed economies show that the policy trend has been shifting towards favouring mergers, this under an increasing understanding that government intervention should be left to a minimum as market behaviour is more efficient in the long run and is constantly expanding in a global economy. It is noted also that in many country's legislations it is not dominance but its abuse which is incompatible with the spirit of dominant position legislation.

3.1.7 Restrictive practice legislation policies

The other policy to promote competition is to limit restrictive practices between firms and their distributors or suppliers which may take such forms as tying, exclusive dealing, description (quantity and price setting) and price discrimination. In many countries, restrictions accepted by two or more parties with regard to the above aspects have to be registered and are to be referred to a Restrictive Practices Court (RPC) which passes a judgement on whether the practice is against the public interest. Because of the existence of unwritten price agreements the RPC is empowered to call up any such arguments for registration.

There are usually several gateways which can be recalled to justify the practice. These are:

- The restriction is necessary to protect the public where the use of the goods requires special knowledge or skill.
- The removal of the restriction would deprive buyers and users of substantial benefits.

- The restriction is a necessary defensive measure against an outside monopoly.
- The removal of the restriction is likely to have an adverse effect on the general level of employment in some area, or is likely to cause a substantial reduction in the export trade.

The RPC is usually helped by lay experts to assess the applicability of these gateways.

The assessment of restrictive practice legislation and its application has not been exclusively positive. Part of the legislation is unnecessary since other legislation exists to protect the public against injury. It is not possible to debate complex economic arguments in a court since many judges lack the technical knowledge. Penalties for registration may not be sufficiently severe to prevent the formation of secret cartels. After many costly negotiations many practices nevertheless become legalized.

There are influential consumer groups and injured businesses which support and lobby for them. Other businesses see government policies designed to promote competition through antitrust policies as hindering economic efficiency. For instance, even if a firm believed that the most efficient way to distribute its products was to guarantee exclusive territories for its distributors, the firm might worry that such a contract might be illegal.

Restrictive practices legislation can be also privately enforced as it allows any firm that believes it has been injured by the anticompetitive practices of another firm to sue the latter, and if successful, the first firm can receive from the second firm several times the value of the damage claimed and attorney fees. There is the advantage here that the private firm – and not the government – is the best-motivated party to take initiative to sue. But there is the shortcoming that a suing firm may tackle its competitor unfairly so as to secure strategic gains.

Policy example 3.1

Airline liberalization

Reciprocal restrictive regulations in the air-carrier industry have evolved historically as a result of fear of the competitive abilities of competing air carriers and national pride from countries to want to have their own air carriers. The last two decades saw more liberalization. The US Airline Deregulation Act of 1978 was the first liberalization move, and this was followed by benefits well documented in Morrison and Winston (1986). The American performance can be used to evaluate future European performance from the liberalization which has taken place since 1998. Good et al. (1993) consider in their analysis (a) cost efficiency and (b) collusive pricing.

Deregulation is expected to let cost efficiency scores converge. Cost efficiency scores are measured relative to the most efficient carrier, this being taken as 100 per cent, after controlling for various environmental variables. From 1976 onwards the different American airlines, starting from an efficiency level of 77 per cent, converged towards 81 per cent in ten years. The European airlines stood at an average of 65 per cent in 1986. If European airlines, as of 1986, would approach the American efficiency level about 16 percentage points can be saved in total operating costs or approximately $4 billion, assuming no change in demand. The 16 per cent gain means a reduction in the airline workforce of 42 000 jobs, and at the average airline wage at the time of $25 000, the efficiency gain is about four times the compensation to the laid-off workers.

Good et al. also examine to what extent the abolishment of collusive pricing practices and capacity-sharing rules, if any, would result in a welfare gain via reduced prices. They do this following Bresnahan (1989). Nash equilibrium in prices implies the simple first-order condition for each carrier:

(3.1) $P = MC - \theta(P/e)$

where P is a price index for the carrier, e is the price elasticity of demand, MC is the marginal cost and the parameter θ measures the degree of collusion. The price–cost margin is zero if θ is found equal to zero, which indicates perfect competition. For θ equal to one, the carrier's behaviour is consistent with the Nash assumption. A value of θ larger than one indicates collusion. Two other equations are regressed, Equations 3.2 and 3.3, and their results incorporated in Equation 3.1, which is then regressed to give an estimate of θ.

Equation 3.2 is a demand equation which generates the price elasticity of demand e, where Q is the quantity demanded,

(3.2) $Q = f(P, X_1, \ldots, X_x)$

P is the price index of the carrier respectively, and the X's stand for other demand-shifting variables such as indices of GDP, consumption, prices of competing carriers, railroads and gasoline.

Equation 3.3 is a total cost function from which marginal cost is derivable. Marginal cost in the first equation is not directly observable, but this can be indirectly specified and substituted from Equation 3.3 which gives a total cost function

(3.3) $TC = f(Q, W, Z_1, \ldots, Z_z)$

where TC is total cost, W is the vector of factor prices and the Z's stand for other cost-shifting variables such as load factor, stage length, and shares of wide bodied and turboprop planes in the fleet.

The estimated value of θ in Equation 3.1 was found to be 0.695 which indicates absence of any significant collusion, but gives also evidence of a set price above marginal cost by some 45 per cent. Should fixed costs be considered, profit margins will be substantially reduced, and this limits the scope for price reductions. Good et al. conclude that the welfare gains from the deregulation of European airlines lie primarily in cost efficiency and not in a dismantling of collusive pricing which hardly exists. In the light of these results it is concluded that European competition policy should encourage formation of strategic alliances among carriers which can make them less costly and internationally more competitive.

3.2 Technology policy

3.2.1 Introduction

There are several contexts in which a government is confronted with actual or potential monopolistic and/or non-competitive behaviour of powerful firms but nevertheless chooses in favour of restricted competition in view of legitimate objectives or because of the limited policy avenues available. Competition policy may give way to technology, industry, environmental, social and regional policy. In this chapter we take technology policy; in other chapters we will consider the other policies.

It is the expectation of large profits in a future monopoly position that make companies invest and introduce new goods and new methods of production. If the management of a company believes that large profits simply cannot be obtained in the future, it is likely to be more reluctant to undertake pioneering investment efforts, thus curtailing the growth rate of the company. Moreover, entrepreneurs facing strong competition may simply lack time for long-term planning and for undertaking more elaborate projects of research and development. Besides, in a situation of heavy competitive pressure, profits are usually so low that little room is left for the internal financing of research and development activities. Hence, it is argued that *restricted* competition creates conditions favourable to rapid growth of cost efficiency in the long-term. But at the same time it is warned that the restricted competition should not lead to a monopoly power which eliminates competition.

The rationale can be elaborated as follows. Suppose company *X* invests in developing a product or process, which it markets later, with the objective of reaching a calculated profit. If other firms *Y* will immediately imitate the new invention, and enter the market, the profits to *X* will fall down much below the stipulated return. Since any firm can foresee that this will occur, few firms will invest in searching for inventions. As long as investor *X* cannot privately appropriate the benefits – since imitator, *Y* cannot be excluded – there is no incentive to invest significantly in technological development. The problem is partly due to the fact that innovations, ideas and technological change contain positive externalities which allow competitor *Y* to benefit from action of *X* without contributing to the cost incurred by *X*. There is also the opposite danger. Firms orient their investment, research and development efforts towards seeking a monopoly position. Suppos-

ing company *X* takes the risk and succeeds in innovating. It can use the advantage strategically for purposes of rent-seeking, in which case conditions of perfect competitive behaviour will not be realized. Because part of the rationale behind technology policy is based on externalities, the review here could also fit in a later chapter on externalities, where we deal with industry policy (see Chapter 5). It is evident then why technology policy and industry policy are so closely linked to each other.

Theoretical insight is still lacking in the resolution of conflict between competition policy and technology policy. For instance, up to which extent should the effort of firms in technological innovations be protected or regulated? Taking no action as regards technology policy by the national government may retard company investment in technological development and growth because of the presence of positive externalities, full protection of the innovating firm may lead to monopoly formation, while imposing a strict short-run competition policy may achieve short-run competitiveness at the cost of retarding growth.

In technology policy we shall address two approaches: the single company approach, and the perspective synergy approach.

In the first approach the state focuses on the innovating firm and attempts to find the right balance between (a) firm behaviour which capitalizes on achieved innovations and causes market imperfections; and (b) firm behaviour that requires incentives: if some future monopoly power cannot be captured by the firm, the firm may not be prepared to invert sufficiently in innovations now.

The second approach accepts the presence of market imperfections but puts more emphasis on the future perspective of alternative technologies. In this approach an evolutionary framework is followed which seeks to find the right balance between: (a) the knowledge cycle; and (b) information synergies.

3.2.2 The innovating firm approach

In this approach the state takes as premises that innovating firms pursue two main channels in realizing technological innovations; *expenditure on research and development* (R&D) and *learning by doing*. The state sees its task as that of directly and indirectly supporting the R&D and learning efforts of the innovating firms, and constraining competition by providing and protecting patents.

In industrialized economies, competition between firms often takes the form of developing both new products and new processes for making old products. Firms devote resources to research (discovering new ideas, products and processes) and development (perfecting, for instance, a new product to the point where it is brought to the market), or R&D for short. Of course, it is noted that *R&D expenditure* is an imperfect measure of innovative input, for money spent on R&D personnel does not tell how creative and well organized the researchers in the given situation are.

Because expenditures on research and development are fixed costs and their advantages can be reaped only much later, large R&D expenditures occur in industries with declining average cost curves up to relatively high levels of output overtime. The presence of fixed costs means that average costs initially decline as firms produce more. Industries with large fixed costs, tend to have lower average costs, larger firms and fewer firms. The large size also provides firms with greater incentives to undertake R&D. Computers, telecommunications and drugs are industries in which R&D is highly important. In these industries, each firm is trying to make new discoveries and bring new products to the market *before* its competitors do and therefore gain the advantages of market power and earn a monopoly profit, even though temporary. The striving for at least temporary

market power is perhaps the principal motivation for expenditures on research and development. When the different companies do the same, the result is often that the industry remains highly competitive.

Some increases in productivity and innovations occur not as a result of explicit expenditures on research and development, but as a by-product of actual production. As firms gain experience from production, their costs fall. *Learning by doing* refers to this kind of technological change. Figure 3.6 depicts a learning curve, showing how the marginal cost of production declines as cumulative experience (output) increases. The horizontal axis represents not one year's output but the sum of all previous outputs. The more experience producing a good, as measured by cumulative output, the lower the marginal cost of producing one more unit.

When learning by doing is important, firms may tend to produce beyond the point where marginal revenue equals *current* marginal cost, because producing more today has an extra benefit: it reduces future cost of production. But more supply in the market may decrease

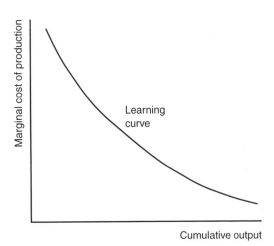

Figure 3.6

price and reduce revenue. How much extra a firm produces depends on the steepness of the learning curve, and the price elasticity of the commodity.

In industries where learning by doing is important, the marginal cost falls as the scale of production increases. Accordingly, these industries have a built-in tendency to be imperfectly competitive, and this is another reason why technological change and imperfect competition often go together. In particular, the first firm to enter an industry has an advantage over other firms. Even if some of what the first company has learned spills over into other firms, not all of it does. Positive externalities show up in a restricted form. Because of the knowledge accumulated by the first firm, its costs can be below those of potential rivals, and thus it may be able to undercut rivals. Since potential entrants know this, they may be reluctant to enter industries where learning by doing has a significant impact on costs. By the same token, companies realize that if they can find a product that provides significant benefits from learning by doing, the profits they earn will be relatively secure. Hence, the race is double-sided. Firms race to be the first to obtain a patent, so too do they race to be the first to enter a product market in which there is a steep learning curve.

3.2.3   Pursued technology policies

A discussion of technology policy and an evaluation of its results requires setting a boundary definition for technology policy. This can be defined as policies that are intended to influence the decisions of firms to develop, commercialize or adopt new technologies (Mowery 1996). Distinction can be made between patent protection of innovations and government policies to stimulate innovations from the supply and demand sides.

In spite of the general advantages of competition in promoting economic efficiency, governments often accept, in view of the above behavioural traits, to constrain competition policy by technology policies which *provide patents*, because without patents, firms would have insufficient incentives to carry on research. This is evident when expenditures on research and development are seen as investment. The incentives of firms to make this kind of investment depend on their ability to realize a return from the investment. In a world with no patent protection, firms would have little incentive to fund R&D. They would simply imitate new inventions, thus enjoying the external benefits of research of others while incurring no costs. Inventors in this situation would not gain market power and thus would have little reason to work at making new discoveries.

Figure 3.7, adapted from Stiglitz (1993), illustrates the economic effects of a patent. Here, an innovation has reduced the marginal costs of production from C_0 to C_1. Before the innovation, the equilibrium price is P_0, which equals C_0. However, an innovator with a patent will drop the price to P_1, just below P_0, and sell the quantity Q_1. Total profits are the shaded area $ABCD$. When the patent expires, competi-

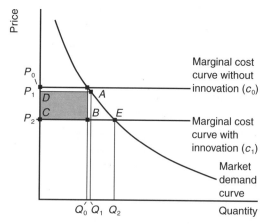

Figure 3.7

tors re-enter the market, price falls to P_2, which equals C_1, and profits drop to zero.

Usually the holder of a patent is given the exclusive right to produce and sell his invention or innovation for a specific period; in the USA this is 17 years. During the time period, other producers are precluded from producing the same good, or even making use of the invention in a product of their own, without the permission of the patent holder, and pay for a royalty.

Not all inventions and innovations are patentable. New products and processes typically are, but many of the benefits of development expenditures, including small improve- ments in existing methods of production that cumulatively account for much of the technological progress in our society, are not. The trick in designing a successful patent system is to provide a big enough incentive for invention, but not such a large and enduring advantage that the benefits of competition become permanently suppressed.

Some firms may evaluate patent races with more scepticism. Competition for patents may be very fierce, even when only a few firms are involved, because it is a race where the winner takes all. However, there are situations where firms would prefer to run their race differently and not to apply for a patent. For example, there are indirect rewards to coming in second. Generally, there is another lap in the race; superior products or processes remain to be discovered. So even if a firm loses one round, what it has learned in the process is likely to be helpful in the next. Thus, the monopoly power granted by a patent for a 15-year period may be of little value, often five years, because the innovation has been superseded by something better.

Another case is when considerations of strategic competition are applicable, such as when there is pre-emptive patenting by incumbent firms. The incumbent may discover a new process or product, patent it, but *not* actually introduce it. Potential entrants are aware that any attempt at entry will be met with the launch of this new product, which will place the entrant at a disadvantage. Thus, pre-emptive patenting can be a highly effective strategic entry barrier. This example shows that intelligent technological and industrial policy must work hand in hand. Evidence of pre-emptive patenting is the type of information that antitrust law seeks in evaluating whether incumbents are abusing their market power.

In other instances, the patent race may actually cause excessive and inefficient expenditures on R&D. Firms may choose to lower total costs of making the discovery by following a more balanced, more paced research programme.

The patent system does not allow inventors to reap all the benefits that result from their innovative activity. Not surprisingly, many firms do not bother to seek patent protection for their new products and processes. To obtain a patent, a company has to disclose the details of the new product or process, and this information may be extremely helpful to its rivals in improving their own R&D programmes. Besides patents are granted on a case-by-case basis, and the questions of what is patentable and how broadly a patent should be defined are subject to considerable uncertainty and legal debate.

Because of these problems with patent protection, some companies prefer to try to keep their inventions a trade secret. A trade secret is simply an innovation or knowledge of a production process that a firm does not disclose to others. Trade secrets have one major disadvantage over patents: if a rival firm independently discovers the same new process, say for making an alloy, it can make use of the process without paying the innovative firm any royalties.

What else other than patent protection can the government do as regards technology policy? There are supply side and demand side oriented policies. Government policies on the *supply side* focus on public R&D spending in universities, public agencies or in launching new technologies with industries. Share of central government funding in total R&D is more important in the USA, the UK and France which have defence-related expenditures. Countries like Germany and Japan are relatively more private-sector oriented in their total R&D expenditure. The benefits of basic research and of public R&D spending in particular occur through complex channels and are difficult to measure. The evidence quoted by Mowery (1996) shows that the contribution by universities to patented innovations that are quickly applied in industry is modest. R&D within public agencies has created new technologies in East Asian countries. Evaluation of the effects of direct financial support to technological innovation within industry for pre-competitive research projects among collaborating firms in the USA and the EU in such sectors as electronics, aviation and information technology gives mixed results. Interviewed enterprises show preference for this channel, however.

Some governments provide tax credits and subsidy schemes to firms engaged in specific technologies. Evaluations of these measures in the USA, Canada and Sweden appear to have induced less additional R&D. Results of German support in microelectronics are, however, found to have a favourable verdict (Mowery 1996).

Public procurement of R&D-intensive products have been found to support the *demand side* for advanced technologies, increase competition and enhance incentives of firms to spend on R&D.

The establishment of technical standards is also found to assist the adoption of new technologies. Governments may also demand technology transfer and the licensing of critical technologies from multinationals investing in the country. This has also been successful in the case of East Asian countries.

Next, there are technology policies for protecting national firms from unfair foreign competition until they can establish themselves technologically, by *relaxing antitrust policies* to encourage, or at least not impede, innovation. Antitrust laws which inhibit firms from engaging in joint ventures may be relaxed so as to allow the engaged firms to share research ideas and the risks and costs of their R&D expenditures or to produce a new product. The arguments in favour of *joint ventures* have to do also with the externalities of R&D. Any single firm knows that if it makes a new invention, other firms in the industry are likely to benefit either directly from imitation, or indirectly from some of the knowledge acquired in the process of making the discovery. Internalization via joint ventures solves the problem of the disincentive to innovate.

3.2.4 The perspective technology approach

The limitation of the innovating firm approach is that it focuses on the individual firm as the sole performer in innovation processes. In contrast, the perspective technology approach emphasizes that although many innovations are motivated by horizontal competition, increasingly more innovations are the result of vertical interactions between suppliers, producers and users. Modern interactive innovations cluster in industries that have a variety of forward and backward economic and technological linkages. Figure 3.8 depicts this relationship.

The perspective technology approach emphasizes that inter-firm co-operation and competition coincide. The appropriate question is not whether to compete and on what but rather on what dimensions to compete and on what dimensions to co-operate. In this approach towards technology policy three notions are important:

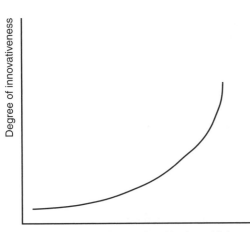

Figure 3.8

- In an economy there should be a *variety* of real innovations representing perspective technologies.
- Given this variety, government should from all innovations/technologies make a *selection* of those innovations/technologies on which it will direct its attention.
- The variety and the selection have a *dynamic* nature and depend on the *endogenous* competition process.

The variety of innovations makes it necessary for the government to select a few focuses of attention. But this selection leads to both positive and negative feedback processes: positive in the sense of innovation encouragement and negative in the sense that certain innovations are excluded, with probably a demotivating influence.

The approach is evolutionary and assumes learning processes and adaptive behaviour. Here government is involved in adjusting policies with the aim of improving the technological performance of the economy. In this policy a distinction can be made between measures which take innovation possibilities as given and measures which aim at enhancing these possibilities.

3.2.5   Perspective technology oriented policies

Technology policies in an evolutionary framework would aim at the stimulation of a great variety of innovations, partly via currently-pursued policies and partly via initiatives to diffuse flexibly-targeted technologies:

- financial subsidies to R&D in the direction of perspective technologies;
- tax incentives for R&D in the direction of perspective technologies;
- flexible patents in the direction of perspective technologies;
- supporting the establishment of contacts between firms which are active in the same research framework; if research is done on a large scale this can lead to scale advantages;
- promoting the dissemination of information via establishment of innovation centres;
- stimulation of periodical reviews and prospects of technology trends by co-operating multinationals and cross-national technological centres.

Furthermore, the approach advises that the government should adopt the right innovation as the standard and should guarantee that this has no excluding influence. Technology policy should also be concerned with deciding how and when selection takes place. Some selection and standardization is necessary, but *timing* is crucial. This requires that the competitor should be monitored closely, in order not to loose track of the innovation waves. Information on firms' market shares and expenditures on R&D is relevant in this respect.

Evidence on contributions of the perspective technology approach to technological development and economic growth is scarce given the fact that policy experimentations with this approach are still young. However, comprehensive studies of the evolution of technology

41

systems do support the contention that the approach opens new and effective policy avenues (cf. Nelson 1994). Furthermore, this approach is supported by empirical findings that succeed in explaining innovation (the proportion of new products in the firm's turnover) by R&D intensity, product life cycle and technological opportunities at the industry level which reflect strategic alliances and interactions between suppliers and users; the more conventional explanations such as market concentration, firm size and entry barriers do not appear to contribute significantly to innovativeness (cf. Bergeijk et al. 1997).

Policy example 3.2

The innovation possibility frontier and the technology policy dichotomy

The importance of recognizing innovation possibility frontiers (IPF) in outlining effective technology policies is emphasized by Metcalfe (1995, pp.424–8). The arguments are:

(a) there is a required critical minimum level of R&D expenditure which must be applied before any innovation can be realized;
(b) there is an upper limit to innovation possibilities within a given period;
(c) as a result, average returns to the R&D innovative effort increase in the beginning but decrease later as the upper limit to innovation possibilities is approached; and
(d) the diminishing returns to R&D is dictated by the current state of knowledge.

An IPF can be defined as a relation between (more) R&D and (less) unit cost, as in Figure 3.9 where X_{r1} is the required critical minimum expenditure, C_{o1} is the corresponding current cost level. The figure also contains C_{L1} which is the lowest cost that can be achieved in the current state of knowledge as circumscribed by the existing IPF_1.

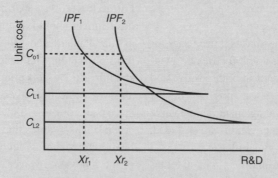

Figure 3.9

The idea of IPF helps to appreciate the two basic approaches of technology policy in this chapter, namely, the single company approach and the perspective synergy approach. In the first approach public policy can induce the firm to intensify its R&D along its given IPF_1 by indirect subsidies, among others. In the second approach public policy can seek to shift IPF_1 to a new innovation possibility frontier which, at the same initial cost C_{o1} would require a higher R&D effort at X_{r2} but allows a lower long-run cost of C_{L2}. However, to apply the second approach the policy maker must act synergetically in identifying the relevant technological areas and developing with the main actors perspective technology scenarios. As the perspective technologies should gain economic significance by displaying existing inferior rivals, the policy makers should encourage experimentation and the efficient selection of innovations in pre-market research settings and later on in market settings. Towards that end the policy makers can play an active role in identifying and supporting the relevant pre-market institutions, enhancing the creativity of innovating firms, and extending the flow of knowledge via integrative and collaborative programmes between research centres and innovating firms. One or the other needs to happen in a cross-national context given the international character of interactions between technological diffusion, foreign investment and foreign trade and the dominant roles which transnational firms play in all three aspects. For a discussion of technological change in the international context see Krugman (1995).

Questions for discussion and further research

1 Review your understanding of the following terms and relate them to each other:
   (a) private interest, public interest, capture;
   (b) managerial slack, rent-seeking; (c) MMC, RPC; (d) innovation possibility frontier, restructuring of R&D.

2 Show in one figure how efficiency and equity effects can be measured under imperfect competition. Show how consumer surplus and producer surplus undergo changes as a result of imperfect competition. An obvious state policy in this context will be to accept imperfect competition, increase the profit tax on producers and use the proceeds to compensate consumers by reducing income taxes. Give an assessment why such a policy is thought inferior and is not usually followed. What are the preferable policies to recommend? If the gains to producers from monopoly power could be distributed to consumers would the social cost of monopoly power be eliminated? Discuss.

3 Baumol states that contestable markets should be free from state intervention. Explain this standpoint. Give an outline of conditions for existence of contestable markets, and supplement by examples. To what extents are the following contestable: sectors with increasing economies of scale, sectors with significant foreign trade? Discuss the statement that the future of competition policy is international.

4 Consider number of innovations, I, as the policy target. Consider market power, M, and linkages, networks etc., L, as possible determinants of I. How do policy makers who advocate the innovating firm approach see the relationship? Draw a graph. How do advocates of the perspective technology approach see the relationship? Draw a graph. Compare both graphs and comment.

Further reading

Basic references for further reading to Chapter 3 are the two volumes of Schmalensee, R. and Willig, R. (eds) (1989): *Handbook of Industrial Organization*, Vols 1 and 2, North-Holland Publishing Co., Amsterdam. A more compact work is Martin, S. (1994): *Industrial Economics, economic analysis and public policy*, Macmillan, New York.

More specific analysis of competition policy, its assumptions and methods, is found in the following selection of four references. See Posner, R.A. (1975): 'The Social Cost of Monopoly and Regulation', in *Journal of Political Economy*, Vol. 83, No. 4f, pp.807–27; Baumol, W.J., Panzar, J.C., Willig, R.D. (1982): *Contestable Markets and the Theory of Industry Structure*, Harcourt, New York; Adams, W. and Brock, J.W. (1991): *Antitrust Economics on Trial*, Princeton University Press, Princeton; Winston, C. (1993): 'Economic Deregulation, days of reckoning for microeconomists', in *Journal of Economic Literature*, XXXI, pp.1263–89.

As background reading to technology policy the following four references are relevant. See Arrow, K.J. (1962): 'The Economic Implications of Learning-by-doing', in *Review of Economic Studies*, Vol. 29, pp.155–73; Freeman, C. (1974): *The Economics of Industrial Innovation*, Penguin, London; Metcalfe, S. (1994): 'Evolutionary Economics and Technology Policy', in *Economic Journal* 104, pp.931–44; Metcalfe, S. (1995): 'The Economic Foundations of Technology Policy', in Stoneman, P. (ed.) (1995): *Handbook of the Economics of Innovation and Technological Change*, Basil Blackwell, Oxford.

Technological growth in comparative systems is the subject matter of two relevant references. See Romer, P.M. (1992): 'Two Strategies for Economic Development, using ideas and producing ideas', in *Proceedings of the World Bank Annual Conference on Development Economics*, World Bank, Washington, pp.63–91; Nelson, R. (1994): *National Innovation Systems*, OUP, Oxford.

Chapter 4

Uncertainty: the case for governance policies

4.1 Introduction

The model of the perfect market economy is a model of indirect exchanges between buyers and sellers who do not personally interact with each other. In an indirect exchange between buyers and sellers, such as the purchase and sale of a standard good like food products consumed and produced daily, the individual consumers make a free choice based on price signals.

Direct exchanges between the buyer and seller is the opposite form of a market. Imperfect information and the degree of uncertainty are much higher here, and become more severe, particularly when such a direct exchange is influenced by an unpredictable behaviour of the direct transactors and when the traded good contains public domain characteristics.

Imperfect information creates uncertainty. In reaction to this uncertainty, micro agents will search for better information as well as for its transmission. Yet there are technical limits as well as behavioural distortions if society relies completely on private reactions. There is a role for market, public and other institutions in remedying these shortcomings. This chapter will treat these remedies under the heading of governance responses.

Imperfect information can be of two types: incomplete information and asymmetric information. The next section demonstrates the welfare consequences of incomplete information. Here we will deal with the search by agents for improved information, the technical limits characteristic of information, and how public policy can remedy them. There is another section which deals with the consequences of ill-intended behavioural distortions resulting in asymmetric information. We investigate here ways of improving informational behaviour, mechanism designs and transaction restructuring.

It will be emphasized that principal-agency theory is basic for the informational perspective towards interpreting uncertainty. A more general framework of looking at uncertainty is the property rights theory. Most discussions in this chapter can be dealt with using both (a) the principal-agency theory; and (b) the property rights theory.

Finally, there is a section which deals with market disequilibrium over time and the institutionalization of co-ordination schemes to combat inherent instabilities.

4.2 The problem of incomplete information

The simple form of imperfect information is that of being incomplete, random and not manipulated by any party. It is shown here how incomplete information on commodity prices leads to welfare losses. The analysis is easily extendible to other informational aspects of the product market, such as improved information about the quality of a commodity and also to the factor market. Figure 4.1 assumes the consumer to be imperfectly informed, with respect to commodity i, whereas the consumer is assumed to be completely informed on other goods (commodity j). The consumer lacks information about the fact that commodity i is available at a lower price from another seller. In Figure 4.1, B_1 represents the consumer's budget line at the known price and B_3 the budget line if he had known about the possibility of purchasing commodity i at the lower price. In the situation that actually prevails the consumer will be able to reach indifference curve I_1. If, on the other hand, he had obtained the additional information, he would have been able to reach I_3. The effect of the missing information was therefore a sub-optimal allocation between i and j at a

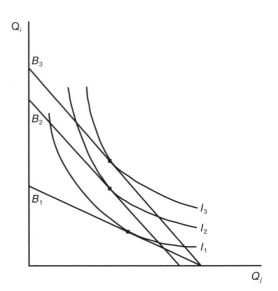

Figure 4.1

lower utility level as shown by the difference between I_3 and I_1.

How do costs for gathering and processing information influence the picture? In principle, the maximum willingness to pay for additional information by the consumer is given by the income reduction, or downward shift of the budget line from B_3 down to the broken line B_2. This shift has the same effects as a reduction in consumer income. The resulting allocation, with information, lies on I_2, which is still more gainful than that on I_1, without information.

Figure 4.1 assumes a hypothetical case in which the consumer always knows what he would get out of an additional effort to gather information at a known cost. Optimum information activity would entail that information should be accumulated as long as the cost of an additional effort to collect information falls short of this maximum willingness to pay for the additional information so collected.

In the real world, however, the consumer cannot normally know the value of an additional effort to obtain information without, in fact, knowing the precise content of the resulting piece of information. But if he knew the content, he would not need to acquire the additional information. Thus, information differs from other commodities in the sense that the consumer cannot have perfect information about the commodity and, at the same time, be willing to demand the commodity. In fact, the consumer often has no idea whatsoever about the outcome of an attempt to obtain further information about, say, the price of a commodity at another source of supply. As the returns on additional acts of information gathering are completely unknown, the optimum level of such acts cannot be determined with the help of conventional methods of optimization. Hence,

economic theory tends to regard individual information gathering under complete uncertainty as rationally bounded and, in a sense, arbitrarily determined.

As for the consequences for the producer, if information is imperfect, prices for homogeneous goods will not necessarily be uniform, since imperfect information allows high-price firms to remain on the market; hence, an equality among producers' marginal rates of transformation will not arise. Moreover, imperfect information may impede equality between true marginal rates of substitution for two commodities and the corresponding price relation (as shown in Figure 4.1).

Policy example 4.1

Immobile markets

A major assumption of competitive equilibrium is that factors of production, and resources in general, are perfectly mobile. Disequilibrium in the form of excess demand or excess supply is assumed to be immediately rectified by the movement of resources in or out of industries.

In reality, in a state of imperfect information, resources are not perfectly mobile. Disequilibrium may exist within markets for some time. This constitutes a market failure, which prevents the economy from reaching maximum welfare. The market failure in this illustration and in the next illustration can be graphically exposed as done in Russel and Wilkinson (1979) and Fitzpatrick (1986).

Figure 4.2 show how the supply curve S interacts with the increase in demand for personal computers, as shown in the demand curve shifting from D_0 to D_1. This leads to a higher price of $P_1 > P_0$ and a higher quantity produced $Q_1 > Q_0$. In theory this increase in output will take place, if not instantaneously, at least very quickly.

In practice, if the computer industry is already working at full capacity, this increase in output cannot be satisfied by the existing capital equipment, chips, materials, and manpower. Rather than increasing immediately, the output, will at best, adjust upwards in due course. The time required can be significant. New factories will have to be financed and built. Plant and equipment will have to be installed. The supply of chips and components will have to be increased. Skilled labour will have to be attracted to the industry and trained. The immobility of all these resources may result in a delay in delivery of several months, a year or more, and disequilibrium will endure. In this context three basic time periods are usually identified. In the very short or momentary run, supply will be very inelastic. With time elasticity will increase. Figure 4.3 shows over time how prices rise immediately from P_0 to P_{01} as a result of a sudden increase in demand from D_0 to D_1. The supply curve shifts in time gradually from S_0 which is a short-run supply schedule to S_1 which is medium term and to S_2 which is long term. This leads gradually to reduction in price towards P_1 and P_2 which is where it finally settles.

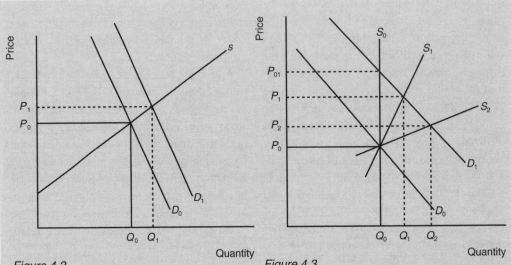

Figure 4.2   Figure 4.3

Under perfect market conditions the movement from equilibrium point Q_0 to Q_1 would take place immediately and smoothly. In practice the transition may be slow and irregular. Similar problems are created when the demand for a commodity falls. The theory assumes that output will fall quickly. Plants will be closed, thereby releasing capital, materials, and labour to be employed in growing industries. However, social and political factors may slow down the rate at which closures take place. The resources which are released – much of it is specialized – may not be suitable for use in the industries that happen to be growing. Growing industries will not necessarily be located in the same areas as declining industries.

The general outcome of the existence of immobility will be a shortage of resources in some industries, in some locations and over time, while a surplus exists elsewhere. Such market failures may require government intervention with the object of improving and replacing the working of the market system. The provision of perspective information, often combined with financial incentives and retraining facilities, can help increase occupational mobility. Through their regional policies, governments try also to reduce the need for geographical mobility by attracting firms to areas with under-used resources.

4.3   Governance responses to incomplete information

4.3.1   The search for and supply of information: some limitations

There is uncertainty about prices and about the nature of the goods being purchased – their quality. When there is uncertainty, there is usually the possibility of reducing it by the *acquisition of information*. Indeed, information

can be seen to be merely the negative measure of uncertainty.

It is appropriate to recall here Arrow (1973). The economic agent can be seen to have at any moment a probability distribution over possible values of the variables interesting to him, information such as present and future prices. He makes an observation on some other variable quality – which can be called a *non-price signalling variable*. Economic behaviour depends not only on the variables usually regarded as relevant, primarily prices, but also on non-price signals which may themselves have little economic significance but which help reduce the uncertainty in predicting other as yet unobserved variables.

From the viewpoint of the society as a whole, prices are signals by which information about scarcities is transmitted among the members of society, but the actual exchange involves non-price signals as well. And this is more necessary if one departs from the assumption of indirect exchanges of standard goods. Under product differentiation actual economic behaviour can be significantly governed by non-price variables which require more information *search*.

Consumers engage in a search for information by looking around for the lowest price, the best deal, the highest quality, and so forth. Thus, information is not merely a good that is desired and acquired but is to some extent a marketable commodity like others, but not fully so. If there are enough searchers, the prices will tend to be the same at each competing store, as long as service is about the same. This means that not every consumer needs to search. Those consumers who do not search are free-riders, so shopping around is an interdependent activity and thus tends to be underproduced. It is likely, then, that the optimal amount of searching by consumers is not reached.

Utility of the consumer is diminished under uncertainty in other ways. Because market information is not equally spread on consumers, some search more than others and, thereby, face higher prices for the same product than others. Markets perform less efficiently when consumers implicitly face different prices for the same product.

Producers also engage in information search. They spend resources on engineering and market research and on acquisition of informa-

tion on the behaviour of other economic agents, including competitors, customers, workers and government. Moreover, there are large and significant exchanges of information through the market. It can be argued that because information is valuable, so one might expect the emergence of a market for it – a place where consumers and producers could purchase, sell and exchange information. This does not happen however. The nature of information makes it more allied to a public than to a private good. Information is not easily tradable since information, by definition, is indivisible in its use; and moreover it is very difficult to appropriate. With regard to indivisibility, it pays a large-scale producer to acquire better information than a small-scale producer, hence causing a departure from the competitive economy. Regarding inappropriability, an individual who has some information can never lose it by transmitting it. If the information is transmitted to one buyer, he can, in turn, sell it very cheaply, so that the market price is well below the cost of production. But if the transmission costs are high, then it is also true that there is inappropriability, since the seller cannot realize the social value of the information. Both cases occur in practice with different kinds of information. The inappropriability of a commodity means that its production will be far from optimal, or otherwise the firm will be induced to implement costly protective measures to obstruct entry. It was shown in the previous chapter that the firm will underinvest in R&D, because the information acquired will become general knowledge and cannot be appropriated by the firm financing the research.

The objective of the producer to maximize profit – which is a basic premise of the perfect market economy – is also adversely affected under uncertainty. Uncertainty upsets this objective. In essence, the demand for and the price of the product which the producing firm face are random. As a result, profit is also random, and as such cannot be maximized. As a substitute for profit maximization, optimal decision-making theory perceives the objective function of the firm to consist of the firm's attitude towards risk, and the firm's perception of the likelihood of various outcomes. The greater the uncertainty, the greater is the departure from risk-neutral attitudes. Furthermore, the more incomplete the information on expected outcomes, the greater is the randomness of profits and the less is the validity of the profit-maximization objective.

4.3.2 Market responses

When information is incomplete or unequally distributed, there are market incentives not only to acquisition of information but also to the emission of signals and exchange of information among agents. In some instances, the buying and selling agents are pulled to each other in a *collaborative* search for information, which often results in changes in governance structures.

Because searching is expensive, agents look for other, cheaper sources of information. Brand names convey information about quality. If the consumer finds a brand of superior quality at a given price, he no longer needs to search for quality. He simply purchases the product with the brand name attached. *Reputation*, based on past searches, is attached to something easily identifiable like a label or name. If the agent notices that the quality declines, or the price increases when the quality does not, the agent will need to search again. Such is the search and reputation behaviour on the consumer side.

Because of the importance of search and reputation, producers have equally an incentive to provide goods that are consistently reliable or of relatively-constant quality to give their brand

name a good reputation. Firms do take advantage of the economizing behaviour by consumers to identify previously-obtained information with a brand name, by differentiating the products they sell, thereby creating markets with characteristics of monopolistic competition.

The costs of searching can also be reduced if products undergo *standardization* and their quality is monitored accordingly by recognized circles.

For some goods, information about quality cannot be produced easily even by search, because no single individual consumes enough of that good to determine its quality accurately, nor does the nature of the good permit use of reputation or standardization. Cases of infrequent purchases of non-standardized goods pose a problem. On the one hand some firms could take advantage of this gap in information and produce goods of lower quality. On the other hand, firms which supply better-quality goods realize that they should accordingly send signals to consumers. This is done by offering a *warranty* on the product's quality.

Finally, *intermediaries* help by decreasing the search time of buyers and sellers as it brings them together. In this sense, information can be purchased in a market.

4.3.3 State responses

The technical limits to the endogenous creation of efficient information via market forces open the way for other types of governance structures via state intervention. Governments often produce and disseminate information on weather, investment, food, education, etc. But governments can go beyond merely providing information, however, by using information about product quality to prohibit the production and use of commodities with detrimental effects.

Four areas of state intervention resulting in the elaboration of governance structures can be mentioned.

1 Economies of scale, typical for information production, imply that decentralized information production is inefficient and that, given the amount of resources consumers want to devote to activities of this kind, an unnecessarily small information output would result from the process. This forms a case for the state to run a nationalized large-scale information industry.

2 Centralized information of the type just mentioned can sometimes be issued and transferred to private users at a charge. For certain types of information, the recipient may be expected to pass it on to others without charge. Thus, information of this kind emerges as a public good and may have to be provided freely and to be financed collectively.

3 In certain cases of persuasive advertising and deceptive marketing practices, legislative and regulative actions can be taken.

4 A reduction of product differentiation may lessen the need for information. This can be carried out without diminishing competition among producers by the introduction of standards jointly agreed upon with producers.

Policy example 4.2

Unstable markets

Instability often occurs when producers do not learn from their mistakes and behave in an unco-ordinated way. Consider there is a time-lag between the making of a production decision and the final delivery of the commodity to the market place. In a given period farmers bring Q_0 tons of produce to the market and sell them at a price of P_0. Assume that the producers look at this period's price to determine the quantity that they will bring to the market the following period. This assumption means that the supply curve S incorporates a time-lag: the next market's quantity will be connected with the present market price. Now suppose that in one particular year the market conditions are altered. Figure 4.4 shows the price fluctuations that would result from such a change. In this case the outcome of the initial movement undergoes a series of fluctuations, over several time periods as the price returns to its original equilibrium level. This is called a converging cobweb, the reason being that the supply curve is steeper than the demand curve.

Assume now a different behaviour. Due to a widespread disease in period 1, the supply of cotton drops to Q_1. This will mean a higher price of P_1. This higher price will encourage the producers to supply more in the next period 2. Too much is produced in period 2. They can sell Q_2 at a price of only P_2. At this low price they will plan to reduce their supply in period 3, and so it goes on.

Where the supply curve is flatter than the demand curve, the price fluctuations will get greater and greater in each subsequent period moving further away from the original equilibrium. This is a diverging cobweb (Figure 4.5).

If the supply and demand curves have the same slope, the price will oscillate between two levels indefinitely without ever returning to the original equilibrium. This is called a perfect cobweb. This simplified analysis provides at least some insight into the fluctuations which can be identified in many markets.

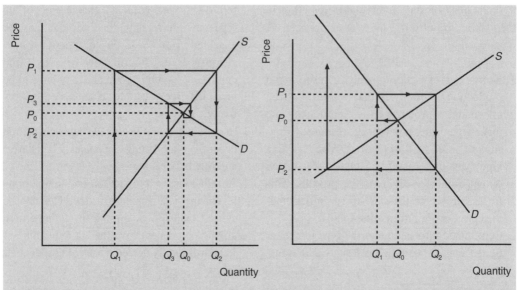

Figure 4.4   Figure 4.5

More efficient information on future markets could eliminate some of the uncertainty regarding prices. However, in the absence of the above, price fluctuations can be diminished by a more direct intervention in the form of a *buffer stock* policy.

A buffer stock involves some form of a central agency setting minimum and maximum price levels. If the market equilibrium price is between the two, the buffer stock does not operate. If the equilibrium price is below the minimum, the minimum price is enforced and all excess supply is bought by the agency and stockpiled. If the equilibrium price is above the maximum, the maximum price is enforced and the agency satisfies the excess demand by selling from the stockpile at this price.

Many practical difficulties are associated with setting up and operating a buffer stock. Storage and the fixing and re-adjustment of minimum and maximum prices are two problem areas. Many controversies surround the question of who should run and finance the agency. Should it be run, for example, by producers, consumers, or the government? An example of buffer stock schemes would include the common agricultural policy of the EU.

4.4 The problem of asymmetric information

Most of the above discussion so far on welfare losses of imperfect information, agents' search for improved information and the technical limits faced would apply to all economic systems, irrespective of their degree of market orientation, because the technical nature of information is as such that uncertainty cannot be wiped out completely. Next to these, there are behavioural factors which characterize interpersonal exchanges, and which can aggravate information failures significantly. These factors lie in the differential information as between contracting parties which can prevent some efficient contracts from being made or well operated.

Market failure due to differential information

is often analysed in the framework of principal–agency theory. Take the case of risk insurance where the population at risk is divided into strata with differing probabilities of a risky event. Suppose that each individual – the agent – desiring insurance knows which stratum he belongs to and hence the probability of risk for him, but the insurer – the principal – cannot distinguish among the insured according to risk and therefore is constrained to make the same offer to all. At any given price for insurance the high-risk agents will buy more, the low-risk agents less, so that the actuarial expectations will become more *adversely selected* than they would be with equal participation by all or than they would be in an ideal allocation with different premiums to different strata. The resulting equilibrium allocation of risk bearing will be inefficient, at least relative to that which would be attainable if information on risks were equally available to both sides. Adverse selection refers to markets where poor quality is likely to predominate, this due to asymmetry of information about product quality between traders and the tendency of traders to select for the cheaper price and lesser quality.

Resolving the above phenomenon of adverse selection may lead to altering the nature of the market transactions from indirect to direct interactions. To reduce the extent of adverse selection, the insurer and insured may opt for medical examinations and a data bank on its clients, since there is a mutual gain to be made. But then the parties to a transaction have closer links. The simple impersonal exchange of money for services is substituted for a closer link where information must be gathered on identified individuals, and not on anonymous customers.

The occurrence of *moral hazard* is closely related to adverse selection. Moral hazard refers to a situation where, for instance, the agent hides information from the principal, and takes actions which deviate from the agreed-upon contract and which benefit the first at the cost of the second. Moral hazard is as such an instance of opportunistic behaviour. An insurance policy, for example, may induce the insured to change his behaviour and take more risks than those against which the insurance is written, and hoping to get refund for damage. Thus, insurance against fire will lead an insured person with selfish motives to be less careful, which will ultimately increase the amount of fire damage payments and ultimately causes an increase in the premiums. This is a social cost, since an irregular increase in fire damage payments to any individual increases the premium for all. Note that the opposite can also occur. The insurer may shirk on its commitments, file a case of misuse by the insured, and refuse to compensate a legitimate damage claim.

Again, economic institutions may compensate by introducing non-market informational devices. In the case of fire insurance, a company may inspect the premises and demand that certain precautions be taken as a condition for the policy, or, at least, adjust the premium according to the observed safety standards.

The general principle underlying the above examples has been set forth by Radner (1968):

> An insurance contract (in the most general sense, including any situation in which the final payoffs to the participants have an uncertain component) can be made only if the conditions under which the contract is to be executed can be observed by both parties. If one will observe a condition but not the other, then the contract cannot hinge on that condition's being satisfied, even though it would be in the interests of both parties – the principal and the agent – to make such a conditional contract if it could be credibly enforced. Whenever some markets are barred from existence, there is inefficiency, which is frequently reflected in strains on other markets …
>
> Source: Radner (1968, pp.31–58)

Adverse selection and moral hazard in insurance are relatively transparent, but the same phenomena exist extensively in the economic system and they can seriously impair the operations of the market. Akerlof (1970) was among the first to call attention to this question. In the market for sale of used automobiles, the seller will in general have more information about the properties of the cars sold than the buyers. Initially, buyers might think that the odds are 50–50 that a car they buy will be of high quality. When making a purchase, buyers would therefore view all cars as being of 'medium' quality. (Of course, after buying the car, they will learn its true quality.) As a result, fewer high-quality cars and more low-quality cars will be sold. This shifting continues until only low-quality cars are sold. At that point the market price would be too low to bring forth any high-quality cars for sale, so consumers correctly assume that any car they buy will be of low quality. Because of adverse selection, low-quality goods drive high-quality goods out of the market.

Moral hazard would occur, for instance, when the car buyer causes car damages due to his bad driving, chooses to shirk and claims guaranteed costless repair from the seller. Moral hazard on the seller's side can also occur where the seller attempts to escape from the agreed-upon terms and avoid genuine repairs.

Risk and uncertainty due to asymmetric information, discussed so far in the framework of principal–agency theory, can be placed *more generally* in the framework of *property rights* theory. Barzel (1989) defines 'property rights of individuals over assets' as 'rights, or the powers, to consume, obtain income from, and alienate these assets'. To obtain income from an asset and to be able to alienate it, exchange is necessary (usually through contracts). People's rights are not constant. Property rights can change as a result of people's own effort at protecting these rights, other people's capture attempts, and government protection.

A commodity or service which is subject to

exchange has many attributes. Some belong to the private domain, others to the public domain. The comprehensive or accurate measurement and monitoring of all these attributes of a commodity is too costly for the exchanges. In other words, transaction costs are very high. Transaction costs are defined here as costs associated with the transfer, capture and protection of rights between the exchangers. Since it is costly to measure all attributes of commodities fully, exchangers will never find it worthwhile to gain the total potential of their owned assets. Only in the case of perfect knowledge would transaction costs be zero, because everybody would know exactly all the properties of an asset, making it easy to transfer a right from one person to another. Because property rights are never completely delineated, the opportunity for wealth capture arises. Whenever an exchange is taking place, some wealth will spill over into the public domain. An attribute of a commodity is said to be in the public domain if it is not charged for on the margin. The buyer and the seller mobilize, each on his own, to capture this public domain wealth.

The maximization of the net value of an asset involves an ownership pattern that can most effectively constrain uncompensated exploitation. When the income stream from an exchanged property is subject to random fluctuations and both parties can gain by affecting that income stream, the delineation of ownership poses some problems. If only one party can affect the income stream, then making him bear full responsibility for his actions will ensure that ownership will be secure. This person is called the 'residual claimant'. However, when both parties can affect the income flow generated by exchanged assets, ownership becomes insecure.

The general principle determining the maximizing allocation of ownership is that the greater a party's inclination to affect the mean income an asset can generate, the greater is the share of the residual that party assumes.

In the property rights model, individuals are assumed to maximize the value of their rights. This implies that whenever individuals perceive that certain actions will enhance the value of their rights they will undertake these actions.

There can be some attributes of commodities which are susceptible to common-property problems. This is the result of individuals having unrestricted access to 'their' part of the commodity. The thesis of Barzel is that:

> the structure of rights is designed to allocate ownership of individual attributes among parties in such a way that the parties who have a comparative advantage in managing those attributes that are susceptible to the common-property problem will obtain rights over them.
>
> Source: Barzel (1989, p.49)

Coase's theorem (Coase 1960) states that when property rights are well defined and transacting is costless, resources will be used where they are most valued, regardless of which of the transactors assumes liability for his effects on the other. A necessary condition for liability is variability. Only in the presence of variability that is too costly to eliminate does liability pose a problem. If property rights are to be well defined, a person who benefits another must be fully rewarded by the beneficiary, and a person who harms another must pay full compensation to the harmed person. By this criterion, a contributor to variability must assume the full effect of his actions if rights are to be fully delineated. In general, both parties to a contract can contribute to the variability in outcome. Since the individual effects cannot be costlessly isolated, property rights, as a rule, are not well defined. As a party's effect on the value of the outcome increases, rights will be better defined if that party assumes a larger share of the variability of outcome, thereby becoming more of a residual claimant.

The property rights approach provides a more general foundation for principal–agent theory. In principal–agent theory the agent has the potential to act contrary to the interest of the principal. The property rights approach can explain why the agent is able to shirk. Because some attributes of every asset are in the public domain, someone will try to capture these. This is also the case for the assets of a firm. The manager, perceiving some attributes of these assets to be in the public domain, will try to capture these. This explains why there is a principal–agent problem. The property rights approach is the more general one, because it can be used to explain a wider range of economic phenomena.

4.5   Governance responses to asymmetric information

4.5.1   Prerequisite conditions for governance structure

Property rights do not only refer to the ownership aspect of an asset but can also include rights and obligations in managing the asset and deciding on its use. Governance relates particularly to these rights and obligations in management and use.

Governance structure is seen by Hart (1995) as a mechanism for making decisions that have not been specified by the contracting parties in the initial contract. For governance issues to arise two conditions should be present: (a) There should be a conflict of interest between different members of the organization or of the contracting parties; (b) Dealing with this conflict of interest through a contract involves very high transaction costs.

Condition (a) states that there is a problem of defining property rights between principal and agent. This could, in theory, be dealt with through a contract. If everything is specified in the contract there would not be residual rights to be decided on. However if transaction costs are very high it is not efficient to write a contract in which everything is specified. Therefore the usual contract will not be complete. Condition (b) refers to the eminence of transaction costs, which can also be analysed in the frameworks of both property rights theory and principal agent theory.

Efficient governance structures succeed in resolving incentive incompatibilities which are typical of principal–agency problems. Stated otherwise, governance deals with allocation of residual rights of control which have not been specified in the initial contract. The more efficient governance structures achieve more efficient allocations of residual rights. We shall review only two areas of governance structures: section 4.5.2 will analyse governance structures in the product market and section 4.5.3 does the same for the factor market (in particular the corporate level). Montias, Ben-Ner and Neuberger (1994) consider other examples. They discuss governance structures which arise in response to problems of agency and undefined property rights in the context of several prototypes of organizations and markets. Williamson (1989) does this in the context of markets.

4.5.2 Mechanism designs in the product market

This section discusses microeconomic policy responses by market forces to uncertainty problems in three important areas: signals can be developed and transmitted with the objective of combating adverse selection and moral hazard, transaction technologies can be redesigned and their costs reduced, and ethical codes can evolve and be instituted to control ill-behaviour. The indirect role of state intervention in regulating these types of governance will be assessed.

Signals

In an ideal world of fully-functioning markets, consumers would be able to choose between low-quality and high-quality objects. The used cars example shows how asymmetric information can result in market failure. The capital market is another very important example. Virtually all extension of credit involves some risk of default. Hence, indebtedness can never be in the form of anonymous promises to pay interest and principal. The purchaser of credit instruments buys them from specific individuals who are responsible; and in general he gathers information about the potential debtors. But how can a credit card company or bank distinguish high-quality borrowers (who pay their debts) from low-quality borrowers (who do not)? Clearly, borrowers know more about whether they will pay than the company does. Given this imperfect information, credit card companies and banks are inclined to charge the same interest rate to *all* borrowers, which attracts more low-quality borrowers, which forces the interest rate up, which increases the number of low-quality borrowers, which forces the interest rate up further, and so on. In fact, credit card companies and banks *can*, to some extent, use computerized credit histories, which they often share with one another, to distinguish 'low-quality' from 'high-quality' borrowers. They eliminate, or at least greatly reduce, the problem of asymmetric information and adverse selection, which might otherwise prevent credit markets from operating. Without these histories, even the creditworthy would find it extremely costly to borrow money.

Asymmetric information is also present in many other markets. The seller knows much more about the quality of the product than the buyer does. Unless sellers can provide information about quality to buyers, low-quality goods and services will drive out high-quality ones, and there will be market failure. Sellers of high-quality goods and services, therefore, have a big incentive to convince consumers that their quality is indeed high. The avenues available to sellers were reviewed already in section 4.3.2, and can be briefly mentioned here. These include exploiting a reputation for quick-servicing, refunding of defective products and alike. Standardization is instrumental in building reputations.

Next in the row are guarantees and warranties which effectively signal product quality and avoid adverse selection. An extensive warranty is more costly for the producer of a low-quality item than for the producer of a high-quality item. As a result, in their own self-interest, producers of low-quality items will not offer an extensive warranty. Consumers can therefore correctly view an extensive warranty as a signal of high quality, and they will pay more for products that offer one.

Transaction technologies

Direct transactions between buyer and seller are explicitly assumed to be absent in the theory of general competitive equilibrium. All exchanges are of the indirect type. This simplification allows markets to clear at no costs of exchange. However, in many markets which require direct negotiations and time-intensive interaction between buyer and seller who are not accustomed to each other and in situations of externalities, transaction costs are fully existing. Consider the example of pollutants. With the establishment of property rights, a market might come into existence if the price that economic agents are willing to pay to get rid of pollutants exceeds the price that other economic agents are willing to accept to absorb pollution. If, however, the transaction cost incurred to negotiate, run and monitor this market over time exceeds the potential profit,

no exchange will take place. As will be elaborated in the next chapter on externalities, a combination of establishing property rights and reducing transaction costs will enhance exchange and the creation of markets.

It seems more likely, however, that property rights and transaction technologies may involve substantial fixed costs and are, therefore, not likely to satisfy the convexity assumptions, which are essential for market success. That is, the amount of resources required to exchange one unit of an uneasily marketable commodity might not be significantly less than the resources required to carry out the exchange of a greater number of units. The marginal transaction cost is therefore diminishing, violating the convexity assumptions required for optimality. Thus, even with the existence of property rights, so long as a market is characterized by transaction costs that violate the convexity assumptions, the market may be inactive and fail to achieve an optimal allocation of resources. Government policy will aim in such circumstances at developing and reshaping transaction technologies.

There is a third type of exchange next to the direct and indirect types. This is a brokerage exchange. The buyer and/or seller involve a broker to realize the deal. Brokerage, as an institution, has had little attention in mainstream theory. Of course, the cost of brokerage is a transaction cost, which is assumed to be absent in received theory.

In practice, brokerage deals are dominant in complex exchanges, and should form an important share of total exchanges. According to some, this type of exchange will play an increasingly significant role in the age of electronic commerce (cf. Vulkan 1999, Shapiro and Varian 1999). Software agents or electronic intermediates – very much acting as intelligent brokers – are now in a position to gather and search through the vast amount of information and offers available on the internet and select the cheapest offers. The software agents can also be programmed so as to negotiate prices and conclude buy (sell) agreements on behalf of their clients. How these developments will affect market designs and competitive performance in the future is still largely unknown.

Ethical codes

One institutional adaptation of the economic system to differential information in markets, where individuals may behave in a selfish manner, is the development of ethical codes and the internalization of certain values which will hence guide interactions between buyers and sellers. Ethical codes, as quoted below, were first introduced by Arrow (1973). Little has been added to these views since then.

> In fact, ethical elements enter in some measure into every contract; without them, no market could function. There is an element of trust in every transaction; typically, one object of value changes hands before the other one does, and there is confidence that the countervalue will in fact be given up. It is not adequate to argue that there are enforcement mechanisms, such as police and courts; these are themselves services

bought and sold, and it has to be asked why they will in fact do what *they* have contracted to do. In any case, the cost of enforcement becomes bearable only if most transactions take place without attempts at fraud, force, or cheating. Further, in transactions of any complexity, it would be too costly to draw up contracts which would cover every contingency. Some aspects have to be left for interpretation when needed, and it is implicitly understood that it will be possible to agree on the meaning of the contract, even though one party loses.

> Source: Arrow (1973, p.149)

If left to itself there is a good chance, but no full certainty, that buyers and sellers, driven by the economic rationale, may evolve codes of conduct to govern their transactions as the need arises. Arrow adds that:

> the evolution of ethical codes is facilitated by the fact that productive units are organizations, not individuals, and individuals are mobile among these organizations. Hence, ethical codes held by individuals, perhaps derived as part of business education, may survive even though detrimental to the profits of the firms because the managerial element can accept a tradeoff between profits and learned ethics, which have been found to facilitate business in general.

> Source: Arrow (1973, p.150)

Policy example 4.3

New governance for the new economy

Reference was made in this chapter to changes in market governance as a result of newly-introduced transaction technologies, such as electronic commerce, internet communication and information technologies, commonly referred to as the 'new' economy. This box reviews related issues in current discussion.

To start with, there are unsettled views on the significance of the new economy. Take, for example, K. Kelly (1998), *New Rules for the New Economy*, Fourth Estate, London, who sees the internet as the foundation for a new industrial order, where place, time and political borders are rapidly becoming irrelevant to the way people conduct their personal lives and business matters. Compare this with C. Shapiro and H.R. Varian (1999), *Information Rules*, Harvard University Business Press, Cambridge, who qualify the phenomenal innovation by maintaining that although technology changes, economic laws do not, and that the impact of the internet should not be exaggerated but be realistically assessed with due consideration of the experience with other significant precedents such as the gasoline engine, telegraph, television, and computer.

So, what is the factual evidence so far on the impact of the new economy? What are the implications for economic welfare? What is the nature and extent of market failures? What kind of governance or other policy responses are required to remedy the failures and how? Drawing on the sporadic empirical evidence and stylizations which are occasionally reported in the financial media, the following can be stated.

1 The internet has reduced profit margins in many markets making it possible for consumers to purchase many goods and services at lower prices, this is particularly true for books, software, travel and financial services. However, the internet is likely to be behind price increases in other goods and services, notably motor cars and supermarket goods. The first effect is likely to be more than the second, so that the total effect enhances economic welfare. There is no need for governance corrections in this respect.

2 The internet experience regarding quality of delivered goods and services, on-site demonstration, maintenance, etc. is mixed and is probably lagging behind that of the 'old' economy. These shortcomings can be rationalized as start-up difficulties, but their solution will require that e-commerce businesses devote more resources and personnel than is currently done to enhance guarantee and reputation. These activities will increase delivery cost and cut on the price advantages sited above. In the long run, market governance will probably be effective in responding appropriately as regards quality and reputation, with the necessary support from law enactments that protect consumers. The coverage of the existing legislation may have to be extended or redefined.

3 The internet tends to produce more price dispersion and more product differentiation. This is made possible by the massive amounts of information about consumer behaviour which firms accumulate via the internet, allowing them to modify the product and the price to meet different tastes and budgets. These developments have positive and negative effects to individual economic welfare: marginal utilities come closer to prices, but there is a drift away from product standardization towards more product uncertainties, and the need for increasingly more information to appraise alternatives and control outcomes. Such information being a public good, its provision would tend to increase the collective tasks of the community/state.

4 The expectation that the internet would eliminate intermediaries and foster direct connections between manufacturer and consumer has not materialized. The opposite seems to be true as consumers tend to delegate more of their search efforts to intermediaries. The search efforts are themselves becoming increasingly specialized information markets on their own. As the size of the monetized exchanges increases, due to conversion of personal search into commercial intermediation, more resources are put to use and the national income increases. There seems to be no governance issue involved here.

5 Some semi-public goods such as telephone communication and television watching, for which consumers pay, may be made available by internet businesses to the consumers at no price if the trend for financing these services through third-party advertisements continues appreciably. Whether the consumer will be better off or not depends on his/her trade-off of a price they pay in case of neutral communication against an advertisement-loaded but cost-saving communication. The more severe problem is that there may not be a possibility

of choice for the consumer with an average purchasing power, if the supply side will dominate the market options. Community intervention in the form of assigning (de)merit goods and implementing regulations and subsidies are the usual responses in such situations.

6 The new economy is forcing a restructuring of industry, not only nationally but also globally. At the national level, some of the established activities like publishing and travel are increasingly challenged by the newcomers. At the global level, banking, software, cable and media businesses are forming cross-sectoral mergers and alliances, as manifested in the merger between AOL and Time Warner, and the joint ventures between Microsoft and AT&T, and the alliances each have made again with many others in and outside USA. The same tendency is also present in Europe. These developments are market driven and can be expected to raise shareholders' value in the long run, and under competitive conditions, higher values imply higher profits from productivity gains, lower costs and market growth. These are all positive developments if indeed competitive conditions can be observed and controlled. It will be very difficult to define, appraise and implement competition policy *cum* technology policy in the new economy. In communication networks, restrictive practices that limit access to competitors and punishments for exiting consumers are very common but it is not simple to pass a judgement on their fairness because of matters relating to indivisibilities and incentives. There are high degrees of interdependence of inputs and outputs causing significant externalities among closely-related activities which stand in the way of clear delineation of the extent of the market and the degree of concentration which a merger or an alliance enjoys. These are unsettled questions in the old economy, and they will only become more controversial in the new economy, as is evidenced by the anti-trust case against Microsoft.

7 The internet technology presently available makes it possible for intruders and hackers to obstruct, distort and misuse communications between agents. This is interpretable as a violation of established property rights arrangements. The evolution of conventional markets needed hundreds of years to develop a system of private property rights and institutions which allows exchanging agents to carry their transactions under more certainty and less risk. A similar exercise in the building of institutions, backed with counter-balancing security-enhancing technologies, is likely to be the governance response in the new economy. Because of the unavoidable externalities in internet use between individual countries in a connected globe, the solution of these externalities would require governance rules at the world level.

8 The internet promotes borderlessness. It highlights the irrelevance of being subject to national regulations in the country in which the agent happens to transact. This has significant consequences for the flow of financial capital, trade registration, tax collection, etc. Some official circles think that the reduction in state revenue may undermine the capacity of governments to rule and meet the collective demand for public goods. Realization of these scenarios will depend on the response of governments in the near future. If, as it is sometimes argued, the state is overgrown and there is a need for downsizing – see Chapter 8 – then the new economy must be a godsend.

Next to the eight aspects reviewed above there are other economic as well as non-economic consequences of a more general nature. For example, the remarkable stock appreciation of new economy companies seems to have taken place at the cost of the old ones who are robbed of financial resources necessary for maintaining their expansion. This lopsidedness can be damaging for the balanced growth of the economy. Economic analysis would

Table 4.1   Financial performance of new and old economy

Selective Stocks		Revenue			Shares		
		1 Year Growth	Revenue/ employees $1000s	Price/ earnings	1 year return	% held by institutions	Market cap $ mil
New Economy							
Cisco	CSCO	50	713	170	96	59	430 432
Microsoft	MSFT	34	712	60	68	42	492 139
Qualcom	QCOM	18	424	306	2618	48	95 258
Yahoo	YHOO	190	737	1561	265	27	82 197
Average		73	647	538	696	44	
Old Economy							
Citi Group	C	−25	337	18	70	64	173 431
Du Pont	DD	13	285	7	27	54	54 399
General Electric	GE	12	381	39	53	53	410 116
General Motors	GM	9	297	8	4	64	57 322
Johnson & Johnson	JNJ	16	295	26	13	60	107 681
Coca Cola	KO	5	692	52	−12	51	126 895
AT&T	T	17	579	28	2	46	151 979
Walmart	WMT	20	181	39	28	37	212 666
Average		8	380	27	22	54	

Source: adapted from www.quicken.com as of 18th February 2000.

recommend that the appreciated new businesses be more active in capital recycling to, participation in, and take-overs of old businesses. There is little evidence as yet that the appreciated capital in the new economy is trickling down to the old economy.

Financial statistics of representative stocks of the 'new' and 'old' economies are brought together in the table above. In some cases the averages are less meaningful because of the high diversity within the segments, nevertheless they give a rough idea of magnitudes of the two segments, showing revenue growth and share performances of the new to be multiples of the old economy. Furthermore, revenue per employee is 1.7 as much, market capitalization is catching up rapidly, though the percentage of shares held by institutions is lagging behind.

As regards non-economic consequences there are many speculations, full of uncertainties, as to the final effects of the depersonalization of agent interactions. As with all innovations, and this applies here too, the upward shift in the production possibility frontier is equally accompanied by an upward shift in risks and uncertainties which are hard to explore ex-ante.

4.5.3   Mechanism designs in the factor markets

This section discusses microeconomic responses to behavioural uncertainty in three areas relating to the factor markets: corporate governance, profit sharing and educational signalling. The need for state intervention will be simultaneously assessed.

Corporate governance

Corporate governance in large firms can be approached as a response to agency problems and property rights problems. Large companies typically have a large number of small shareholders. Although these shareholders have residual control rights, they are too small, and there are too many of them, to exercise this control effectively. In practice every-day decisions are taken by management. Small shareholders have little incentive to monitor management. Monitoring involves costs. The benefits of monitoring (e.g. higher efficiency) however accrue to every shareholder. Hence every shareholder is inclined to free-ride. Very little monitoring will take place in such a situation, giving managers an opportunity to pursue their own goals at the expense of the goals of the shareholders (usually profit maximization). Corporate governance deals with this situation by designing mechanisms to constrain management of a company.

More generally, when capital is treated as a single asset, then shareholders are the residual claimants to the profits which are generated by this asset. Since property rights are never fully delineated due to high transaction costs, some attributes of this asset are in the public domain; other people will capture these attributes, because these are not charged for on the margin. Managers can use the firm to increase their own status by investing in large, but potentially unprofitable projects. Because this attribute of the firm is not priced, it will be overused, at the expense of the shareholders. Corporate governance deals with these issues, trying to make the use of these attributes costly to managers. Corporate governance will constrain managers, in order for them to act in the interest of the shareholders. We will now turn to some mechanisms that are designed to combat managerial slack and control management.

The *board of directors*, chosen by shareholders to monitor management, is one important mechanism. The board's incentive to act only in the interest of the shareholders is, however, limited, given the fact that some members of the board are usually also members of the management team. Outside directors who do not have shares of the company do not have an incentive to monitor, because they would not gain financially if the company would operate more efficiently. Because they are often very busy people they must rely on information given to them by management. This leaves little room for monitoring. As outside directors may sometimes owe their positions to management they could be feeling loyal towards them and would not risk their own position.

If a shareholder thinks the current board of directors does not monitor management well enough, he could try to set up a *proxy fight* by having another group of persons elected in the board. In this case there is a free-rider problem. This shareholder incurs cost, while every shareholder will benefit from his action. With a large group of shareholders, most shareholders will be inclined not to gather information about the proposed new board, because their own vote will not make a difference. They are therefore more likely to vote for the board in place. If management is allowed to use company funds to promote their directors, then it is more costly for a shareholder to convince other shareholders that they should vote for the alternative board.

Large shareholders is another machanism. They have more incentive to monitor the managers, because they benefit more from it. This incentive is not large enough, though, because even large shareholders do not benefit for 100 per cent from monitoring the management team. Large shareholders might also be inclined to use their power to improve their own position at the expense of other shareholders. When a large shareholder is an institution, another principal–agent problem arises, because the person who does the monitoring for the institutional shareholder might have other goals than the shareholders of the institution.

A *hostile takeover* is, in theory, a very powerful mechanism for disciplining management, since the rewards of a takeover accrue to the person(s) taking over an underperforming company. However, the rewards of a takeover may not be very large for three reasons. First, small shareholders may not have an incentive to sell their shares to the raider, in order to gain from the improved efficiency after the takeover. Second, if the raider faces competition from other bidders, the price of the company may be driven up, lowering the net gains of the takeover. Third, the management could improve the efficiency of the company after the bid has been announced, hence raising the value and the price of the company. If the raider is aware of these factors he may be disinclined to take over the company. The pressure on management is therefore reduced.

Debt can serve as a device to limit the extent of inefficiency in a company. If a company has a large debt, it has to be efficient enough to be able to repay the debt. This could provide an incentive for management, but only if their jobs are at stake in case of a bankruptcy. If this is the case, the managers will be forced to be efficient.

Another mechanism which corporate founders may use is to choose *statutory rules* that maximize total surplus. It is not clear that statutory rules will encourage companies to internalize the right externalities. The case for government intervention with regard to externalities is not strong, however. The government is generally not as informed as the companies involved, so with regard to unforeseen events, government intervention is also not very useful.

Finally, *business reoganizations* includes leveraged buy-outs, management buy-outs and buy-ins, employee stock ownership plans and the like. These involve simultaneous changes in the ownership, financial structure and incentive structure of firms. Thompson and Wright (1995) argue that this corporate restructuring can be seen as a response of Anglo-American capital markets to the governance problems they encounter.

Corporate restructuring is a device which restores active governance by creating incentives to monitor senior management. Thompson and Wright (1995) have studied leveraged buy-outs (LBO). An LBO involves a private company, which acquires a publicly-quoted corporation. The equity of the private company is usually subscribed by a specialist LBO association, institutional investors, and the management of the bought-out corporation. A large part of the deal price is met by borrowing. This restructuring has strong implications for corporate governance:

- There is a reconcentration of equity in the hands of insiders or with institutions with a close association with the new firm. Because the institutional investors went through the initial buy-out transaction, they have a thorough knowledge of the new company and therefore have the ability to monitor management.

- The involved substitution of debt for equity reduces managerial discretion and acts as a commitment device for management, because they have to perform well enough to be able to repay the debt.
- Many buy-outs involve incentive schemes for management, as well as for employees, such as shareholding schemes.

Corporate restructuring make firms more efficient, because management has incentives to maximize profits. The performance of the firm is improved by the restructuring in three ways:

- Management efforts towards cost minimization are increased. Since most restructuring activity is concentrated in mature, low-growth industries, where it is difficult to motivate managers with conventional reward systems, restructuring represents methods of injecting new incentives to management.
- Unprofitable diversifications are reversed. Mature businesses, with free cash flows, tend to engage in unprofitable diversifications. A debt-financed restructuring transaction can be used to commit the firm to raise the cash flow. Unprofitable diversifications will be divested.
- The response time for adaption to market conditions is reduced. With a large debt and strong incentives, the corporation is forced to adapt quickly to changes in economic conditions.

Several empirical studies, quoted in Thompson and Wright (1995), have examined consequences of LBO deals. They usually find large gains in share prices for shareholders. Substantial mean improvements are also found in profitability and cash flow measures over the interval between one year prior to the transaction and two or three years subsequent to it. In LBOs with significant insider participation, there is the possibility of systematic underpricing. The evidence on this is not conclusive, however. Evidence strongly supports the view that capital investment falls immediately following the LBO and that LBO firms reduce spending on R&D.

Some argue that restructuring could lead to revision of implicit labour contracts, thus transfer value from employees to equity owners, but evidence by Kaplan (1989) and Opler (1992) on this does not indicate major transfers. Furthermore studies by Wright et al. (1992) found that job losses occur most substantially at the time of the change in ownership. Because restructuring transactions typically substitute debt for equity, they tend to reduce corporate tax liabilities. Studies suggest that tax savings do account for a small fraction of the value gains from LBOs.

The general conclusion is that corporate governance structures change when economic conditions change. Firms themselves are well capable of creating a governance structure necessary for profit maximization. The case for statutory rules is weak. Government intervention with respect to governance issues is not to be welcomed, because it will limit a firm's capability to adapt to a changing world. Firms are restructuring when it is necessary.

These general conclusions may require relativation depending on the specific country, corporate culture and the specific sector. At the country level, Anglo-American capital markets are known to emphasize exit, which refers here to the ease of selling stocks. In these markets there is usually little incentive to monitor management, because of free-rider behaviour of small shareholders. Shareholders are more mobile and they can let a company go dead by withdrawing from it. In the EU and Japan there is more of an investor voice of large shareholders in corporate decision-making. In these countries the concentration of equity voting power, active participation of large investors and the important position of banks provide an incentive for monitoring management. At the sector level the applicability of corporate restructuring transactions seems to be restricted to low-growth industries. Industries which experience rapid technological or market change may require greater managerial flexibility.

Profit sharing

The second example relates to the world of work. The property rights theory argues that it may be advantageous for the workers to become residual claimants where their actions are especially costly to supervise, otherwise suppliers of labour are severely restricted in their insuring ability. Owners of labour are more likely to enter into contracts in which they are required to guarantee the difference between their market wage and their actual wage than they are to enter into contracts that require them to guarantee other possible effects of their behaviour. Equity capital is a factor specializing in guarantees. A firm may be seen as a set of contracts guaranteed by equity capital.

Recent work on principal–agent theory, as quoted in Bhargava (1994), has provided theoretical justification for the claim that profit sharing enhances worker efficiency. There have been a few empirical studies which used relatively small samples of profit-sharing firms and found that the average rate of return on capital is considerably higher in profit-sharing firms than in non-profit-sharing firms. However, more recent work by Bhargava (1994) shows that the rise in profitability is limited and is a one-period rise when the firm shifts from non-profit to profit sharing.

Jensen and Kervin (1990) investigated a relationship between base salary plus bonus for top executives and stock market performance: this is found to be very weak in both the United States and United Kingdom, suggesting that incentive mechanisms are not very strong. Furthermore, the link between wider measures of compensation and performance does not seem strong. It is this weak link that generates the widely expressed concerns about designing appropriate compensation for top executives and related issues of mechanism designs in the context of corporate governance.

Educational signalling

The third example relates to the world of education. Observation of the productive quality of newly-recruited educated labour is costly to employers. Hence, it pays employers to use signals of ability in education emitted by graduate students, at no cost to them, in making this selection of future employees. In turn, however, this creates an incentive for the student to continue his/her education beyond that level which he/she would otherwise desire and beyond the level which is socially desirable. In this way the educational system becomes an industry which sells signals to students that are in turn emitted to the world, while the primary intended function of the educational system is the acquisition of knowledge and skill. These undesirable outcomes are manifestations of asymmetric information and may rightly call for state intervention to institute appropriate governance structures.

Policy example 4.4

Enterprise governance in transition economies

Governance in privately-owned small firms is straightforward, as the owners are usually the managers. When owner and manager are separated as in corporates, the need for monitoring by the first of the second raises complex issues of governance designs. The case of state enterprises is even more complex as the owners, i.e. the people, delegate their rights to politicians and bureaucrats who in turn exercise monitoring on enterprise managers. Decision making can become highly politicized.

When governments privatize, policy choices are made as regards ownership arrangements, these are either outsider owned or insider owned. Outsider-owned privatizations are implemented via selling shares to the general public at the stock exchange, competitive sale to or takeover by another firm or an investment fund, domestically or foreign. Insider-owned privatizations take the form of management–employee buyouts.

Privatization in Western Europe are of the outsider type, privatization in the transition economies of Eastern Europe followed a mixture of outsider and insider governance with more emphasis on the latter. As the table below shows, Hungary and Estonia transferred about 40 per cent of state ownership to outside owners. The Czech Republic distributed equal access vouchers to citizens which is primarily an outsider-oriented policy; the new owners were encouraged to place their vouchers in competing investment funds which monitored the privatized companies. Russia followed the insider-owned policy. This is rationalized on the grounds that the transition economies have no stock markets to float initial public offers, the public lacks purchasing power, there are no high-performing domestic companies to take over the ailing state enterprises, selling to foreign companies is felt to be against the national interest and would raise unsolvable negotiations on asset valuation. Faced with strong economic and political pressures, domestically and internationally, to take action, Russia implemented a sort of management–employment buyout of state firms. These firms were effectively controlled by their managers anyway and responsible ministerial authorities. In most cases, the state retained a share of about 20 per cent. The other contrasting example is that of Poland which emphasized ownership by municipalities and semi-public bodies and maintained strong links between management and state.

Most economists hold the view that enterprise governance and performance after privatization are more successful if privatization is done through outsider instead of insider ownership, i.e. Aghion and Blanchard (1996). A great deal depends also on what happens to financial restructuring in the years after privatization. Earle and Estrin (1996) report that the Czech Republic stands after five years of privatization as the only transition economy where the majority of firms have outside ownership. At the other extreme is Russia where recent evidence from Filatochev et al. (1997) shows insider ownership to continue dominating with a slight shift from employees to management, the share of employees being reduced from 47 to 46 and that of management increasing from 19 to 20 per cent. The share of the state has fallen down from 23 to 14 per cent, and this was to the advantage of private individuals, industrial groups and institutional external investors which increased from 11 to 20 per cent.

Table 4.2 Privatization responses in transition economies

Country	Sale to outside owners	Equal-access vouchers	Management–employee buyout	Other incl. restitution, semi-public	Still in state hands
Czech Republic	5	50	–	5	40
Estonia	60	3	12	10	15
Hungary	40	–	2	16	42
Lithuania	–	60	5	–	35
Poland	3	6	14	23	54
Russia	–	11	55	–	34

Source: adapted from World Bank (1997), *From Plan to Market, World Development Report 1996*, OUP p.53. All data refer to medium-size and large firms, and are as of the end of 1995. All figures are percentages of total based on capitalization values of privatized firms as a share of the value of all formerly state-owned firms, except for Russia and Poland where the base is the number of firms.

4.6   Incomplete markets

The theory of competitive equilibrium simplifies the operation of the market system by assuming certainty at no costs. This comes down to envisaging a static world with an infinite mobility of factors and products and a stable and instantaneous clearance of supply and demand, no costs of exchange, negotiations, transport etc., no money, and no risk associated with an uncertain future. There are absent and unco-ordinated markets which are not able to clear over time, due to the absence of one or the other of the above aspects.

Perfect information on the part of the economic agents in the case of intertemporal markets is not credible. Even though there is a strong profit incentive for some economic agent to set up a market for future commodities, i.e. commodities that will not be delivered until some future date, yet such markets fail to come into existence and this might be traced to some of the factors reviewed earlier. For example, markets for contingent commodities might involve nonconvex transaction technologies. Fixed costs or set-up costs in security and insurance markets would imply nonconvexities that could account for the non-existence of equilibria in these markets. Alternatively, economic agents might perceive futures contracts as being quite risky and there might be a lack of buyers for such commodities. In this case, futures markets would be characterized by the problems of small numbers of buyers and sellers – thinness – and non-competitive results would hold. Incomplete markets are also characteristic of situations of externalities and collectivities, as will be clear from the next chapters. Government intervention directed to instituting and increasing the size of the market will very much fit in these contexts.

Two markets are considered in the illustrations to this chapter: immobile markets and unstable markets. These market failures call for government interventions aiming at creating and facilitating quick market clearance over time.

Questions for discussion and further research

1 Review your understanding of the following terms: information search, non-price signalling variable, transaction technologies, ethical codes, public domain, proxy fight, LBO, immobile markets, unstable markets, incomplete markets, conditions under which governance issue emerge.

2 Explain graphically and by an example from consumption behaviour, how substitution and income effects interact as a result of more and better information.

3 The cost of buying a good can be different for two buyers in spite of paying the same purchase price. Give various explanations of how this can happen making use of Arrow's notion of non-price signalling variables. Relate this notion to adverse selection. What is the market response to these anomalies? What can the state do to improve market performance in this respect?

4 Why is profit-sharing likely to resolve agency problems, whereas wage payment will not? Why is it sometimes profitable for the firm to pay an efficiency wage which is higher than the competitive wage?

Further reading

Several topics in this chapter are treated at greater length in the following three references. See Laffont, J.J. (1998): *The Economics of Uncertainty and Information*, MIT Press, Cambridge, Mass.; Hirschleifer, J. (1971): 'The Private and Social Value of Information and the Reward to Economic Activity', in *American Economic Review*, Vol. 61, pp.561–74; Mirrlees, J.A. (1974): 'Notes on Welfare Economics, Information and Uncertainty', in Balch, M., Mcfadden, D. and Wu, S. (eds) (1974): *Essays in Economic Behaviour Under Uncertainty*, North-Holland Publishing Co., Amsterdam.

On imperfect information and behavioural responses, the following three references approach the issues from a game theoretic point of view, and are most directly connected with the topics in Chapter 4. See Levinthal, D. (1988): 'A Survey of Agency Models of Organizations', in *Journal of Economic Behaviour and Organization*, Vol. 9, pp.153–85, Dixit, A. and Nalebuff, B. (1992) *Thinking Strategically*, Norton, New York; Milgrom, P. and Roberts, J. (1992): *Economics, Organization and Management*, Prentice Hall, New Jersey.

An institutional approach to the issues of uncertainty, information and governance are elaborated in the following three references. Governance response to uncertain behaviour and related transaction costs was first treated in a comprehensive way in Williamson, O.E. (1975): *Markets and Hierarchies*, Free Press, New York. The property rights paradigm is systematically treated and illustrated in Barzel, Y. (1998): *Economic Analysis of Property Rights*, CUP, Cambridge. A classical article on uncertainties and externalities is Coase, R.H. (1960): 'The Problem of Social Cost', in *Journal of Law and Economics*, Vol. 3, pp.1–44.

On corporate governance, a compact treatment is that of Hart, O. (1995): 'Corporate Governance, some theory and implications', in *Economic Journal*, pp.678–89. The more detailed study is in Hart, O. (1995): *Firms, Contracts and Financial Structure*, OUP, Oxford. Another book which discusses governance issues from an international perspective and in the context of comparative economic systems is Keasey, K., Thompson, S. and Wright, M. (eds) (1997): *Corporate Governance*, OUP, Oxford.

Chapter 5

Externalities: industrial policy and environmental policy

5.1 On characteristics of goods

The typical good that has been analysed in previous chapters shares two characteristics: *excludability* and *rivalry*. In this and the next chapters we deal with non-excludable and non-rival goods.

The excludability characteristic of a good makes it possible for consumers and producers to engage in mutually beneficial exchanges. If consumer A can exclude consumer B from consuming a unit of bread, and consumer B can do the same with respect to meat, the exchange of bread for meat may be the only way in which both consumers can achieve preferred commodity bundles. There are, however, goods that have a *non-excludability* characteristic. Air pollution is a good which is non-excludable in consumption and production. Consumers cannot exclude pollution from the air that they must consume.

The rivalry characteristic of a good makes it possible that the consumption or use in production by one economic agent of a particular unit of that good precludes the simultaneous consumption or use in production by other agents of the identical unit. Two consumers cannot both consume the identical unit of bread or meat. A good with this property is called a rival good. There are, however, goods that do not have this *non-rivalry* property, but are characterized by collectivity. For example, two or more consumers can simultaneously consume the same unit of national defence, street lights and air at no extra cost. Each consumer consumes the total amount available and there are no additional costs involved.

A good which is both rival and excludable is called a *pure private good*. These goods form a major share of economic activity but it is difficult to specify how big this share is. The other types of goods together can be as significant in extent. We turn to these from now on. In this and the next chapter we analyse the consequences for the nexus between competitive equilibrium and Pareto-optimal allocations of goods that are non-excludable and those that are non-rival. These phenomena were referred to in the introductory chapters, as *externalities* and *collectivities*, respectively. In this chapter we deal with policy responses to externalities in the form of industrial and environmental policy. In the next chapter we turn to policy responses to collectivities in the form of public goods and merit goods. But first we discuss linkages between the different characteristics of goods.

The possible linkages between excludability and rivalry are summarized in Table 5.1, where the following four cases are identified.

Case 1 (rival and excludable) is the clear-cut example of what is known as a pure private good. A meal is rival and is consumed exclusively by either individual A or B; once A buys it he is entitled to exclude B from sharing it. General equilibrium theory as outlined in Chapter 2 deals primarily with private goods.

Case 2 (non-rival and excludable) illustrates a situation of the private provision of goods which have a public good content and the public provision of goods with a private good content. As an example, consider a school or a library with a capacity crowd of 2000 persons. Up to this capacity, attendance is non-rival. It is made excludable by requiring enrolment or entry fees. The same argument applies to theatres, museums and libraries. As an example of a good provided by the government but which has a private good content, consider the

national health service: this is non-rival up to its capacity, but excludable in the sense that the beneficiaries of medical care can be identified – this means that the government is able to choose to some extent who shall benefit from the health service. Insurance schemes guaranteeing unemployment benefits or for maintaining income at retirement age would also fit in this category, and depending on design can be also formulated as a public externality. As stated earlier, the next chapter will be devoted to these cases and will treat social provisions in health and education as well as social insurance.

Case 3 (rival and non-excludable) is the case known as semi-public good. If government would upgrade skills through training programmes, employment of this factor in production is non-excludable but is rival. The same applies to use of and benefits from industrial infrastructures and a large range of forward and backward linkage effects resulting from industrial policy.

Case 4 (non-rival and non-excludable) is the clear-cut example of what is commonly known as a pure public good, like defence, police and lighthouses. All agents can consume them at no additional cost. Other goods that qualify here are the beneficial outcomes from environmental policy.

In real life, there are few pure private or pure public goods. A public good may have some private good content: for example, a motorist crossing a bridge in peak-hour traffic affects the supply of bridge-crossings to other motorists by contributing to congestion and delays; in this

Table 5.1 Characteristics of goods

	Excludable	Non-excludable (i.e. externality)
Rival	Case 1 – pure private good	Case 3 – semi-public good
Non-rival (i.e. collectivity)	Case 2 – semi-public good	Case 4 – pure public good

case, the marginal cost of supply is zero for low levels of use, but exceeds zero for higher levels. Similarly, a private good may have some 'publicness': for example, watching a television at home (basically, a private good) has some public good content as neighbours and friends may also be invited to watch.

Externalities (read as non-excludability) and collectivities (read as non-rivalry) in the form of public goods are not mutually-exclusive concepts. An externality can be either rival or non-rival and a collectivity can be either excludable or non-excludable. For example, pollution, which is an externality, is substantially non-rival since the sufferings of A from poor air quality does not diminish B's discomfort. On the other hand, appreciation of someone's flower garden, which is also an externality, might be substantially diminished by the crowding effect of large numbers of sightseers. Similarly, collectivities like libraries or public health vaccination programmes are recognized as non-excludably beneficial to all persons in the community. On the other hand, admission to a library or treatment in a medical centre can be made excludable since individuals can be excluded or charged an entry fee.

Such observations of real-life situations show that there is a whole range of *mixed* goods, with various degrees of excludability and rivalness, whereas pure public and pure private goods are but extremes of these situations.

5.2   The problem of externalities

In Table 5.1 we associate externalities with goods which are non-excludable. An externality may therefore generally exist when a decision variable on buying or selling of one consumer or producer cannot be excluded from entering directly into the utility or production function of some other consumer or producer.

This can be expressed by the expression $U^A = U^A(x_1^A, \ldots x_n^A, y^B)$ where utility U of individual A depends on excludable goods x ranging from 1 to n, consumed by A, as well as some non-excludable activity y carried by individual B. To be of value for economic policy the application of the notion of externality requires further scrutiny. For a thorough but at some points repetitive discussion of externality in the history of economic thought, see Papendreou (1994).

In real life, producers depend upon other producers and upon consumers in their attempts to maximize their profits. Thus their behaviour via the goods they produce and consume can hardly be described as being without side-effects. Consumers depend upon other consumers and producers in the attempt to maximize their utilities and so their behaviour generates side-effects and involves interdependence. A great deal of economic interdependencies are incorporated in the exchange economy and these result in the market prices and resource allocations which are observed. To the extent that these market prices are assumed to be Pareto-optimal there should not be a policy concern here. The policy concern of externalities relates to economic interdependencies which are not incorporated, or so to speak, not effectively internalized in the exchange economy. So, which side-effects should fall under externalities? These are side-effects which are: (a) conventionally recognized as economically relevant, and (b) not internalized and remain uncompensated. Externalities are, therefore, those conventionally recognized gains and losses which are sustained by others as a result of actions initiated by producers or consumers, or both, and for which no internalization takes place as yet. It must be noted that interdependence alone is not sufficient to constitute an externality. In the above equation, y^B must be conventionally recognized as economically relevant for U^A and also be shown that there has been, as yet, a failure to internalize it in the decision-making process via payments or otherwise on account of any gains or losses.

The notions of recognition and internalization are closely related. Recognition means that the inter-property rights of parties involved in a side-effect are made explicit. Once made explicit, internalization mechanisms will develop which can be applied later. Internalization takes several forms: (a) unification or merger of the parties involved, (b) private contracting, (c) creation of new markets in which the property rights are exchanged, and (d) state intervention intended to correct the privately-determined market prices to their social values. These are discussed below.

A competitive-equilibrium allocation is not Pareto-optimal as long as the one agent does not take the economic externality caused to other agents into account in his decision making. The competitive-equilibrium solution to the resource allocation problem will not be Pareto-optimal due to the fact that the production of good i has a direct side-effect on the technology set for the production of good j (e.g., pollution of the environment). This side-effect can be viewed as a commodity for which there is no market. Under conditions of low transaction costs an agreement could be reached by the two producers of i and j so that they maximize profits while taking into account the economic externality. As a result a Pareto-optimal production allocation could be achieved. For example, with only two producers and an easily-identifiable externality, an incentive exists for unification: a merger and joint-profit maximization.

Private contracting, covenants and arrangements whereby each producer pays for the externality rendered by other producers is another internalization mechanism. If the pro-

ducers can organize themselves for this purpose and if the externalities are priced correctly, the production decisions would satisfy the marginal conditions for a Pareto-optimal allocation.

An alternative solution is to find an institutional mechanism that decentralizes the production allocation. The producer of a positive (negative) externality cannot exclude consumers or other producers from benefiting (losing); consequently, it is impossible for him to sell (buy) the positive (negative) externality and the appropriate market fails to come into being. This scenario suggests another way of characterizing externalities; namely, as the lack of a 'property right', which in turn explains the non-existence of a market that is needed for Pareto-optimality. Suppose that a market for the externality is created. This might happen because the producer is given property rights over the environment. Alternatively, the producer of i might be geared to a mechanism for paying the producer of j to restrict his polluting production process (thus repairing the damaged environment). The emergence of a market results in the establishment of a market price for the externality. Markets that are established by the conferral of property rights are sometimes referred to as 'artificial' markets.

A final solution lies in state intervention. One remedy, first suggested by Pigou (1924), is the use of externality taxes and subsidies by the government. This remedy avoids problems of too high transaction costs that may prevent unitization covenants or artificial markets from correctly pricing an externality commodity. The government taxes beneficiaries of positive externalities or generators of negative externalities and subsidizes generators of positive externalities or victims of negative externalities. The government may transfer the tax revenues to the externality victims – also referred to as the parties with externality rights – in accordance with the marginal losses attributable to the externality. Such transfers are not, however, required to achieve a Pareto-optimal allocation. Given full convexity and many buyers and sellers, the establishment of either artificial markets or taxation schemes generates the identical allocation of resources.

However, there are difficulties which indicate that whatever allocation is reached, this may not be a Pareto-optimal allocation. First, either solution requires a clear definition of which economic agents have the rights to the externality. The optimality of the resulting allocation is not affected by whether the rights are given to the economic agent responsible for the externality or to the economic agent affected by the externality. On the other hand, the endowment of the rights to the externality obviously affects the resulting distribution of income and disagreement on the resulting distribution may hold up the creation of an exchange. Second, it is not sufficient merely to subsidize (tax) the economic agent affected by the external diseconomy (economy) without taxing (subsidizing) the agent responsible for the external diseconomy (economy). Pareto-optimality requires that the agent responsible for the externality takes this into account in his decision making. Third, the above discussion assumes that the consumer or producer with the property rights correctly informs the government of his marginal loss, rather than overstating it. This problem is discussed in more detail in the next chapter in the form of consumers attempting to get a 'free ride' for public goods. That is, consumers might attempt to conceal their true preferences for a public good if they believe that they can thereby reduce their share of the cost of producing the good. Fourth, in the presence of non-convexities in the production (or consumption) of externalities, which can be very common, a taxation scheme, like artificial markets, is not necessarily a remedy for the externality.

It is possible that for some reason an economically legitimate side-effect is not recognized. This is in opposition to the view held by some economists that the collective decision to recognize a side-effect is fully consistent with a collective economic rationality. The reasons can be many: imperfect information; higher incomes over time and place may lead to higher valuations of well-being and recognition of such negative side-effects as environmental pollution; transaction costs that go with the recognition of a side-effect can be too high for the time and place. Besides which, since recognition requires a specification of the property rights of the transacting parties, and such a specification has as a consequence a redistribution of property and income, it can happen that the group which is to be disadvantaged may not permit recognition if this group has a sufficient coercive power. Take, for example, air and water pollution which were a common-day experience already from the early days of industrialization, but the externalities involved were not recognized as such until much later. With rising incomes attention goes to higher needs which increasingly take the form of merit goods. The delay in the recognition can be also reasoned in terms of imperfect information, very high transaction costs or obstacles due to a powerful position of the losers *vis-à-vis* a weak position of the gainers.

The above discussion is schematically set in the sketch below of Table 5.2, showing where a side-effect would call for an economic policy.

Two additional comments need to be made. First, an externality was defined as a side-effect, either good or bad, that results whenever a person or firm making a decision does not consider social costs or social benefits of the particular decision, and, as a consequence, directly affects the utility or profits of other consumers or producers. Note that the 'activities of decision makers' is not only intended to

Table 5.2 Scheme for the identification of externalities

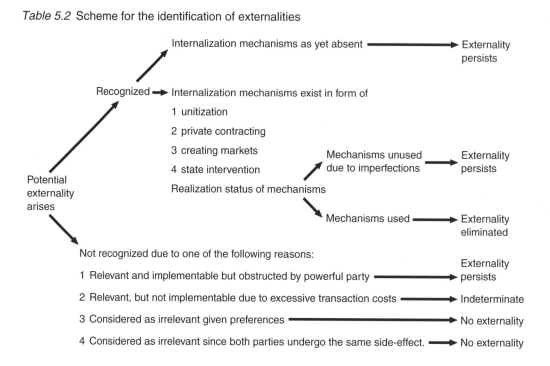

mean the actually-materialized activities but also potential activities which are not executed because of the involved externality effects.

Second, externalities can be positive or negative. A common example is air or water pollution; this is an output of one producer that enters into the utility or production functions of other consumers or producers. This example is a *negative externality* since the consumption of pollution reduces the utilities or profits of consumers or producers, respectively. An example of a *positive externality* is the often-cited case of bees and nectar. Bees raised by a producer of honey pollinate the trees of nearby producers of fruit. In this way, the profits of fruit producers are directly related to the number of bees kept by the honey producer. Similarly, a display of a flower garden in a shopping centre is a positive externality to shopping consumers who pass by. Examples of relevance for economic policy are the development of the railway system and seaports which allows industry and commerce to

flourish, or the setting up of an iron and steel industry which allows the exploitation of many forward and backward linkages.

This chapter will deal consecutively with industrial policy as an example of positive externalities, and environmental policy as a response to negative externalities.

5.3 Positive externalities: some principles

Some significant examples of positive externalities may be given. In connecting the factory site to an emerging seaport with significant export perspective, the operating firm X will appraise the building of a road connection based on its own benefits and costs. Other firms Y located along the road can be expected to use it and have a better chance to export and grow. The social benefits of the extended road system is thus the sum of advantages to X and Y, and this is much more than the willingness of X or any individual firm to pay for the additional road mileage. An action plan by all benefiting firms to contribute to the construction costs of the road system will internalize the external effects and assure that the road extension is carried out. Another example is of the firm which protects its own employees from contracting an infectious disease and considers to offer to inoculate other inhabitants in town as well at no cost. There is here again a positive externality which is not paid for. If the inhabitants would be ready to pay a very small cost, the firm, or the municipality, can become more enthusiastic to carry out the inoculation. Or, if more education reduces costs of skilled workers and makes people less prone to engage in criminal activities, then the market price of education should reflect these positive social effects, but as it does not there is a tendency for underspending in education. Similarly, if individual *A* spends time creating a beautiful garden, *A* gets to enjoy it, but others benefit indirectly from those who pay for the goods as well. In each of these examples those who do not pay for the good receive an *external benefit* at no extra cost, and this may discourage the payers from producing the good.

A positive externality is thus a side-effect that exists whenever the social benefits associated with a particular decision are not fully considered by the person or firm making the decision. In Figure 5.1, the demand curve, D_0, summarizes the market participants' individual willingness to pay for road extensions, that is, the private marginal benefit (MB_p) obtained from road extension. (It is the horizontal sum of each individual's willingness to pay for additional roads.) However, D_1 summarizes the *social* marginal benefit of roads (MB_s), including the benefit to others when other firms are connected to the road. In Figure 5.1, the social marginal benefit of the road extension (MB_s) is greater than the private benefit (MB_p). That is,

the social marginal benefit is equal to the private benefit plus the external benefit provided to others:

$$MB_s = MB_p + \text{marginal external benefit}$$

In the presence of the externality, the market equilibrium is Q_0 and P_0. If consumers of roads, inoculations, education or garden watching were compensated for the utility they rendered to other producers and consumers, however, the market equilibrium would be Q_1 and P_1. The market price would be higher and more of these goods and services would be both produced and consumed. The situation can be analysed in terms of its efficiency and equity effects.

Efficiency effect

At the market equilibrium in Figure 5.1, the market price, P_0, is less than the social value of the commodity, which can be measured by [MB_s at Q_e]. That is, the marginal cost of producing additional commodities is less than the marginal social value that those commodities provide. The market outcome is inefficient: the market price is too low, too few scarce

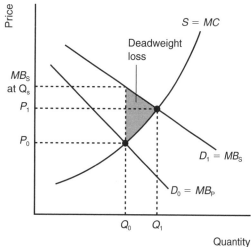

Figure 5.1

resources are being devoted to this activity and too little is being produced, compare quantities Q_0 and Q_1. This inefficiency has a deadweight loss of the size indicated in the figure.

If the use, consumption or enjoyment of a commodity creates benefits for those who do not purchase it, the marginal social benefit of additional use (MB_s) is greater than the marginal private benefit (MB_p) that those who pay for the commodity receive. The market equilibrium is at (Q_0, P_0), but the social optimum is at (Q_1, P_1).

If the value of the positive externality can be determined accurately, then a subsidy equal to this amount to the purchasers of the commodity whose consumption created the externality will increase both the consumption and production of the activity, and move the economy toward a more efficient use of resources and avoiding the deadweight loss. Governments pursuing individual policy can provide energy use to industrial firms at a subsidized rate, thus lowering the cost of production for industry and, therefore, increasing the number of investing and expanding firms and a realization of the external effects to the benefit of other users of the output. In the case of a positive consumption externality, the subsidy equivalent to the difference between MB_p and MB_s could be provided to the consuming firms as an incentive to increase their activities. Alternatively the producers can be subsidized, shifting the supply curve to the right, and leading to the similar effect of a higher quantity.

Equity effect

This cannot be fully traced in Figure 5.1 because the transfer between producers and consumers is not as relevant in this context. The transfer effect would have to be analysed with the following two states and two parties in mind. The two states are the current state in which too little is produced and a prospective state in which Q is increased to its social optimum. The two parties are consumers and producers alike of the commodity who pay for it, and consumers and producers alike who do not pay, but could become payers in a prospective state. Note that if the positive externalities are exclusive, there will always be some non-payers who benefit.

5.4 Positive externalities: some examples from industrial policy

5.4.1 Introduction

Commonly, industrial policy would refer to government actions which aim at growth and change either via a general shift of productivity or enhanced activity across the board, or via a reallocation of means in the economy in such a way that current and new activities with better perspectives (high rates of social benefits to social costs) get higher weights at the cost of other activities which are less attractive (low rates of social benefits to social costs). The first channel is often called the neutral approach, the second channel is the targeted approach.

The neutral approach to industrial policy in the sense of a stimulation across the board takes the form of generic instruments such as standardization, provision of information, investment in science, technology, human and physical infrastructure, and the setting up of financial institutions, and judiciary systems.

The targeted approach to industrial policy in the sense of consciously influencing reallocation of production among activities makes use of four broad policy areas:

(a) exploitation of positive economies of scale and/or economies of scope;
(b) strategic trade and investment policy in relation to sunrise industries;

(c) economic restructuring in response to sunset industries and regional development; and

(d) encouragement of business clusters of linked technologies, industries and firms.

This list is not exhaustive as other chapters have touched upon other related areas of industrial policy.

While economists do not disagree on the state's role as regards the neutral approach, targeted industrial policies are considered to be controversial as they interfere with the market forces. This deployment requires careful handling to assure that the expected welfare gains are realized.

5.4.2   Exploitation of economies of scale and economies of scope

The literature on economic development was first to recognize that economies of scale were a limiting factor on the ability to establish profitable industries in developing countries. Economists working on development advocated the 'Big Push' model in which co-ordinated investment to exploit economies of scale at the plant level and an elastic supply of factors of production interact to yield pecuniary external economies of scope, and generate growth forces with real welfare significance. The argument for co-ordinated investment is well established and is due to Rosenstein-Rodan (1943). Imagine a country in which 20 000 unemployed workers are put into a *large* new shoe factory. They produce and they receive wages substantially higher than their previous income in natura, and consequently enhance purchasing power. This investment is likely to be unprofitable in isolation but profitable if *accompanied* by similar investments, production and income in many other industries. Several conditions need to be present: first, that there are

economies of scale, that the factory must be established at such a large scale; second that industries feed each other back because they are accompanying each other; third that the required workers can be drawn elastically from among the unemployed or other poorly-paid activities; fourth that industry policy should not be directed to the supply side of the economy only, but should also be demand oriented to assure enhancement of purchasing power.

If industry policy leads to a greater supply (the supply curve shifts to the right) and to a greater demand (the demand curve also shifts to the right), the ultimate effect is a larger traded quantity and a lower price, and a higher level of economic welfare, as shown in Figure 5.2.

This section will elaborate further on economies of scale, discuss economies of scope, and reflect once again on the interaction between the two types of economy.

The conditions for *economies of scale* were discussed in section 3.1.2, Chapter 3. Suppose that these conditions exist. An industrial policy which governments can pursue in this context is encouraging more enterprises to combine together to generate the potential increasing returns to scale. To be successful it will be necessary, on the supply side, to establish that

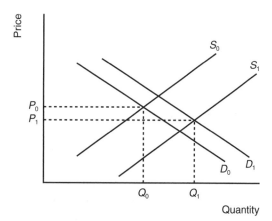

Figure 5.2

the enterprises have sufficient knowledge, financial means for investment, that their scale is large enough to specialize, and that the dimensional factor is relevant. On the demand side it is necessary to establish that the potential demand is sufficiently high. If neither is the case, co-operation constructions like horizontal integration and network relations are perhaps necessary in order to realize this larger scale. Because such constructions tend to limit competition, the industrial policy needs to be well balanced.

As for measures on the supply side, governments sometimes act to reduce indirectly the cost of production. High fixed costs, which are necessary in the case of entry in a modern sector with scale advantages are often an impediment, especially in high-risk activities where the fixed costs may ultimately turn into *sunk costs*. Fixed costs can be reduced via public investment in infrastructure or granting subsidies. Lower wage tax is another instrument.

As for measures on the demand side, without potential demand for the specific industry it is of course pointless for governments to engage in industrial policy. In this respect governments sometimes take action to stimulate demand for the created production capacity along the following fronts:

1 stimulation of forward and backward linkages so as to shift demand upwards by supporting economic activity in complementary sectors;
2 promoting marketing activities of the firms concerned;
3 directing government consumption towards the created production capacity;
4 redistributing income to stimulate private demand and stimulating export in order to sell the additionally created supply at the international market.

The idea of *economies of scope* is based on the existence of one input factor which an enterprise possesses and which is a necessary ingredient for the production of one of its outputs, but can also be used, without affecting the production costs of the 'first' output, for the production of one or more other outputs. This input factor is characterized by its *chainable* nature and therefore has a complementary influence.

Economies of scope can be achieved by means of clustering. Clusters are combinations of enterprises which co-operate with the aim to realize, among others, cost savings, common product standards and synergy effects.

The advantage of clustering is the stimulation of *forward* and *backward linkages*. This results in other so far not profitable parts of the industry being drawn across the 'profit threshold'. Through the newly arisen linkages it is possible to operate on a larger scale, which facilitates specialization. As a consequence the dependence on foreign competitors decreases.

Industry policy can be aimed at bringing these linkages into being, strengthening existing ones and exploiting them to generate positive externalities. Policy should stimulate the right linkages in order to realize economies of scope. Input–output analysis is helpful in identifying the right linkages, as well as an analysis of (future) competitors, especially when the benefits exceed the costs.

Here again the supply side is stimulated, and as noted above when discussing economies of scale, the demand side should also be considered. However, demand develops partly autonomously because linkages join developers and users. If the government still observes a *demand gap*, it can still try to create them in the same way as in the case of economies of scale.

Economies of scale and scope *can* interact with each other. There is an interesting complication with important consequences for industrial policy. Examine the following definitions of backward and forward linkages. An industry creates a backward linkage when its demand enables an upstream industry to be established at minimum economic scale. The strength of an industry's backward linkages is to be measured by the probability that it will push other industries over the threshold.

Forward linkages can also involve an interaction between scale and market size; in this case the definitions should include the ability of an industry to reduce the costs of potential downstream users of its products and thus, again, push them over the threshold of profitability.

The policy problem when economies of scope are considered as a separable policy area from economies of scale, is different from the policy problem when both economies of scope and scale are viewed simultaneously.

Viewing linkages, per se, emphasizes intermediate goods rather than final demand as the motor for industrial development, and hence industrial policy could better focus on a few strategic industries rather than seek an economy-wide 'Big Push'. Furthermore, approaching the problem this way would suggest that appropriate key industries can be identified by analysing linkages in input–output tables. Investment in the key industries is then advisable.

The other view considers economies of scale and scope together. Figure 5.3, adapted from

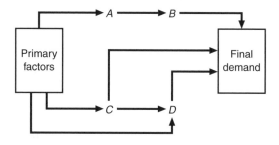

Figure 5.3

Krugman (1992), sketches an input–output structure to demonstrate this interdependence in the policy problem. Imagine that there are four industries – *A*, *B*, *C*, and *D*. *A* is a pure intermediate good industry, and *B* makes no direct use of factors of production. By contrast, *C* sells part of its output directly to final demand while *D* uses primary inputs as well as inputs from *C*. Any classification using the input–output table will suggest that *A* has stronger forward linkages than *C*, and that *B* has stronger backward linkages than *D*. But what if *A* and *B* are characterized by constant returns, while *C* and *D* are characterized by economies of scale? Then it could easily be that there is a co-ordination problem for *C* and *D* – that neither industry will emerge unless assured of sufficient scale of the other – without any corresponding problem for *A* and *B*.

In other words, lots of entries in the input–output table tell the analyst little about which industries might actually play a catalytic role for the economy. According to this view, it seems best to regard linkages as strategic complementarities that arise when individual goods are produced subject to economies of scale.

5.4.3 Strategic trade and investment policy and the sunrise industries

One concern of industrial policy is with the rise of industries and the firms within them. *Sunrise* industries are the emerging new industries of the future. Sunrise industries are identifiable for each country separately. What is good for one country can be bad for another.

Four types of market failure are usually put forward to justify the case for a sunrise industrial policy, or what is sometimes called strategic trade and investment policy (STIP). First, banks may be too risk-averse, or too unfamiliar with the new business, to lend the money needed through the early loss-making years.

Second, the market may be slow to provide the relevant training and skills; for until the industry exists, people cannot perceive the need for developing such skills, but without the skills, the industry cannot exist. Third, there may be important positive externalities when similar producers locate in the same place. Fourth, rent-seeking incumbent firms may obstruct entry in a sunrise industry by erecting strategic entry barriers to preserve and enhance their market power.

If markets get it wrong, and do not create sunrise industries, can the government do better? It is too far-stretched to assume that politicians can do better than trained businessmen in industry and finance. Rather, if such industrial policy is to be attempted, it seems preferable to diagnose the cause of the market failure and provide a generalized incentive which market decision makers then take into account, when undertaking their professional analysis. The situation can be different in a developing country where a generalized incentive is wasted because of a 'thin' structure. In this case, concentrated support to chosen sectors can be more relevant.

Governments are eager to support a protective policy of sunrise industries during their infancy phase. The government can offer protection to infant or young industries with good future perspectives, which however lack the necessary means to continue their existence without government support. Here, protection means that enterprises are protected by the government against (potential) competitors. Protection can also counterbalance possible monopolies outside the industry concerned. The government can realize this protection: by means of tariffs and regulations (import restrictions and prohibitions). It is important to introduce and stop protection at the right time. If, for instance, the case of the infant industry is considered, the timing of stopping government

protection is crucial. In guiding government in its decision on when to stop protection, several analytical studies can be conducted, such as revenue analysis, cost analysis and market shares.

Market failures favouring state intervention apply in international competition between large firms across countries and over time, as is demonstrated from the airline industry in the early 1990s. The incumbent American aeroplane manufacturers Boeing and McDonnell-Douglas dominated the world market. The European entrant, Airbus Industrie, who was at the time a relatively recent entrant still building up its product range, is a case in point. The governments behind the Airbus (France, Germany, Spain and the UK) pursued STIP. They engaged in launch aid to help with R&D, and placed long-term orders for the Airbus. The Europeans were uncertain that McDonnell-Douglas would stay in, and provide effective competition to Boeing, hence the commitment to launch Airbus, encourage competition and allow travellers getting the benefit of cheaper planes; for otherwise, they risked buying American planes in the future at highly set non-competitive prices. They were right in their uncertainty for the two American companies integrated later into one company. The pre-commitment was also meant to warn the American incumbents that European governments will not allow Airbus to be bullied out of the industry by a price war or customer monopoly. This has worked out as well. At the end of the decade, the American incumbent and the European entrant have now roughly equal shares of world orders for bigger aeroplanes. Positive external effects of having an airline industry supported the joint venture as well, and such benefits are now being realized. The quantitative significance of these benefits to the EU countries and to the US at large have been modelled in a three-actor model over three decades by Neven and Seabright (1995). Their results show that the STIP pursued by the EU countries brought gains to the EU producers at the cost of the US producers. This was accompanied by cheaper planes but not to the extent expected because the advantage of economies of scale had to be shared by producers in EU and US. If the world demand for large planes was higher, the cost advantage would have been more.

Policy example 5.1

Airbus assessment

The launching of the Airbus by four European governments, its subsequent sharing of the market for large passenger aircrafts with American incumbents, and the changing structure of the industry and prices have been simulated by Neven and Seabright (1995). This box will review the main features of their model, analysis and results which together serve as a useful and effective method for assessing the impact of industrial policy and adding insight as regards policy making.

The model describes a stylized history of the market for large civil airliners since the 1960s, dominated for the large part by Boeing until Airbus was launched in the 1970s. They have now roughly equal shares. The authors divided the history into six periods named *A, B, C, D, E* and *F*; which correspond roughly with the introduction of different aircraft categories/eras and decisions based thereupon. They distinguished between four aircraft types, index *i*. The model contains three producers, index *j*, these are Airbus (AB), Boeing (BA) and McDonald Douglas (MD).

Basically, the model consists of five equations. Equation 5.1 states that the price of aircraft *i* offered by producer *j*, P_{ij}, is equal to the annual cost of the aircraft to the operating airline K_{ij}, this being appropriately depreciated by depreciation rate δ and discounted using real interest rate ρ.

(5.1) $P_{ij} = K_{ij}/(\rho + \delta)$

Equation 5.2 makes K_{ij} dependent on three terms: first, operational costs of aircraft *i*; second, the output of aircraft *i*, and third, the outputs of related aircrafts which are chain linked. The central variable here is output, i.e. the number of airplanes Q_i.

(5.2) $K_{ij} = \alpha_{ij} + \beta_i Q_i + \gamma_i(Q_{i+1} + Q_{i-1})$

Equation 5.3 defines in turn Q_i as the sum of outputs of *i* over the three producers *j*.

(5.3) $Q_i = Q_{i1} + Q_{i2} + Q_{i3}$

Equation 5.4 treats the cost of manufacturing all aircrafts by producer *j*, M_j, as a function of learning effects λ, chain-linked scope effects σ, fixed costs ζ_{ij}, vintage-specific costs ν_{ij}, output Q_{ij} for each *i*, and accumulated output Q_{ij}^* for each *i*, so as to capture learning effects. The equation is specified here in a general form.

(5.4) $M_j = \text{function } (\lambda, \sigma, \zeta_{ij}, \nu_{ij}, Q_{ij}, Q_{ij}^*)$

The fifth equation defines profit of the firm R_j.

(5.5) $R_j = P_{ij}Q_{ij} - M_j$

In this model the variables R_j, M_j, P_{ij}, K_{ij} and Q_{ij} are as yet unknown while Q_{ij}^* is a predetermined lagged variable. All other parameters are given and were estimated from various sources. Substituting Equations 5.1 to 5.4 in 5.5 gives an equation of profit R_j in terms of Q_{ij} and data. This is an equation set for $j = 1, 2, 3$. Differentiating this equation set and making the outcome equal to zero yields a system of simultaneous equations in the three variables Q_{j1}, Q_{j2}, Q_{j3} and data.

The first objective of the authors is to calibrate in a basic run what happened in the past with regard to prices and outputs of the four aircraft categories, i, and the distribution of this output on the producers, j. They do this by solving backwards. For example, the authors solve first for period F (late 1990s) which relates to decisions on aircraft type $i = 4$ (replacement of Boeing 747 and equivalents), making use of historically given data on the other aircraft types. And similarly for period E (late 1980s) which relates to decisions on aircraft type $i = 3$, they use given data from previous periods together with the (rationally anticipated) equilibrium solution for $i = 4$ in period F. And so on, as a result, a basic run calibration is obtained by combining backward data with forward equilibrium output solutions conceived as rationally expected.

The second objective of the authors is to run counterfactual simulations on the basic run with the purpose of examining the effect of European industrial policy as regards the Airbus on the structure of the world airline industry, competition and prices. In the table below, the base run, which included the three producers for most periods, is compared with alternative scenarios: $j = BA$, $j = BA \& MD$, $j = BA \& AB$.

Table 5.3 Simulation results for major producers of large airlines

period/type	P_i $m				Q_i planes			
	base run	BA	BA, MD	BA, AB	base run	BA	BA, MD	BA, AB
A 1960s SRNB	33	35	32	36	3627	3540	3806	3265
B 1960s LRWB	127	138	127	138	1296	1161	1308	1152
C 1970s MRMB	66	74	69	65	2841	2586	2709	2947
D 1980s SRNB	29	40	32	32	6021	4499	5675	5594
E 1980s LRMB	102	114	113	106	1236	1101	1086	1189
F 1990s LRWB	125	143	126	125	1507	1280	1507	1512

Source: adapted from Neven and Seabright (1995). Abbreviations: SR, MR, LR for short, medium and long range. NB, MB, WB for narrow, medium and wide body, respectively.

As can be seen from the table, prices P_i are generally lower in the presence of Airbus as a competitor (base run) than in its absence. The output of planes Q_i is also higher in the base run showing that with less competitors the output is restricted. The results indicate that MD played a less significant role in implementing results in the latter years. Note in this connection that, in 1998/99, MD was taken over by Boeing.

5.4.4   Restricted competition in lagging industries and region

Contrary to the sunrise industries, sunset industries present a different policy problem. These are the industries in long-term decline. Usually, a sharp shock in the declining sector signals the extent of the structural adjustment required to bring the sector back to solvency. Governments differ in their response. Some governments consider the unemployment effect of closing businesses and act counter to international competitive tendencies. There are, of course, successful examples of industrial policy that sought and implemented long-term efficient rationalization of a sunset industry.

Closely related to the policy problem of the sunset industries is that of economically less-developed regions. Large population centres with their differentiated economic activity make it possible for labour laid-off by one firm or industry to be absorbed by the expansion of other firms; hence, an efficient utilization of resources is allowed for more or less continuously. There are contexts in which free competition and efficient allocations are not feasible and where the government does not have sufficient power to alter such contexts. For example, small and economically backward areas may have only a limited number of employers, a limited absorption of the local labour, and creation of employment opportunities is given top priority by the local government. This may easily develop into a situation where firms more or less count on protection, and become sheltered from the effects of outside competition.

The same holds when an individual country, particularly if it is small, is unable to intervene into the affairs of a giant multinational company, for such a policy might have far-reaching implications both in terms of employment opportunities and the inflow of foreign exchange.

5.4.5   Business clusters

In their study of key industries general economists focused on economies of scale and scope. The identification and support of key industries has been approached by business economists in a different way, in what is referred to as business clusters of linked technologies, industries and enterprises.

Six success factors at the firm level have been distinguished in the literature (cf. Guerrieri and Tylote 1993 and Nooteboom 1993):

(a) internal co-ordination, namely InterFunctional Co-ordination with Production and R&D (IFCPR);
(b) interfunctional co-ordination with marketing (IFCM);
(c) vertical interaction across hierarchical borders (VIHB);
(d) external interaction (EI) with suppliers, customers and other relevant enterprises;
(e) knowledge infrastructure (KI): that is, suitable expertise in research and education;
(f) patience money (PM): that is, money for risk-bearing long-term investments, with a distinction between visible (fixed assets, R&D) and invisible investment (curing child diseases of innovations, training, marketing and market research, distribution and service).

If for specific industries an indication can be made of the relative significance of each of these success factors, and if for a specific country and its business culture it is possible to indicate the presence or absence of these success indicators, then a picture can be drawn for that country of the business clusters in which it is likely to be most and least successful, see policy example below.

Identification of clusters is one thing, design and implementation of a support package is another matter. Which links should be created between which industries and firms, and how should this be done? The conditions pose a paradox: on the one hand there should be intensive rivalry, on the other hand good co-operation. This is not necessarily contradictory, but how can it be organized, and what should be the task of the government here? It can be directly seen how this aspect of industry policy overlaps with and reinforces Chapter 3 on monopoly, competition and technology policies.

In the first place, there should be a technology policy and an industry policy in which technology areas, and, related to this, families of production sectors in mutual interdependence, are key notions. Attention should be focused on relations of critical demand and high-level supply, and of mutual strengthening and support.

Second, support of individual firms is desirable only if key linkages are concerned in a constellation of technology and sectors. This often concerns medium-size, not large companies. If the government offers support in order to strengthen the potential for the future, it should be possible to convince banks and possibly even future buyers of the goods and services of financing such activities.

Apart from this exceptional direct support of individual firms the broader tasks of the government in promoting business clusters are as follows:

- contributing to the financing of R&D in key technologies in selected technology/sector constellations;
- strengthening of vocational and higher education in these areas;
- clearing institutional obstacles for innovation, especially in institutions and enterprises owned by or related to the government itself;
- clearing stalemate situations regarding the co-operation of market parties, especially in the field of standards and other factors with external effects of scale or scope;
- evaluation of cartels on the basis of pragmatic considerations, not of ideology: getting rid of undesirable cartel-like constructions which hamper the dynamism of development and competition but allowing those with a social function. It should be noted that one cannot say in general whether cartels are good or bad. They can be justified as ways to avoid prisoner's dilemmas, but can also just protect vested interests.

Policy example 5.2

Business clusters

Guerrieri and Tylote (1993) have developed a matrix which gives, per selected industry, an indication of whether or not the six success factors mentioned in section 5.4.5 are of special importance (Matrix A). This is a first step in identifying business clusters at country level.

In a second step, countries can be evaluated on the success factors as well, as Guerrieri and Tylote did in Matrix B. In such an evaluation, due consideration needs to be given to the following limitations. IFCPR and IFCM are often negatively correlated: technically-oriented managers often spurn marketing, and vice versa, financial/commercially-oriented managers shun technique. VI can be approximated by power distance. The KI-score should not only depend on the level of research and education, but also the connection between education disciplines and the needs of the business community.

The score for PM is generally higher in countries where financing is provided to a large

Table 5.4 Matrix A Cross-section between success factors and industries

	Mech./ electr.	Electronics		Food	Chemicals		Instruments
		hardware	software		bulk	spec.	
Interfunctional co-ordination with production and R&D (IFC1)	X	X		X	X		X
Interfunctional co-ordination with marketing (IFC2)		X	X	X		X	
Vertical integration (VI)	X	X				X	X
External interaction (EI)	X	X	X			X	X
Knowledge infrastructure (KI)		X			X	X	X
Patience money (PM)	X	X	X			X	X

Table 5.5 Matrix B Cross-section between success factors and countries

	Netherlands	UK	Germany	Switzerland	USA	Japan
Interfunctional co-ordination with production and R&D (IFC1)	+	−	+	+	0	+
Interfunctional co-ordination with marketing (IFC2)	0	+	−	?	+	+
Vertical interaction (VI)	+	0	0	0	−	+
External interaction (EI)	0	−	+	+	0	+
Knowledge infrastructure (KI)	+	0/+	+	+	0/+	+
Patience money (PM)	0	−	+	+	+	+

Table 5.6 Matrix C Outcome for the Netherlands

	Mech./ electr.	Electronics		Food	Chemicals		Instruments
		hardware	software		bulk	spec.	
Interfunctional co-ordination with production and R&D (IFC1)	+	+		+	+		+
Interfunctional co-ordination with marketing (IFC2)		0	0	+		0	
Vertical integration (VI)	+	+				+	+
External interaction (EI)	0	0	0			0	0
Knowledge infrastructure (KI)		+			+	+	+
Patience money (PM)	0	0	0			0	0

extent by banks, private capital, cross-wise participation and reinvestment of profits than in countries where capital is attracted primarily via anonymous share markets. In general, the latter are more focused at utilizing the present short-run profit potential of an enterprise than the creation of future potential.

In principle, for any one country these factors are determined by history, culture and the structure of society, and therefore cannot be easily changed. Yet knowledge infrastructure (KI) can be influenced by tuning the size and direction of vocational and higher education and research to sectors which are of national importance. The co-ordination with R&D and marketing can, in the longer run, be influenced by integrating both technical and commercial strategical and organizational aspects in one course of education.

A third step has been derived by Nooteboom (1993). By combining the results of Matrices A and B, a third Matrix, C, is obtained displaying the scores on the six success factors for national industries in specific countries. Large deviations from the present industrial structure would, of course, be highly uncomfortable, but deviations are likely to be more marginal. In sectors which are dominated by one or only a few enterprises, sector-wise rankings can be replaced by evaluations of the concerned individual firms. Matrix C is an example of the outcome for the Netherlands. It is feasible to verify the validity of this outcome by examining the past performance of corporates belonging to the respective clusters.

5.4.6 Assessment of industrial policy effects

In general, two approaches to industrial policy were identified, namely the neutral approach which stimulates activity across the board and a targeted approach towards specific sectors. In this section the empirical evidence on the success and failure of industrial policy will be reviewed. We will especially focus on the United States, the United Kingdom, West Germany, Eastern Europe and Japan.

Although the United States is known to avoid industrial policy, technology policy in the USA is active and has not been neutral. The approach adopted by the US government can be described as a 'mission-oriented' approach to promoting industrial technological change in the post-war period (cf. Ergas 1986). The goal is to achieve a technological breakthrough in specific areas, so that entirely new industries using this technology come into being. The mission-oriented approach is associated with activities that carry a high cost for the first mover, compared to the relatively low cost of diffusion (copying) once the innovation has been made. This approach has led to the creation of prestigious projects with disproportionally high costs, especially in the area of the military and aerospace. Civilian applications of related innovations came much later and in a limited extent. Another example with a mixed performance is the development of the semiconductor industry (cf. Audretsch 1993). In the beginning of the 1960s, the contracts for integrated circuits came from the government. By the end of the decade, as the technology spilled over, the computer industry replaced the government as the major buyer of semiconductors. The government has not been able to capture the rents accruing from the investments made, and is no longer in a position to influence the future direction of technological research in this area.

Industrial policy in Western Europe is mixed. British industrial policy is based on a liberal philosophy, that industrial performance is best left to the private sector, assisted only at the margin by state activity. As a result, the British industrial policy fits best into the neutral approach. It is difficult to assess the performance of British industrial policy, since one needs to know how the economy would have fared otherwise and no material of this kind is present.

Germany has applied both approaches to industrial policy. Declining industries were targeted for support, either to maintain the current level of output, or to adjust to new conditions in the industry. Examples are agriculture, the railroad sector and housing. On the other hand, the most successful sectors (in terms of export performance), like the moderate technological intensive industries, have in general not received governmental support. The success of these sectors is mainly due to the neutral industrial policy of investment in industrial infrastructure and workforce. So, the success of Germany does not reflect targeting policies but rather the policies of investing in a skilled workforce and infrastructure, which can be considered as an indirect form of industrial policy, leaning more towards a neutral approach.

The industrial policy of Eastern Europe can be seen as another example of a heavily-targeted policy that failed. Eastern Europe's industrial policy is characterized by state ownership of economic assets, centralization of these assets and a planning system to allocate their use. Furthermore, large-scale production (mass production) was regarded as the only efficient way of production. This focus on large-scale production has led to a high concentration of industries, which has shaped the comparative advantage in Eastern Europe in the past. Eastern Europe's industrial policy can be regarded as a targeted approach towards industries where large-scale production and concentration are important. However, the policy has not been useful for promoting international competitiveness in high-technology and information-intensive markets, where entry and exit are very conducive to innovative behaviour.

Japan has mostly used the sectoral approach to industrial policy. In the mid-1950s industrial policies focused on the heavy and chemical industries, whereas in the early 1970s the attention shifted to knowledge-intensive industries.

In the 1980s under pressure from the USA and the EU, MITI (the Ministry of International Trade and Industry) took industrial policy measures to prevent trade conflicts with foreign governments. Recently the focus is on deregulation and restructuring of areas that are criticized by foreign governments as being protected. At the same time, throughout the years the Japanese government has given assistance to small and medium-size enterprises (SMEs).

Economists are divided over whether Japanese industrial policies have been successful or not, but most argue that the Japanese targeted approach has made no contribution to the Japanese growth. This is demonstrated by Beason and Weinstein (1996) and El Agraa (1997) in a ranking of thirteen Japanese industries by their annual output growth in the period 1974–90 from highest to lowest. The industries were also ranked by significance of industrial promotion measures they received. Four measures were reviewed: (a) subsidies share in sectoral output; (b) share of Japan development loans (JDL) to the sector in total loans to the sector; (c) effective tariff rates of protection for the sector; and (d) tax relief by sector.

The results showed that some of the sectors with low growth rates received relatively high support. For example, the mining sector which had an annual growth of 0.19 per cent ranked highest in subsidies and JDB loans. On the contrary, the highest growth industry like electrical machinery (ranked at 1) did not receive much support from the government industrial promotional measures (ranked at 8). Pooling all sectors together gave negative correlation between sectoral growth and sectoral support. It is also observed that the application of promotion measures across industries has not been very systematic: some sectors received high support in terms of one instrument but low support in terms of the other (e.g. textiles). The conclusion is that high growth industries do not seem to have received as much support as did the low growth industries.

What can be concluded from the national experiences? The evidence on neutral industrial policy shows that it can work out fine. It shows the importance of enhancing factors of production in gaining competitive advantage. Capital, technology and raw material can easily be replaced, which is not true for labour. Thus the quality of labour always seems to be the focus of a successful neutral industrial policy. The targeted approach is functional but only to a certain point, after which the protected sector should be made open to competitive forces. Sectors that have received support have not always been successful, and similarly successful sectors have not been targeted by industrial policy. The case for state support of infant industry, typical of early phases of industrialization in developing countries, is a special one.

Little or no attention is given to analytical or empirical assessments of the equity effects of the various types of industrial policies. Some speculation can be made nevertheless. If the targeted sector is one with a high labour intensity, has a sunset perspective or is located in a depressed or developing region, positive equity effects can be expected. Otherwise, equity effects accompanying other industrial policies may go in all directions.

5.5 Negative externalities: some principles

Negative externality is a side-effect that exists whenever the social costs associated with a particular decision are not fully borne by the person or firm making the decision. Pollution is an example of a negative externality. Land degradation, overgrazing or deforestation, polluted air, acid rain, garbage deposited along roadsides, or blowing in the wind, or toxic wastes leaking into water supplies, all exist because particular consumers and producers do not fully account for the costs associated with their decisions. The costs are *external* to their decisions and the result is a negative externality.

It is important to be precise about the nature of the externality. The negative externality does not arise because producing goods also produces by-products that require disposal – any decision to produce more is virtually always a decision to produce additional by-products. Almost every industrial activity has by-products that cannot be sold but must be disposed of, including garbage, chemicals, dust, gases, tailings, and so forth. Some of these by-products can easily become mixed with the water used in production; others are easily vented into the air above a plant. As a consequence, air and water frequently become convenient disposal places for industrial by-products. The problem occurs because the person making the decision to produce more does not consider the costs *to others* of the by-products as long as they can be easily – which is to say freely – dumped in the air or water. Such costs to others can become recognized as relevant. The affliction of pollution of all sorts was always there but the recognition of a certain type as a cost to others is not universal but differs in place and time. Today it is recognized that garbage, chemicals, dust and gases in the air and water, degrade the environment, and may very well create serious health hazards. As a consequence, air and water pollution impose costs on those who live or travel near industrial plants.

When a side-effect associated with a decision is not fully accounted for by agents making the decision, it will not be reflected in the market price. The price will be 'wrong' and an inefficiency will result. If, because some benefits or some costs are external, willingness to pay for additional output does not reflect the full value or the full costs of additional output are not considered by decision makers, the full effects of private decisions will not be reflected in the market price. Thus, the market will produce the wrong outcome and resources may not be put to their best use.

Figure 5.4 illustrates the market effect of a negative externality. In this figure, it is assumed that, although producing the commodity has an associated negative externality, there are no externalities directly associated with consuming it. That is, the willingness to pay for additional output accurately reflects all the benefits associated with consuming a good. On the other hand, disposing of by-products without paying for their disposal (by dumping them into the water or into the air, for instance) implies that *private* marginal cost (MC_p) – that is, the marginal cost that firms actually incur – is less than *social* marginal cost (MC_s) – that is, the social marginal cost of producing the commodity from society's perspective. The difference, of course, is the cost of the externality that is imposed on someone in society but that the firms do not have to pay. That is,

$$MC_s = MC_p + \text{marginal external cost}$$

A competitive market will produce Q_e when the horizontal sum of the marginal cost curves over all firms is MC_p. If Q_e is supplied to the market, the equilibrium price will be P_e. By contrast, if firms actually paid the true social cost to dispose of their by-products, the horizontal sum of the marginal costs over all firms would be MC_s, and the market would have an equilibrium output of Q_e and an equilibrium price of P_h. The market price would be higher, and less would be both produced and consumed. Notice that the externality is caused by what appears to be a free method for firms to dispose of by-products. Society essentially subsidizes the producers, in this case by the difference between

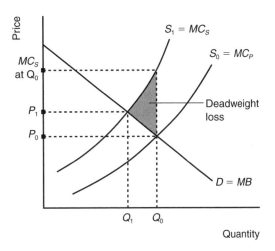

Figure 5.4

MC_s and MC_p. The situation can be analysed in terms of efficiency and equity effects.

Efficiency effect

If there is a negative externality, the true marginal cost of producing Q_0 is measured by [MC_s at Q_0]. Consumers pay only P_0 for this output, however. At the market equilibrium, as a consequence, the true marginal cost is *greater* than the market price, and hence, greater than the amount that consumers would be willing to pay for additional output. That is, consumers pay less than it costs the economy to produce this additional output, when all costs, both internal and external, are considered. Put simply, it is as if the economy was using x in scarce resources in order to produce y of additional satisfaction, whereby $x > y$. Thus, there is a deadweight loss equal to the shaded area. When there is a negative externality, the economy is using too much of its scarce resources in producing too many goods which are less valued.

89

Equity effects

The issue of equity relevant here is not that of the distribution of total surplus between consumers and producers, but between the group of consumers and producers taken together who are causing the pollution to the group of consumers and producers together who are suffering from the pollution without being compensated for. The format of Figure 5.4, while suitable for discussion of the total surplus between consumer and producer – such as in Chapter 3 and 4 on monopoly and competition – is not suitable for tracing equity effects in case of external effects.

5.6 Negative externalities: some examples from environmental policy

5.6.1 The search for the 'right' prices and 'right' quantities of environmental protection

Market prices are important because they convey information. If market prices do not incorporate the correct information because of an externality, individuals will be led by the market price to make the wrong decisions. The problem of environmental damage can then be seen as a problem of 'wrong' prices. The challenge for sensible public policy, then, is to get the prices 'right.' It is a search for the right quantities with the right prices, implying that there is an optimal amount of environmental damage (and environmental protection) and optimal prices to be paid for such a balance between 'goods' and 'bads'.

Environmental policy can be approached from the perspective that air, water, land, forests and other dimensions of the environment are public goods. The following example illustrates the basic ideas involved. Consider a city faced with the problem of air pollution. No anti-pollution legislation exists and the price

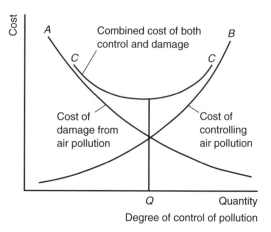

Figure 5.5

system is clearly failing to provide any control. This is hardly surprising as the activity of reducing such pollution fits the above definition of a public good very closely. Any reduction in air pollution will simultaneously benefit all residents whether they pay anything towards it or not. Hence it displays the property of non-excludability. The benefits provided by less air pollution will not be diminished by the number of people who experience them. Hence it displays the property of non-rivalry. Environmental protection is then a public externality which is a positive sign and stands in contrast to pollution which is the public externality but has the negative sign.

These two characteristics would make the activity of reducing pollution 'uneconomic' as far as any private firms are concerned, but there is also the requirement to devote resources to the reduction of air pollution. The question is, then, how much of the community's scarce resources should be devoted to the reduction of air pollution? Cost–benefit analysis can help provide an answer.

The degree of control is required to expand for as long as the total benefits exceed the total costs. The optimum degree of control is reached as soon as the total cost is equal to the total benefit. Figure 5.5 expresses this idea. The optimum degree of control is shown as that which minimizes the total costs of control and damage. Curve *A* shows how the total cost of damage due to pollution decreases as the degree of control increases. Curve *B* shows how a greater degree of control will cost the community more. By adding the two curves together, curve *C* is obtained. The optimum balance between costs and benefits is achieved by a degree of control that will minimize the total cost to the community. This optimum degree of pollution control (*Q*) does not eliminate all pollution; there is thus such a thing as an optimum amount of pollution.

It was stated earlier that the ways open for society to assure that 'right' prices hold are via a variety of market solutions or via state measures. These will be treated below in separate sections.

5.6.2   Market solutions

Market responses to negative externalities include creating markets via forcing unitization, facilitating private contracts, and defining and enforcing property rights.

1   Unitization

One solution to the externality problem in some settings is facilitating single ownership or unitization of the separate activities that are connected by the externality. For example, if a factory owner also owned all of the land affected by the smoke and other pollutants created as by-products of the factory's production, any increase in by-products would lower the value of the land. Therefore, the owner of both the land and factory would have to consider the effect of a decision to produce more at the factory (that would increase his factory income) on the value of land that he owned

(where pollution would tend to decrease the value of the land and the income from land sales or rentals). Unitization is the creation of single ownership and control of resources whose uses might conflict to create an externality. Unitization does pose one problem, however. Creating a single owner for the different activities may create a firm with market power. Then solving one problem – an externality – creates another problem – a monopoly.

2   Private contracts and covenants

Most often, property rights are defined and protected by the government. Sometimes, however, property rights can be created and transferred at a low cost by private individuals. Certain kinds of negative externalities can also be eliminated by private contract. These kinds of contractual arrangements, known as restrictive covenants, are often used for land-use control in new housing developments. Restrictive covenants are private agreements among a group of landowners about how each owner can use his or her land. Covenants limiting land use for residential purposes, precluding apartments or agricultural uses, are common. Covenants sometimes place restrictions on the architectural design and size of a home, as well as on the kind of landscaping that must be maintained.

3   Creating markets via property rights

Situations characterized by missing or incomplete markets are likely to face problems of externalities. For example, firms may be tempted to dump pollution in the air because there is no market where dirty air can be disposed of or clean air can be purchased. Without such a market, firms are not forced to consider the full opportunity costs associated with their production decisions. Such markets often fail to develop given the nature of the by-products and the absorbing environment. For example, firms dispose of by-products in the air because air is a common property, and is not easily convertible into private property.

Because lack of ownership creates externality problems, an externality problem can sometimes be solved, if technically feasible, by establishing ownership of previously unowned resources (cf. Coase 1960). A property rights arrangement of some sort can, in some circumstances, effectively deal with pollution. The government can decide how much pollution of a certain sort is acceptable. It can then create 'rights to pollute' by allowing this predetermined, fixed amount of pollution to be marketed. A firm then has one of three choices. First, it can purchase the right to pollute by paying the market price. Or, second, it can adjust its production to a lower level than the prescribed amount. Or, finally, it can adopt a new, low-pollution technology, if available, or install pollution-control equipment to lower its pollution.

As long as pollution can be monitored, its source identified, and its rights easily traded, a market in pollution rights will limit it to the amount determined by the government, and do so in a cost-effective way. That is, firms that cannot easily decrease the amount of pollution they produce will either have to purchase the right to pollute, close down, or install pollution-control equipment. Those that can easily adjust their pollution output can choose to do so rather than purchase an expensive right to pollute or adopt an expensive new technology. As a consequence, pollution will be reduced the most by firms that can reduce it for the least cost, and reduced the least by those firms for whom the costs would be the greatest.

In the above examples, the externality problem is eliminated by creating property rights. This solution is not quite as simple as it

seems, however. Although in certain circumstances there is a 'natural' way to define the property rights, in many settings it is not clear who is entitled to receive which rights. Should a firm have the right to use the air for disposal so that individuals must purchase less pollution from the firm? Or, should individuals have the right to clean air so that firms must purchase air for disposal of by-products from individuals? Apart from the problem of defining property rights, there is the difficulty of enforcing and transferring property rights, which are costly activities. For example, if a steel mill owns the rights to the air around it, the people living in a neighbouring town might find it difficult to organize in order to purchase clean air from the mill, even if they were willing to pay for it. Everyone in the community must participate in the transaction, and the process of transacting with a large number of purchasers of a single property right is frequently difficult. On the other hand, if the air rights belong to the community, and the steel mill wants to purchase the right to pollute, the steel mill must transact with everyone in the community, but some members may hold out for a higher price. When a single good ('the right to use the air for disposal') must be purchased from a large number of joint owners, the transaction costs often undermine any possible trades. In addition, it is not simply a matter of deciding who should have what rights, but deciding *who should decide*. Who should be given the power to determine who has which property rights?

Despite these problems, private ownership is pervasive in modern society and internalizes many externalities that would otherwise exist. If property rights and ownership can be defined and enforced effectively, decision makers are forced to consider all of the costs or benefits associated with decisions. The conclusion is that while ownership automatically internalizes the costs and benefits of decisions, creating and monitoring property rights remains difficult in many areas.

5.6.3   State measures

Even if there are market remedies to some externality problems, when transaction costs are high, these remedies frequently fail. Then, property rights cannot be effectively defined, transferred from lower-valued uses to higher-valued uses, or enforced against producers of externalities. In such cases, direct legal, regulatory or fiscal remedies are often pursued.

1   Nationalization

The firm can be nationalized and operated at the socially-desirable prices and levels of production and external effects.

2   Government-mediated negotiations

In cases where the number of parties involved is small, negotiations among these parties may lead to settlements which regulate future external effects. Government may initiate and/or mediate in such negotiations, provided the conditions for settlements are favourable.

3   Tort law and liability

In many countries negligent behaviour makes a person liable to pay damages. Faulty goods, negligent surgery, careless driving and so forth create liabilities that force manufacturers, surgeons, drivers, and others in similar situations to calculate the full costs associated with their activities; they will be subject to lawsuits if their behaviour is negligent and imposes costs on others. The same would apply to negative environmental externalities incurred by person A or person B, in so far that that effect is recognized by society as a liability. The body of law that deals with such matters is tort law. If the liability determined is consistent with the value of the external cost, tort law can move the economy toward a more efficient use of resources.

These kinds of lawsuits shift the private marginal cost curve toward the social marginal cost curve by forcing persons involved in activities to consider the costs that they might impose on others; they must pay these costs if they are sued and found negligent. As a consequence, individuals and firms are more careful.

4   Emission fees

An *emissions standard* is definable as a specific legal limit set by state agencies on the quantity of pollution that an individual activity is allowed to dump into the environment, while an *emission fee* is definable as a tax charge imposed on each unit of a polluter's emissions above the emission standard. When excess emissions go above the standard permitted, the involved firm has to pay the tax and this imposes costs on the firm. An increase in marginal production costs via the tax moves a market plagued by a negative externality toward the standard emission and the efficient output.

Setting standards is attractive because society can determine precisely how much pollution it will have. Of course this needs to be done carefully because if the standard is set too high, it leads to a market outcome in which too little, rather than too much, is produced. If the standard is too low, too much, rather than too little, is produced. Similarly, the rate of the emission fee should correspond with the marginal external cost.

Such taxes on pollution are attractive for several reasons. First, they not only move a market toward a more efficient equilibrium but also, if they change with changes in the quantity or type of pollution, they provide incentives for polluters to find cost-effective means of lowering pollution. This means that firms that cannot find particularly effective ways of lowering the amount of pollution caused by their production simply pay the tax, thus increasing their costs. Firms that can adopt pollution-reducing techniques more easily have an incentive to do so, however, because they can partially or fully avoid paying the tax. This choice is important because there is no reason to believe that every producer or every production process will be equally good at reducing pollution. In general, polluters tend to reduce their emissions as long as marginal costs of such reductions fall short of the fee. They reach equilibrium where the marginal cost equals the fee. In this way, the marginal costs of reduced emissions tend to be equal among all sources of emissions.

Second, the cost of achieving a specific amount of pollution reduction can be minimized if the marginal costs of pollution control can be set equally for all activities that create the pollution. This is a simple, yet effective, rule for deciding how a particular target level of pollution reduction should be allocated among the many producers of pollution to keep the costs of pollution control at a minimum. That is, this criterion can be used to select the most cost-effective pollution-control policy, even when it is not possible to determine whether the target level itself is efficient. (Remember that determining the efficient target level requires assessing the benefits of production, and the costs of by-product disposal.)

Third, in a sense, if firms are taxed on the basis of the pollution that they create, there is a market for pollution. A firm can either buy the right to pollute from the state by paying the tax, or it can avoid the tax by reducing its pollution. If it pays the tax, its costs will increase and it will produce less, including less pollution.

Fourth, these emission fees lead to favourable effects in the long-term. Research activity will then concentrate on developing new methods of production aimed at economizing on the now more expensive factor of production. At the other extreme, if all firms in a perfectly competitive industry unavoidably produce the negative externalities, the emission fees will remain in the long-term, thereby causing the prices to increase. In this way, prices will 'inform' the consumers about the true social costs of producing these commodities. Moreover, increased prices will reduce demand for the products and hence reduce output as well as the volume of negative externalities.

5 Regulation methods

The firm may be prohibited from producing more than a specific quantity. Alternatively, the level of emissions may be regulated or the use of specific production processes may be banned. Also, plant location may be controlled by zoning laws. Regulation measures can be used to achieve almost the same results in terms of effecting incentives to reduce negative external effects if it can be made flexible enough and, in particular, if it is the amount of effluents rather than the amount of output that is regulated. But if flexibility is low, incentives will be ineffectual or absent; the company's interest in adjusting production methods and developing new ones diminishes, of course, if the volume of production is not allowed to increase.

6 Combining emission fees and regulation methods

In an economic evaluation of regulation methods and emission fees, the latter is usually preferred. A socially-efficient distribution of reduced emissions is attained where the marginal costs of such reductions are the same for all emission sources. This result can often be attained by using emission charges. It is partly in view of this fact that the charge approach is considered more likely to promote social efficiency than the regulation approach.

In practice, government policy prefers physical regulations to emission charges. A policy effect which can be monitored and attained with certainty, such as in regulation, is particularly valuable when environmental damages are expected to increase dramatically if this level is surpassed. In contrast, the effect of charges on emission volumes is less certain. One reason is that the cost structure of polluting firms, which determines the effect of charges imposed on them, may be essentially unknown to the policy maker.

Efficiency may be achieved by *combining regulatory instruments with emission fees*. Two examples can be given. The first example is simply to combine an *upper limit on emissions with emission fees*. This generates incentives for polluting firms to reduce emissions whenever such measures are fairly inexpensive. A second example is to provide existing polluters with tradeable emission *permits* which state a maximum amount of a specific kind of air pollution. As these permits can be sold to others such as new or expanding firms, a market and hence market prices for permits tend to be established. The existence of such a market will spur firms to economize with emissions for the same reason, in principle, as when fees are imposed by government. This is obviously true for those who engage in purchasing such permits. But it is also true for firms that initially received permits at no cost; they would abstain from making a profit if the market price for a

permit unit were allowed to exceed the value of this unit when used for the firm's own emissions. Thus, the result of allowing trade with emission permits is that the total volume of emissions judged to be acceptable by the authorities tends to be used in a socially-efficient way.

Whether emission fees, regulation methods or both are followed, the effectivity of environmental policy depends ultimately on the extent of compliance of firms and the ability of the regulators to enforce the regulation. In general terms, a profit maximizing and risk neutral firm will comply if the cost to the firm of complying with regulation, C, is equal or less than the penalty for noncompliance, which consists of the probability that the noncompliance is detected, p, and the penalty for noncompliance, P. Thus, $C \leq pP$. If the left-hand side in this equation is lower, the firm will comply. Raising p or P by government will promote compliance, but full compliance will not be feasible in view of costing, budgetary, technological and legislative constraints in the sphere of enforcement of regulations. Enforcement costs can be seen to be a part of the abatement costs, see Figure 5.5, and should, therefore, be considered in determining the optimum degree of pollution control.

Harrington (1988) studied compliance and enforcement in the real world. For the USA it was found that while authorities often choose not to pursue deserved violators, firms tend to comply most of the time. Several explanations are posed: voluntary compliance, penalty leverage, and regulatory dealings. Furthermore, the cost to the violating firm in terms of losing goodwill in the market place is usually much higher than the penalty P. Compliance avoids such a damage to the firm's position.

Policy example 5.3

The Kyoto Protocol

The Kyoto Protocol (KP), negotiated in December 1997, is the first international treaty to limit emissions of greenhouse gases. KP offers an illuminative example of environmental policy in several respects. To start with, the table below gives a summary of emissions and targets by participating countries.

Table 5.7 Emissions and targets of the Kyoto Protocol

Countries	Actual emission 1990 (gigagrams CO2)	Projected emission 2000/actual emission 1990	Kyoto target 2008–12	Share in total emissions (%) in 1990
United States (1 country)	4 957 022	104	93	36.00
European Union (15 countries)	3 288 667	103	92	24.05
Other OECD (9 countries)	2 065 119	109	98	15.35
Transition economies (13 countries)	3 364 259	81	103	24.60
Total (38 countries)	13 675 067	98	95	100.00

Source: adapted from Barrett (1998)

First, Figure 5.5 argued that the optimal environmental policy would require equalization of the marginal cost of abatement to that of damage. KP fulfils this condition. For example, KP studies, implemented by the Clinton Administration in 1998, estimate the marginal cost of meeting the Kyoto targets by the participating countries at about $18 per ton. The global marginal damage of the emissions is valued at a similar level.

Secondly, the Kyoto targets are expressed in net emissions, this allows effective use of alternative instruments. Net emissions are equal to greenhouse gases emitted by industrial activity less gas removals through forestry, which is very effective in absorbing these gases.

Thirdly, additional degrees of freedom are introduced by including, along with carbon dioxide, other gases that cause greenhouse effects. Abatement of a ton of nitrous oxide, for example, is put as equivalent to abatement of 315 tons of carbon dioxide.

Fourthly, KP requires that the targets in the above table be met over the five-year period 2008–12 on average, and not every year. Countries are also allowed to carry forward additional reductions they achieve to a future control period. This provision makes country participation attractive as it allows trading over time.

Fifthly, and most important, KP also allows trading over space. A country in which abatement cost is higher (USA) can trade its emission target with another where abatement cost is cheaper (Russia), and the environmental effect will be the same for the globe since where abatement takes place is of relevance to the earth climate as a whole. This provision will help create a global market for trading environmental burdens.

Sixthly, KP allows project-based joint implementation by participating countries, in which one country receives emission reduction units for undertaking projects in another country that reduce net emissions. KP extends the joint-implementation provision to African, Asian and Latin American countries. In this way an incentive is created for implementing abatement in the developing world, and persuading countries of the developing world to endorse the protocol, and as can be gathered from the table, at no emission reduction target for them until 2012. This is based on the understanding that for many years to come the developing world needs to intensify its industrial activities in a catching-up growth process, and cannot be subjected to emission reductions.

There are obstacles as well. As the above-mentioned 38 countries, or more, participate actively in reducing their emissions, non-participating third world countries will acquire comparative advantage in the polluting industries which will tend to shift from the North to the South. Emission will increase in the South so that some leakage is unavoidable. The leakage in the South has been estimated at about 10 per cent of the abatement in the North. A greater obstacle is that shifting industry can hurt some parties and these may lobby for protection in the North.

Aspects of implementation and inspection are not yet worked out, and the difficulties involved should not be underestimated. But there is a demonstrated willingness to go ahead with KP. At the meeting of the KP Framework Convention in Buenos Aires, November 1998, the total number of countries signing the agreement reached 60. It is expected that the agreement will become legally binding in 2001.

5.6.4   Experience with assessment of methods in environmental policy

Currently, the economic evaluation of environmental effects is done mainly at the project level and uses cost–benefit analysis and environmental assessment. In practice, policy responses need to be related to the specific circumstances of each market failure; in many cases, more than one market failure will be involved: indivisibilities, externalities, collectivities and failure to incorporate uncertainty, risk and irreversibility. This commonly gives rise to complex inter relationships in the context of environmental policy. Among other things, this necessarily involves a case-by-case approach to the policy problem. The cost–benefit analytical framework is not always easily applicable under the circumstances. Furthermore, because environmental issues involve significant economy-wide effects and externalities there is now increased attention for the modelling of benefits and costs of environ-

mental effects in a general equilibrium framework. Such a framework allows a simultaneous appraisal of alternative policies, not only state measures but also market responses. The next section includes an illustration of the kind of models used by Persson and Munasinghe (1995), among others.

In valuing environmental costs and benefits, a number of methods can be used. The major ones are market value approaches, household production functions, such as the travel cost method to particular recreational or amenity sites; hedonic price methods, such as real estate valuations of disamenity. A promising alternative is direct questioning, notably the contingent valuation method (CVM). CVM involves sample surveys to determine via appropriate questionnaires the willingness to pay by respondents for hypothetical environmental programmes of projects (WTP) or willingness to accept compensation for their loss (WTA). In direct questioning the questionnaires need to be developed in ways which reduce the element of free-riding by respondents, as for instance, was done in the Clarke and Groves surveys (cf. Clarke 1971 and Groves 1970).

Since many benefits from using environmental resources are incurred in the short-term and the costs experienced over the long-term, the intergenerational incidence of costs and benefits needs to be addressed. The time horizon and the discount rate can be crucial in policy evaluations. On the one hand, the higher the discount rate, the greater the apparent willingness to pass costs on to future generations; a rate at or above the opportunity cost for capital, for example, would make the present value of future costs of global warming seem small. On the other hand, lower rates favour larger, often environmentally-damaging, capital investments like nuclear power plants. Some analysts favour, wrongly, using special discount rates when evaluating environment-related projects. This is distortive. The right way for considering environmental effects in policy evaluations is by inclusion of the combined costs of control and damage of the environment whereby the two costs should be viewed as substitutes along the lines of Figure 5.10 above. For a further discussion, see Pearce (1998).

Next to the pure efficiency aspects there are also the equity aspects. Efforts to find the solution to the equity or compensation problem can be seen as an inquiry into the *property rights* system of society. Is it the polluter or the pollutee that has the formal right to use a particular resource – a park area, water shed or 'air shed' – or is it both (common property)? To take a concrete example, do smokers or non-smokers have the right to use the air in a conference room? In most cases, property rights are specified by tradition, contracts or otherwise by law which will hold for long periods and remain relatively non-disputed, so that the compensation problem is settled. For a discussion of the political economy of the redistribution effects of a change in property rights, see Papendreou (1998).

National environmental issues are heavily loaded with externalities across countries. For example, there are trade aspects (such as trade barriers protecting environmental resources, but also trade in wastes); cross-border pollutants (acid rain); biodiversity (the whale, tropical rain forests); and global environments (climate change, ocean dumping). There is also the fear that environmental costs will make local producers uncompetitive in the international market or lead to outflows of investment capital to countries with lower environmental standards. The issues involved are well elaborated in Chichilinsky (1994). For a well-documented case study of the Kyoto Protocol, which is the first international treaty to limit emissions of greenhouse gases, see Barrett (1998).

Policy example 5.4

CGE modelling of natural resource management

Some market performances which appear to be successful and some well-intended development projects and/or economy-wide policy reforms may be found to cause significant environmental damage when analysed more deeply. An ideal approach in this context is a computable general equilibrium (CGE) modelling analysis that traces the economics of both non-environmental and environmental effects, and design-complementary measures that remove the environmental damage. CGE models with environmental components have been applied, among others, to air pollution in Sweden (Bergman 1990), overgrazing in Botswana (Unemo 1993) and deforestation in Costa Rica (Persson and Munasinghe 1995). The current illustration reviews the work of Persson and Munasinghe.

Deforestation in Costa Rica is caused indirectly via agricultural and industrial demands and directly by logging and by squatting. When squatters clear common property land they are rewarded for their services by the 'buyers' of this land who become 'owners'. The sub-optimal use of land is, in this context, due to an insufficient definition of property rights. Persson and Munasinghe introduce in their model property rights next to state interventions such as taxes and subsidies.

The general part of the model consists of an economy with trading and non-trading sectors. For each sector there is a production function in terms of primary inputs of capital and labour and intermediate inputs, as well as a market equilibrium condition for supply and demand whereby prices of non-traded sectors are equal to producer prices plus indirect taxes. Factor market equilibrium for labour and capital is modelled with supply given and demand derived from the production functions of the various sectors including the activities of logging (g) and squatting (q). There is also a market equilibrium for foreign exchange, which is essentially kept as exogenous.

The particular part of the model which relates to deforestation can now be summarized. Assuming for deforestation from logging d_g a log-linear production function with as factors of production capital K and labour L:

$$d_g = K_g^\alpha \cdot L_g^\beta \quad , \quad \alpha + \beta < 1$$

Under profit maximization and undefined property rights, the demand for capital and labour are:

$$K_g = \left[\frac{P_k}{\alpha P_f (L_g)^\beta} \right]^{\frac{1}{\alpha-1}}, \qquad L_g = \left[\frac{P_l}{\beta P_f (K_g)^\alpha} \right]^{\frac{1}{\beta-1}}$$

where P_k and P_l are factor prices and P_f is the user price of forestry logs.

When property rights are well defined so as to value forests higher, the opportunity value of the forests, represented by $H(d_g)$ and assumed exogenous to the model, will be considered by the logging companies. As a result the newly-modelled demand for capital and labour can be rewritten as:

$$(5.6) \quad K'_g = \left[\frac{P_k + \dfrac{\partial H(d_g)}{\partial L_g}}{\alpha P_f (L_g)^\beta} \right]^{\frac{1}{\alpha-1}} , \qquad L'_g = \left[\frac{P_l + \dfrac{\partial H(d_g)}{\partial (L_g)}}{\beta P_f (K_g)^\alpha} \right]^{\frac{1}{\beta-1}}$$

And the new equations for deforestation from logging d'_g and the production of logs Q_g becomes:

$$(5.7) \quad d'_g = Q_f = \left[\frac{P_k + \dfrac{\partial H(d_g)}{\partial L_g}}{\alpha P_f (L_g)^\beta} \right]^{\frac{\alpha}{\alpha-1}} \cdot \left[\frac{P_l + \dfrac{\partial H(d_g)}{\partial (L_g)}}{\beta P_f (K_g)^\alpha} \right]^{\frac{\beta}{\beta-1}}$$

In addition, there is a market equilibrium condition for logs which equalizes demand to supply:

$$(5.8) \quad \frac{\partial C_g}{\partial P_f} = Q_f + X_f$$

where C_g is a cost function and X_l is the available supply for net export of logs.

As for deforestation from squatting this is formulated as a decreasing production function of the factor labour L_q:

$$d_q = (L_q)^{\gamma}, \qquad \gamma < 1$$

Under undefined property rights squatters will clear land until marginal cost equals marginal revenue, so that the demand for squatters is:

$$L_q = \left(\frac{P_l}{\gamma P_s}\right)^{\frac{1}{\gamma - 1}}$$

where P_s is the user price of cleared land. When property rights are well defined so that every squatter will now own his previously grabbed squatting plot, deforestation will occur until marginal costs equal marginal revenue under a profit function regime π which deducts $H(d_g)/(1 + r)$ from revenue and cost. Here H is the future value of the forests and r is the interest rate. The newly-modelled equation for labour demand Equation 5.9 becomes:

$$(5.9) \quad L_q' = \left[\frac{P_l + \dfrac{\partial[H(d_q)/(1 + r)]}{\partial L_q}}{\gamma P_s}\right]^{\frac{1}{\gamma - 1}}$$

And the total deforestation by squatters is changed from $d_q = \left(\dfrac{P_l}{\gamma P_s}\right)^{\frac{\gamma}{\gamma - 1}}$ to d_q' as in Equation 5.10:

$$(5.10) \quad d_q' = \left[\frac{P_e + \dfrac{\partial[H(d_q)/(1 + r)]}{\partial L_q}}{\gamma P_s}\right]^{\frac{\gamma}{\gamma - 1}}$$

The market equilibrium condition for cleared land can be written as a demand from the agricultural sector, derivable from a cost function C_a and P_s, that equals the initial stock of cleared land S plus deforestation by squatters d_q' as in Equation 5.11.

$$(5.11) \quad \frac{\partial C_a}{\partial P_s} = S + d_q'$$

The model further contains a definitional equation of 'Green GDP' which is the sum of factor incomes and indirect taxes less a term reflecting the value of diminished deforestation as in Equation 5.12.

(5.12) Green GDP $= \Sigma(\text{factor incomes} + \text{indirect taxes}) - \Delta(d_q' + d_g')H$

where H is the future value per unit of forests.

The model is furthermore solved by maximizing consumer utility:

(5.13) Max $U = \ln[\Pi_i(D_i)^{b_i}]$

with $\sum_i b_i = 1$ and subject to $Y - \sum_i P_i D_i = 0$, b_i where b_i is the expenditure share on good i, D_i is the domestic final demand of good i, and Y is disposable income. The model contains additional equations for D_i and Y.

The model is employed to simulate the effects of (a) defined property rights and (b) tax changes on logs, labour, and sectoral products. The results, after defining property rights, show a reduction in deforestation from squatting and high sensitivity of results to values of H and r. The results of tax changes show that where deforestation from logging declines, total deforestation will nevertheless increase due to indirect linkages captured by the general equilibrium analysis. The contraction of the logging and forest industry sectors causes a shift of resources toward agriculture, and as agriculture expands, deforestation increases. The analysis underlines the advantage of a CGE modelling of environmental policies because it allows the simultaneous appraisal of property rights issues and conventional state interventions, and it does so with due consideration of the existing economy-wide linkages.

Questions for discussion and further research

1 Review your understanding of the following terms: interdependent utilities; artificial markets; unitization; sunrise and sunset industries; STIP; emission fees; green GDP; CVM; WTP versus WTA; economies of scale in production and in consumption, include examples; economies of scope in production and in consumption, include examples.

2 All countries are involved in one form of industrial policy or another. Distinguish between a neutral and a targeted approach to industrial policy, and give examples. What is the empirical evidence on the success of the two approaches in Western Europe and Eastern Europe? What is the economic rationale for a targeted approach in the growth process of a developing economy and how can such a policy be modified to meet criteria of allocational efficiency at the global level?

3 Opinions differ on appraisal methods in environmental policy. Comment on the following two statements:
In the appraisal of environment-related development projects policy makers should discount future benefits and costs at a higher rate than other development projects. The optimal level of pollution is not the same for rich and poor countries.

4 Discuss using graphs the relationship between damage costs and abatement costs of environmental pollution and comment on the optimum degree of environmental pollution. Discuss whether there are also optimal degrees of policies regarding competition, technology and industry, and how to define their optimality.

Further reading

One of the most influential articles on externalities is Coase, R.H. (1960): 'The Problem of Social Cost', in *Journal of Law and Economics*, Vol. 3, pp.1–44. Another influential article in the same journal is Demsetz, H. (1964): 'The Exchange and Enforcement of Property Rights', in *Journal of Law and Economics*, Vol. 7, pp.11–26. Consideration of externalities next to other market failures is in Arrow, K.J. (1970): *The Organization of Economic Activity*;

issues pertinent to the choice of market versus non-market allocation are discussed in Haverman, R.H. and Margolis, J. (eds) (1970): *Public Expenditures and Policy Analysis*, Markham, Chicago.

For an extensive study of economic thought on externalities see Papendreou, A.A. (1994): *Externality and Institutions*, Clarendon, Oxford.

Industrial policy in a competitive market is treated in various levels of detail in the following selection of four references. See Caves, R.E., Porter, M.E. and Spence, A.M. (1980): *Competition in the Open Economy*, Harvard University Press, Mass., Audretsch, D.B., Yamawaki, H. (1988): 'R&D Rivalry, Industrial Policy, and U.S.-Japanese Trade, in *Review of Economics and Statistics*, Vol. 70.3, pp.438–47; Evans, A. and Martin, S. (1991):

'Socially Acceptable Distortion of Competition, EC policy on state aid', in *European Law Review*, Vol. 72.3, pp.389–405; Smith, A. (1987): 'Strategic investment, multinational corporation and trade policy', in *European Economic Review*, Vol. 31, pp.89–96.

For supplementary reading on environmental economics and environmental policy see, respectively: Bromley, D.W. (1991): *Environment and Economy*, Blackwell, Oxford; *Oxford Review of Economic Policy* (1998), Vol. 14, No. 4, special issue on environmental policy. For more comprehensive treatments, see Baumol, W.J. and Oates, W.E. (1988): *The Theory of Environmental Policy*, CUP, New York; Cropper, M.L. and Oates, W.E. (1992): 'Environmental Economics, a survey', in *Journal of Economic Literature*, Vol. XXX.2, pp.675–740.

Chapter 6

Collectivities: social provision and insurance schemes

6.1 Public goods

If certain goods are not profitable, the market system will fail to produce them. If, nevertheless, such goods are collectively considered as necessary by a community, then production must be undertaken despite the negative signals of the price mechanism. Under these circumstances it is usually the government which plays an active role in the provision of goods with collectivity characteristics. Public goods fall into this category, for they display two basic properties that together make their provision on a profitable basis very difficult.

The first property of a public good is that it cannot be supplied to one consumer without simultaneously being supplied to others. It is in this sense that the public good is an extreme example of externality. When the good is provided for one individual, it will bring external benefits to many others. This property is known as *non-excludability*.

The second property is that once the good has been supplied to a single consumer there is no additional cost in supplying it to others. The supply of benefits generated by the good are in no way depleted no matter how many people use it. This property is known as *non-rivalry*.

Pure public goods need to display both total non-excludability and total non-rivalry. In practice this is not always the case. Roads are often given as an example of a public good even though tunnels, bridges and some stretches of monitored motor highways can operate in such a way that people who use them can be charged and those unwilling to pay excluded. However, the practical difficulties that would be involved make the major part of any road network in essence non-excludable. The characteristic of non-rivalry may break down when a road becomes congested. Charging transporters a price at crossroads may reduce the congestion problem, but once again the practical problems mitigate against such schemes. Hence, the public good is often given as free while a general tax is levied to finance it.

6.2   Merit goods

At best the concept of merit goods is simply an example of other types of market failure. At worst some argue that there is no such thing. Those who see the merit good as no more than a specific example of other types of market failure suggest that individuals fail to appreciate the full benefits of such goods because of a lack of information. Where consumer ignorance regarding all the potential internal and external benefits is the problem, merit goods can be seen in terms of a failure to provide enough information. A similar view stems from the fact that a common characteristic of merit goods is that they provide more external than internal benefits. In this way market failure in the form of underproduction can be attributed to the existence of externalities. These points emphasize the overlapping nature of market failures. Where there is market failure the concerned good may show varying degrees of more than one type of market failure.

There is another view which defines *merit goods* as goods that the median voter, or a majority of the population, knows and asserts to have greater benefits for individuals than the individuals themselves realize and that this assertion is faithfully followed by the politicians and government who are appointed by the population at large.

This view looks at merit goods as the result of a public choice, which is not different from that of electing a legitimate government. All that is happening is that the population collectively imposes its collective interests on the rest of the population via the institution of the government. The merit good gets a collective legitimacy and, defined as such, can be categor-

ized as a public good. Income maintenance at a minimum level and various types of social insurance are merit goods which are transformed into public goods via collective legitimacy. It is then non-excludable by law and the benefit of the merit good – being a merit good – is non-rival. Similarly, when attending 12 years of basic education, or scanning for potential cancer, are announced as merit goods, and with the required capacity being made available for all, both are transformed into public goods. If individual *A* becomes better off from using either merit good, this will not rob individual *B* from doing the same, and the commodity, service or entitlement under discussion is then a truly non-rival good.

6.3   The problem of collectivities

The two aspects of the definition of public goods provide the two reasons why the market mechanism fails to operate satisfactorily in the case of such goods.

The first aspect, non-excludability, results in the problem of 'free-riders'. People will not like to pay for goods which they think can be acquired free, while private firms cannot provide goods free of charge. One solution is for such goods to be provided by private collective action in the form of non-profit-making institutions. The more common solution is through public collective action where government authorities take the lead to supply the goods.

In general, the free-rider problem becomes more serious as the size of the group of potential consumers increases and, as a consequence, the likelihood that the market will provide the public good decreases. For small groups, free-riding can be detected and prevented more easily. For large groups, however, free-riding by any particular individual is detected and prevented less easily. Thus, for example, if only two parties keep an eye on the natural resources of the community, free-riding is easy to detect and perhaps offset. If four parties share in that, however, it is more difficult to know exactly who is defecting. With eight parties, it is even more difficult. Hence it can be expected that pillage would be a bigger problem when there are more, rather than fewer, parties.

As a consequence of free-riding, the demand for a public good understates the true value of the good to a group of individuals. Worse still, the amount that individuals might be willing to pay *in the market* does not reflect how much they value any additional production of the good. This arrangement contrasts with a competitive market for private goods, where demand reflects the market participants' willingness to pay.

The second aspect, non-rivalry, in effect means that the cost of supplying an extra user with the good is zero. The benefit enjoyed by the second, third person (and so on) from the street lighting has not resulted in an increase in costs, nor has it reduced the amount of light available; in terms of the Pareto criterion, it would be inefficient to charge a price. Indeed, when any extra user can benefit from the good at no extra cost to society, charging a price would clearly discourage some potential users and result in a loss of total benefit to society. As there are by definition no costs involved in serving additional consumers, a price should not be charged for these services. But with a zero price and non-zero production costs, output cannot be determined in the usual way by demand and supply on a market.

It is clear that competitive equilibrium is not Pareto-optimal in an economy with a public commodity. One 'solution' to this problem emanates from the insight (originally attributable to Lindahl) that, as in the case of externalities, the Walrasian equilibrium is characterized by too few prices to decentralize a Pareto-

optimum. Consequently, Lindahl (1919) suggested the construct of 'personalized prices' of public commodities – different prices for different agents for the same commodity. An economy with personalized prices is a fictional one which, however, provides insight into the appropriate role of a government in engineering an optimal allocation of resources in an economy with public commodities. Because of the importance of the 'pseudoeconomy' with personalized prices, we shall briefly describe its formal structure.

The equilibrium is called a pseudoequilibrium because there is no rational reason for such prices to arise in an economy with price-taking agents. Indeed, if the public commodity is also non-excludable, as is the case for most important examples (individual members of a society cannot be excluded from the benefits of national defence or public health programmes), there is no mechanism available to the producer for imposing the personalized prices on the consumers. It is this feature of an economy with public commodities that rationalizes the intervention of the government in order to assess the consumers for their shares of the cost of producing the public commodity.

The importance of the foregoing analysis is that if the government chooses the set of personalized commodity-specific tax rates and the public commodity prices appropriately, decentralized decision making on the part of producers and consumers results in a Pareto-optimal allocation even in the presence of public commodities. It is not possible to demonstrate that this result holds for more general tax systems. That is, unless taxes are differentiated by each public commodity and each economic agent, equilibrium cannot be shown to be Pareto optimal.

The existence of externalities and public commodities perhaps constitute the most compelling case for government intervention in competitive markets. Fundamentally, this is because there is no natural reason for the appropriate markets (those needed to generate Pareto-optimal allocations) to arise. This explains the terminology 'artificial markets' (for externalities) and 'pseudoequilibrium' (of a public-commodity economy). Even if the government creates externality markets by assigning property rights, such markets are unlikely to decentralize Pareto optima because of the existence of fundamental non-convexities. Thus, the analysis of externalities may point toward tax or subsidy schemes as the solution and the analysis of public commodities may point toward personalized prices, or taxes, as the solution. Unfortunately, these proposed solutions are not panaceas; two fundamental problems must be addressed: (1) providing incentives for producers and consumers to reveal truthfully their technological rates of transformation and marginal rates of substitution, respectively, and (2) determining the equilibrium taxes/subsidies. These problems correspond closely with two policy decisions described previously in Chapter 3 as the investment-production decision, and the pricing-financing decision. We shall come to both in a while.

Incentive compatibility

The decentralized planning procedures mentioned above require that private economic agents provide correct information to the centre about their demand preferences and production technologies. However, private agents have an incentive to misrepresent their preferences or technologies. For example, a producer, by exaggerating the damage to his productive capacity of a negative externality, increases the externality tax and hence increases the subsidy paid to him by the government. Similarly, if a consumer understates his marginal rate of substitution between a public commodity and a

private commodity, his personalized price will be reduced by the government. That is, it is advantageous to understate one's willingness to pay for a public commodity, thus paying a lower personalized price and enjoying a 'free ride' at the expense of others. The result is that the production of public commodities is too low. The problem becomes that of designing a resource-allocation mechanism that is individual-agent-incentive compatible.

Determination of taxes/subsidies or personalized prices

Suggested procedures for finding the optimal taxes/subsidies are typically dynamic systems describing the exchange of price or quantity information (or both) between the government and the private economic agents (consumers and producers). The economic agents respond to the information offered by the government by providing information about their preferences and technology sets. The latter information, in turn, is used by the government to revise the price or quantity information supplied to consumers and producers, and so forth. Such dynamic processes can be shown, under certain conditions, to converge to an optimal state of the economy.

The following example highlights the above issues and lays down basic links between general equilibrium theory and game theory in treating the problem of collectivities. Assume there are many farmers, a, owning their own farmland, i, and they share a desire for building and using a common road, j. Assume a marginal rate of transformation (MRT) of two units of farmland to one road. To obtain 'general' Pareto-efficiency it is not necessary that the marginal rate of substitution (MRS) between farmland and road for each farmer should be two. If there are 20 farmers it is, in principle, sufficient for each to give up 0.1 of farmland to have full use of the common road. For 'general' Pareto-efficiency to be realized in the context of public goods it is not necessary that $MRS^a_{i,j} = MRT_{i,j}$, but rather $\sum_a MRS^a_{i,j} = MRT_{i,j}$ where a denotes farmer and i, j the goods. The efficiency problem is, therefore, transformed to one of reaching a satisfactory distribution among the farmers. Whether it is feasible or not to reach agreement on the allocation of costs and benefits to the individual farmers depends on the prospects of collective action.

The co-ordination problem can be presented along the lines of a prisoner's dilemma. Let the only two existing farmers, a and b, assess the consequences of each one's initiative to build a non-excludable road on his own or collectively. In the example below, total cost of building the road is eight, while the benefit of using the road per farmer is twelve. The two strategies give four combinations of net benefits in Table 6.1. A co-operative decision to collectively build the road gives a highest total benefit (8, 8). This may not occur, however, as long as the individual returns from acting as a free-rider are higher, and it is very likely that no road will be built at all given the relative individual returns. Intervention of a third player whose objective is to maximize the collective benefit, i.e. government, can enforce (or facilitate) the construction of the road. Of course this government has still to solve the distributive problem of allocating costs and benefits to the individual farmers in correspondence with their respective revealed preferences.

6.4 Practical approaches to resolve the problem

The non-excludability characteristic of a good makes it impossible to charge a price for the good, while the non-rivalry characteristic makes it undesirably inefficient. A good for which there is no price will not be supplied by private enterprise. If such a good is considered necessary, the obvious solution is that the government secures its provision. In many cases this is exactly what happens, even though some goods only conform to a diluted definition of a public good, they fit well as merit goods, e.g. health and education.

The decision problems faced by governments are of two types. They can be denoted by the investment–production decision and the pricing–financing decision, see also Chapter 3. First, in the absence of the market mechanism the government needs to decide what amount of a given public good to provide. An application of a cost–benefit analysis can be helpful in reaching a decision about the extent of the activity by calculating the full economic costs and comparing them with the full economic benefits. To enable such a comparison to take place, all costs and benefits have to be expressed in monetary terms. Great practical difficulties lie in the estimation of benefits, which are value-judged by the interested parties and are subject to free-riding influences. Second, the pricing–financing decision, if optimally done, would require differential pricing and financing contributions per individual user. Here too, there are practical difficulties in monitoring individual use.

In determining the demand for a public good, it is assumed, as in general for private goods, that the individual consumer is able to specify, at least approximately, the value he attaches to the marginal increment of a public good. Directly or indirectly, this value may be expressed in

Table 6.1 A game theoretic presentation of the problem of collectivities

Farmer b / Farmer a	Build road	Do not build road
Build road	(8,8)	(4,12)
Do not build road	(12,4)	(0,0)

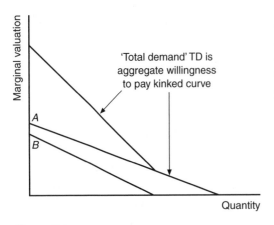

Figure 6.1

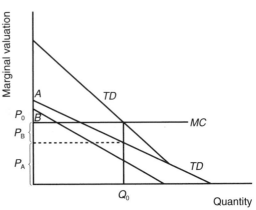

Figure 6.2

money, as illustrated by the curve of consumers *A* and *B* in Figure 6.1. In other words, if a price were charged for this service, the individual's demand curve would have the appearance indicated. The principal difference as compared with private goods, however, arises in the determination of the 'total demand'. Since a public good is, by definition, a good that can be consumed by one individual without reducing other individuals' possibilities of consuming it, the total demand is calculated as a vertical summation of the individual demand curves of *A* and *B*, in contrast to a private good where total demand is calculated by horizontal summation of the individual demand curves. The total demand for a public good is then obtained as an aggregate willingness to pay kinked curve, as illustrated in Figure 6.1.

If the total demand for a given public good is known, the socially-efficient output of the good occurs where the marginal cost for producing the good is equal to the sum of all the individual valuations of a marginal increment of the good. Formally, the optimum condition for the production of a public good is equality between the sum of individual marginal rates of substitution, and the marginal rate of transformation with respect to this good and an arbi-

trary private good. This means, using previous symbols, that

$$MRS^A_{1k} + MRS^B_{1k} = MRT_{1k}$$

where commodity 1 is a private good and *k* denotes the public good. Compare the corresponding condition for two private goods:

$$MRS^A_{12} = MRS^B_{12} = MRT_{12}$$

In Figure 6.2, which describes a special case in which marginal costs are constant, Q_0 represents the efficient output. In terms of public policy, this peculiar demand curve means that if a community wants to provide a public good, it should determine the dollar value of the public good to each of its members (each person's willingness to pay), add up these dollar values and if in a cost–benefit analysis the production costs are less than or equal to this dollar value, provide the public good.

How the total costs for Q_0 are distributed between consumers is not a matter of efficiency but purely a question of real income distribution. One particular distribution alternative, of interest mainly in those cases where the desired income distribution can be attained with specific means, deserves mention. If the cost per unit of the public good is distributed among the consumers according to their marginal valuations at Q_0, P_A and P_B, respectively, and if the consumers regard the fees for the good calculated in this way as prices for the public good, they will clearly find themselves in an equilibrium position (a so-called pseudo-equilibrium) corresponding to that existing in markets for private goods. In other words, with given 'prices' P_A and P_B the consumers prefer quantity Q_0 to all other alternative quantities. This method of charging also means that the sum of the fees per unit corresponds to marginal cost; and, in this particular case of constant marginal costs, the total receipts exactly cover total costs.

We have seen that, under the assumption that the individuals' valuations of public goods are known, the existence of such goods does not lead to any complicated analytical problems. The real difficulty is related to the realism of the assumption that consumer valuations of the public good are known or can be ascertained. If the government, in an attempt to achieve an efficient volume production of a public good along with a distribution of payments indicated above, asks consumers how much they are willing to pay for marginal changes in production, there are great risks that the answers will be consciously distorted. If the individual consumer understands that an increase in production will not cause him to pay any noticeable increase in taxes or a special fee, he may tend to answer with an *exaggerated* demand for the public good relative to his true demand. (Such an understanding can exist, for example, in general statements or simple interview studies concerning desires for better roads, increased police protection and the like.) On the other hand, if the individual knows that he will really have to pay in accordance with his expressed willingness to pay and, moreover, that he is one of a great many consumers, he knows that he has complete control over how much he

himself will have to pay but that he has meagre possibilities for affecting the *total* demand. In this situation he may attempt to take advantage of the expressed willingness to pay of others and indicate a low willingness to pay (the so-called 'free-rider problem'). Thus a tendency to *understate* the true willingness to pay for public goods would arise.

It has been shown that the problem of getting consumers to reveal their true valuations is solvable only approximately or with fairly sophisticated approaches, practicable only in certain special situations. In the absence of a general solution, 'informed guesses' by the political representatives of the people have to serve as the basis for most decisions about the volume and distribution of payments for public goods. But these informed guesses may be influenced by political motivations and bureaucratic interests which are external to the final consumers. It is possible, then, for the government, like the market, to underproduce the public good or, unlike the market, to tax and subsidize too much and overproduce the public good. Just as with the problems associated with positive and negative externalities, for public goods, it is difficult to obtain the efficient outcome precisely because the market and the state fail to produce the information necessary for allocating resources efficiently.

Because of the problems of exclusion and appropriate pricing, governmental entities frequently provide public goods. When the government can tax all of its citizens, the free-riding problem is diminished in relevance. Taxing everyone means that everyone has to pay for the public good. In addition, because the government can tax individuals and then subsidize the production of the public good, the pricing problems associated with public goods are also eliminated. That is, with a subsidy, a public good can be provided at a zero price to consumers.

Government intervention needed to offset the free-riding and pricing problems associated with public goods is, however, necessarily coercive. As long as individuals can free-ride on private or governmental provision of a public good, they will not reveal their true preferences for it. The only remedy to the free-riding problem is to force individuals to behave in ways *not* consistent with self-interest. That is, all citizens have to pay such taxes whether or not some of them value the public goods provided by the government. Therefore, if it is determined that the public good should be provided, taxing individuals who benefit from it but who would otherwise free-ride is a coercive but necessary remedy.

The coercive nature of taxation and public provision implies that some individuals who really do care about the public good will be taxed too little. This discrepancy occurs because taxes are not based on willingness to pay. Thus, forcing individuals to pay a 'fair share' is difficult: government provision almost always unintentionally redistributes income. The lengthy public debates about how much should be spent on national defence or how much should be spent on parks, roads, fire and police protection, and so forth, reflect difficulties in obtaining informed guesses of the real needs, as well as the concerns associated with the redistributive effects of the associated taxes.

There are some cases in which a public good need not be delivered at zero price. A *public good* can be *transformed into a marketable good* (to be produced and sold by a public *or* private enterprise) through different, more or less expensive mechanisms of distribution. In other words, a public good may be transformed into a good from which the non-paying consumer is excluded. For example, as is well known, there are instances where a non-zero price (toll) is charged for the utilization of

certain uncongested roads – a public good. In other cases, there are technical possibilities for achieving such a transformation, but for reasons such as cost these possibilities have not been exploited. This applies, with some exceptions, to 'Pay TV' broadcasting, where it is technically possible to allow only those who pay for a certain programme to watch it on their receivers. Cable TV may be seen as a counter example but it is most often used with payment for monthly viewing, not with payment per programme.

The advantage of excluding those who do not pay for access to a public good is that the problem of determining total demand is eliminated or is at least considerably reduced. The disadvantage is, of course, that a price is introduced in spite of the fact that the marginal cost of adding another consumer (automobile driver or TV viewer) is zero, and this in itself implies inefficient resource allocation. In other words, in each separate case this disadvantage as well as the cost of charging a price has to be weighed against the advantages of gaining information about the total demand for the good.

Another way to make the public good private is to tie it to the provision of a service that requires payment. For example, TV signals are tied to the sale of advertising services. Advertising services are essentially a private good. If a firm does not purchase advertising time, a TV station does not provide the service of airing the firm's advertising. What a TV station sells, then, is not TV programmes, but the ability to get viewer attention. TV programmes are merely a way of delivering advertising services. In a very real sense, it is the advertisers who consume the TV signals and not the public. For the public, watching TV becomes a positive or negative externality.

Because the interests of advertisers probably differ substantially from those of consumers, there is no reason to expect that the involved externalities are solved to the optimal satisfaction of both watchers and advertisers.

6.5   Social provisions

This section will introduce the sort of policy questions to be resolved in two areas of social provisions: education and health. It is noted that there are programmes in these sectors which fit fully with the definition of public goods, while other programmes are neither non-rival nor non-excludable by nature, but when considered as merit goods they will share the definition of being non-excludable and non-rival.

A great deal of the controversy on policies for health care and education reflect differences in opinion regarding the extent of market failures due to the applicability of problems of externalities and collectivities. The assumption of perfect information necessary for market efficiency hardly applies, too. The distribution of education and health on the population is also known to be correlated with socioeconomic status which complicates matters further. The controversies are furthermore accentuated by measurement problems of private and social costs and benefits in both sectors.

In spite of the controversy on policies, it is true for all countries that private and public resources are linked together in education as well as in health, and have resulted in mixed and stable balances over time. In most countries, movement from these balances towards more market- or more public-oriented solutions is a slow process. Sectoral reforms here are typical for the long-term.

Health

Private markets allocate efficiently only if the *standard assumptions* hold, i.e. perfect information, perfect competition and no market failures such as externalities or collectivities. To what extent do current systems of medical care conform with the standard assumptions? To begin with, individuals are not perfectly informed about the nature of the product (in analytical terms, their indifference map is not well-defined). If consumers are to make rational choices, they need to have the necessary information, and also the competitive power to enforce their decisions. The provision of information on a scale sufficient for rational individual choice may be too costly, in which case decisions about treatment must be delegated to doctors. Minimal intervention takes the form of regulation, e.g. only individuals with approved qualifications are allowed to practise medicine. But where the information problem is serious, the performance of the market may be so inefficient that more extensive state involvement, either through substantial regulation of private production, or through public production and allocation, might be a better solution.

Health care conforms only minimally with the assumptions necessary for market efficiency. The imperfect information and unequal power of consumers, externalities, collectivities and technical difficulties with private medical insurance cause serious problems on the demand side of a hypothetical private market; non-competitive behaviour by doctors can cause problems with supply, and third-party payments cause inefficiency via both demand and supply. *A priori*, there is an overwhelming presumption that an unrestricted private market will be highly inefficient, and also inconsistent with widely-held notions of social justice. This view is confirmed by empirical observation. Countries with little public involvement in health care, or which adopted careless *ad hoc* modifications to private systems, typically experienced sharp, unplanned increases in expenditure. Efficiency requires, at a minimum, considerable regulation and state financial involvement. No system of health care can be perfect – the real issue is to develop an accountable system which is the least inefficient and inequitable form of organization.

In developing such an accountable system, attention needs to be given to defining the nature of the maximand, valuation of improved health, causal links between sickness condition, health care and improved health, and the comparative advantage of privately and publicly medicated health care delivery systems by sickness condition.

There is no conventional definition of the maximand in health and how to measure improvement in it. Recently, the Quality Adjusted Life Year (QALY) has been gaining more ground among public policy and health economists. Normal health is assigned 1, the score going down the poorer the health of the person. One QALY is one year equivalent of normal health. Figure 6.3, level 1, shows QALY over time for a reporting patient with particular sickness conditions and with a QALY of 0.4, who does not undergo treatment

and dies in year x. If treated he recovers doubly to a higher health score of 0.8 and lives longer, y more years, as shown in level 2. The area of the benefit is given by the difference between levels 1 and 2, or simply the difference ΔQALY. Figure 6.3 also shows the costs incurred for the treatment which can be expected to concentrate in the beginning and stabilize thereafter. These costs can be discounted. The expression ΔQALY/cost is a benefit–cost ratio which can be calculated for various diseases or sickness conditions. The reciprocal expression of cost per QALY gained per disease treatment is more apprehensive for policy makers in allocating health provisions. There are presently such estimates for treatments of cancer, heart and kidney diseases and various body injuries (Barr 1998). Comparable appraisal methods are found in Culyer (1980).

Education

Measurement problems dominate educational policy. There are two major sets of problems in measuring benefits: (a) the maximand standing for the concept of what 'good' education is and how to value it; and (b) the causal links between education and educational benefits to the individual in terms of production, income, and consumption.

The nature of the maximand raises a number of problems. Families and educationalists have widely different views about what is precisely meant by good education. The valuation of educational benefits such as consumption benefits (i.e. enjoyment of the educational process itself), production benefits and income benefits pose complex measurement problems. Besides, there are alternative causal links and each alternative implies a different viewpoint and a different state policy.

Causal links are disputable. Human capital theory explains the demand for education in

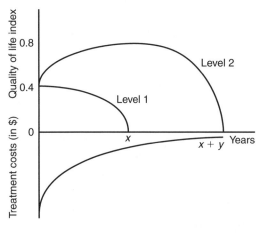

Figure 6.3

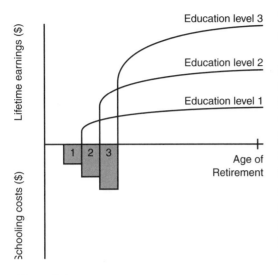

Figure 6.4

terms of its production and utility benefits. It is argued that an individual who acquires more education becomes more skilful and productive. Education is seen as a form of investment analogous to improving machinery. From the individual viewpoint, such investment is profitable to the extent that it increases future income by more than its initial costs (including foregone earnings). Empirically, there is a strong correlation between an individual's education and his lifetime earnings, as shown in Figure 6.4.

Incurring schooling costs, in say educational level 3, is an investment which is transformed in a higher lifetime earning profile typical of graduates of educational level 3. Discounting the stream of future less foregone earnings due to educational level 3, and dividing this by the discounted school costs of level 3 gives a cost–benefit ratio for level 3. Such cost–benefit ratios can guide economic policy with respect to allocation of public provisions between educational levels 1, 2, 3, etc. Alternatively, an internal rate of return can be derived from an equalization of discounted costs and benefits.

The similarity between Figures 6.3 and 6.4 for education and health respectively is noted.

The job competition model, also known as the screening hypothesis, challenges the human capital theory by arguing, first, that education beyond a basic level does not increase individual productivity and, second, that firms seek high-ability workers but are unable, prior to employing them, to distinguish them from those with low ability. The problem is analytically similar to adverse selection in insurance markets. The job competition model questions the causal link between higher education for the business sector and increased individual productivity. Put another way, the model calls into question the production and utility benefits of higher education, and views public expenditure on higher education with reservation. An illustration in this chapter reflects on the policy implications of the human capital and job competition models.

Another policy problem relates to the respective roles of private enterprise and the public sector in supplying various types of educational demand. These roles undergo periodic reviews and reforms. For instance, one policy problem is with regard to the optimal mix in vocational training between in-company training and institutional training. Large firms which organize company training face the risk of poaching of trained persons by other firms. The non-excludability character of the acquired skills is a disincentive for firms to engage in in-company training. This can be remedied by providing a training subsidy. Institutional training is also necessary in view of the infeasibility of company training in small and medium-sized firms. These firms, in turn, are called upon to partially finance institutional training and training subsidies.

A second policy reform concerns distribution of vouchers to students which they can use at the school of their choice. The efficiency effects of vouchers for schools are unclear *a priori*. Empirical testing of efficiency effects is not yet well developed. In equity terms, vouchers are likely to increase inequalities in the distribution of education, and in particular to benefit the middle class at the expense of lower socio-economic groups.

A third policy reform concerns a well-designed loan scheme which would enable higher education to expand appreciably. Such a scheme can contribute to expansion (improving macro efficiency) and open up capital markets facing students (a micro-efficiency gain). Loans

can also improve equity by improving the chances of working-class attendance and by reducing the regressivity of higher education finance.

Finally, the equity criterion applied to education is enhanced by a reduction in inequalities in the quantity and quality of school education by social class. But there might be limits to the extent to which this can be achieved solely within the confines of the educational system. To the extent that inequalities in education are the result of broader inequalities, progress in the former will depend in part on improvements in the latter.

Policy example 6.1

Educational policy appraisals
Models of human capital (HC) versus job competition (JC)

Under simplified assumptions of all earnings explainable by education, constant streams of yearly earnings, constant schooling costs, and, following the model of human capital, the private internal rate of return to investment in educational level k, RHC_k, becomes a cost–benefit ratio as in Equation 6.1:

(6.1) $RHC_k = (WAG_k - WAG_{k-1})/(WST_{k-1} + COS_k) \cdot n_k$

where:

WAG_k = annual average earnings of workers with completed educational level k
WST_{k-1} = initial average earnings of workers who forgo educational level k, i.e. starting wage
COS_k = annual average schooling cost
n_k = foregone years of earning, or simply duration of educational course k

The impact of additional education on enhanced earnings is incorporated in the JC model in an indirect way by allowing education to give access to an upgraded occupational mix with higher labour productivities and higher earnings. The private return here, RJC_k, is expressed in Equation 6.2:

(6.2) $\sum_{T=1}^{w} \sum_{q} (\lambda_{qk,t} WAG_{q,t} - \lambda_{qk-1,t} WAG_{q,t})(1 + RJC_k)^{-t} = \sum_{t=1}^{n} \sum_{q} (\lambda_{qk-1,t} WST_{q,t} + COS_{k,t})(1 + RJC_k)^{-t}$

where:

WAG_q = annual average earnings of occupation j
WST_q = initial average earnings of occupation j, i.e. starting wage
λ_{qk} = proportion of workers with education k in occupation q
w = number of working years after completing education k

Equation 6.2 allows for variable occupational wages over time and for changing compositions of the occupational–educational matrix of which λ_{qk} are elements. Changing compositions over time in the present context are equivalent to occupational mobility. If, for the sake of simplification, the parameters in Equation 6.2 are assumed to occur at a constant rate, this equation can be reduced to Equation 6.3 which is comparable to Equation 6.1.

$$(6.3) \quad RJC_k = \sum_q (\lambda_{qk}WAG_q - \lambda_{qk-1}WAG_q)/(\lambda_{qk-1}WST_q + COS_k)n_k$$

Estimates have been made in Cohen (1994, p.120) of rates of return following the two models for Indonesia in the 1980s making use of occupational and educational cross-sections, earnings and costs. The results for RHC_k and RJC_k are shown below.

Table 6.2 Alternative labour theories giving different education returns

Educational level k	Primary	Secondary	Higher
RHC_k	.254	.164	.162
RJC_k	.164	.087	.050

Rates of return following job competition differ from those following human capital in two respects. First, RJC_k are generally lower than RHC_k. Second, the reduction in returns is more pronounced the higher the educational level, which reflects a biased applicability of the screening hypothesis for the higher level of education.

It is likely that the functioning of the labour market situation contains elements of both models. In any case, validation of the JC model would recommend that governments shift their financial support from upper to lower educational levels.

A more integrative approach towards both models would be to nest the two hypotheses, thereby allowing earnings to depend on education, occupation, their imperfect interactions as regards screening and selection, and a host of individual characteristics such as age, gender, background, experience, etc.

6.6   Insurance schemes

Social insurance is concerned with protection in the face of stochastic contingencies. The two main types of social insurance are: (1) unemployment insurance, and (2) retirement schemes; this is basically *income smoothing* which relates to life-cycle effects connected with retirement or the presence of dependent children.

Unemployment insurance

The rationale for state intervention in insurance schemes can be highlighted by answering several questions. Are efficiency and social justice assisted by state involvement in insurance markets? In particular, would individuals in a private market buy the *socially-efficient* quantity of insurance against the causes of income loss covered by national insurance? This breaks down into three separate questions:

(a) why people insure at all;
(b) why the state makes membership of national insurance compulsory;
(c) why the state provides such insurance itself.

Why, first, do people insure at all? A rational risk-averse individual will insure voluntarily against unemployment so long as the value of certainty exceeds the net cost of insurance.

Why, second, is membership of national unemployment insurance compulsory? The standard argument for voluntarism is that it is efficient for an individual to make his own decision so long as he bears fully the costs of so doing. It might be argued that he should be free not to insure against income loss because of unemployment or ill-health. If he then loses his job and starves that is his fault. The flaw in the voluntarism argument in this case is that it overlooks the external costs which non-insurance can impose on others. Suppose someone chooses not to insure, and then loses his job. If society bails him out by paying a non-contributory benefit, the external cost falls upon the taxpayer. Alternatively, if he is given no help he starves, which imposes costs on others in a variety of ways. First, non-insurance may bring about not only his own starvation, but also that of his dependants. There are also broader costs, including the excess of the individual's lost output over his consumption; any resulting increase in crime; and the financial costs of disposing of his body, or the health hazards if it were left where it fell. Additionally, though more arguably, it is possible to specify a psychic externality, where people do not like the idea of a society which allows people to starve. If so, the individual's death from starvation imposes external costs by reducing the utility of others directly. In sum, the major efficiency argument for compulsory membership is that uninsured losses due to unemployment, illness or industrial injury may impose costs on others, including dependants like spouses and children. As a result, unemployment insurance acquires the status of merit good and joins the list of semi-public goods.

There is an analogy with automobile insurance, which is also compulsory in most countries. But, quite correctly on efficiency grounds, compulsion is limited to insurance to cover the damage one might inflict on *others*. One can choose whether to take out insurance to cover damage to his *own* car or person. To continue the analogy, the state makes car insurance compulsory, but does not supply insurance itself. Why, then – this is the third question – does the state provide national insurance for unemployment? This question brings us back to Chapter 4, to the discussion of the circumstances in which private insurance markets are efficient. In particular, we need to look at the supply conditions, namely that the probability of the insured event must be independent across individuals, less than one, known or estimable, known equally to all parties (i.e. no adverse selection) and exogenous (i.e. no moral hazard). Efficiency arguments about the appropriateness of public provision hinge on whether these five assumptions hold in the cases of the risks covered by national insurance and this can be separately applied for unemployment and retirement pensions.

Should the system be national? The efficiency arguments rest on externalities justifying compulsion, and technical (mainly information) failures on the supply side of the insurance market, justifying provision.

In evaluating the incentive effects of social insurance two questions predominate: is the system itself a contributory cause of unemployment?; and does it reduce the rate of saving and capital accumulation (the latter issue being particularly relevant in the case of pension schemes)? Empirical evidence is mixed on both questions, which manifests the presence of many economic interactions which are difficult to separate.

As for *equity issues* it can be argued with regard to horizontal equity, that national insurance gives everyone equal access to income support. However, not all groups receive equal coverage. With regard to vertical equity there are two sets of questions. First, how redistributive is national insurance? The major difficulties include many measurement and conceptual problems. A definitive answer would require general equilibrium analysis of the joint incidence of premiums and benefits. No such work exists, so we must be content with more rough-and-ready answers. Employment insurance premiums for most people do rise disproportionately with income for all except the highest earners. Unemployment benefits are also redistributive, in as much as those with lower incomes pay smaller contributions, generally for fewer weeks, and receive unemployment benefit more frequently than someone with a higher income. Sick pay is redistributive to the extent that claims are more common among the lower paid.

Another disputable aspect is whether benefits are pitched at the right level. This raises two further questions. First, largely an efficiency matter: whether the level of benefit is that which would have been chosen voluntarily by a hypothetically perfectly informed, rational individual. This is the issue, discussed earlier, of whether national insurance provides the optimal quantity of insurance. Second, we need to consider the level of insurance benefits relative to the poverty line.

Pension schemes

From an individual viewpoint, the economic function of pensions is to redistribute consumption over time. By contributing to a pension scheme an individual consumes today less than he produces, so as to continue to consume when he has retired and is no longer producing. In principle, an individual can transfer consumption over time in two ways, he can store current income in a Funded Scheme; or he can exchange current income for a claim to future income via Pay-As-You-Go.

In a funded scheme (frequently organized in the private sector by insurance companies), premiums are invested in a variety of financial assets, the return on which is credited to its members. When an individual retires, the pension fund will be holding all of his/her past premiums, together with the interest and dividends earned on them. This usually amounts to a large lump sum which is converted into an annuity. The annuity is then the individual's pension. Funding, therefore, is simply a method of accumulating money, which is exchanged for money at some later date. Most occupational schemes are of this type.

Pay-As-You-Go (PAYG) schemes are usually run by the state. They are contractarian in nature, based on the fact that the state has no need to accumulate funds in anticipation of future pension claims, but can tax the working population to pay the pensions of the retired generation. Almost all state pension schemes today are PAYG, the only major exceptions in the OECD countries being the earnings-related component of the state pension in Sweden and Japan. An illustration in this chapter appraises policy implications of alternative pension schemes.

Efficiency requires that individuals buy the socially-efficient real level of pension. The theoretical conditions under which private insurance markets achieve this result were discussed in Chapter 4. The three major policy issues are why people insure at all, why the state makes membership of a pension scheme compulsory, and why it provides retirement pensions itself.

The private market provides pensions efficiently only if the standard assumptions of perfect information, perfect competition and no market failures hold. On the demand side it is not unreasonable to postulate well-informed consumers, not because individuals are necessarily able to acquire information themselves, but because they could purchase it from an insurance broker. On the supply side it is necessary to consider separately the five technical conditions which must hold if the private market is to supply insurance efficiently:

(a) the probability of living to a given age for pensioner *A* is independent of that for pensioner *B*;
(b) the probability is known and less than one;
(c) data on mortality rates are available and reliable;
(d) there is no problem of adverse selection – by and large, people do not know when they are going to die; and
(e) moral hazard is not a problem either, with suicide costly to the individual.

The initial conclusion, therefore, is that there is no technical problem with private pension provision. This, however, overlooks inflation. An individual can purchase a future consumption bundle which is efficient in terms of quantity and quality only if he is able to guarantee the real value of his future pension. This can occur without intervention only if the private market can supply insurance against unanticipated inflation. Such insurance is not possible for two reasons. First, the probability of pensioner *A* experiencing a given rate of inflation is now independent of that for pensioner *B* – the rate of inflation facing one pensioner will (by and large) face them all. There is no possibility of winners compensating losers and so insurance is impossible. In addition, the probability distribution of different future levels of inflation is neither known nor estimable.

Thus inflation is an uninsurable risk, and private-sector hedges offer incomplete protection. If pensions are to be protected against inflation, such protection must come from government. Thus there is an efficiency argument, at a minimum, for state intervention to assist private schemes with the costs of unanticipated inflation once pensions are in payment. The state is able to offer such a guarantee because it can use current tax revenues on a PAYG basis. This will introduce a PAYG element even into the purest funded scheme. It should be clear that an indemnity against inflation, if publicly provided, is not true insurance (because it cannot be), but a form of tax/transfer.

We turn now to *equity* aspects. Horizontal equity concerns goals like a guaranteed minimum standard of some commodities, or equal access to them. These occur without intervention where individuals have perfect information and equal power, a line of argument which lends little support to public provision of pensions. If individuals did not have perfect information, they would generally be able to buy it. At most, there is a case for regulation of minimum standards. The fact that individuals do not have equal power lends further support to minimum standards. There is then the vertical equity argument that the state should provide pensions because otherwise the poor could not afford them. If they react aggressively there is an externality. The society may then collectively confer pensions on the poor as a merit good.

Generally speaking, equity reasons for public provision coincide with efficiency arguments. These arise out of the inability of the private market to offer protection against inflation, giving an efficiency justification for public provision at least of the indexation component of pensions, and possibly (depending on the outcome of the funding versus PAYG debate) of the entire pension. Once a commodity is publicly provided on efficiency grounds, it is not inappropriate to finance it redistributively. In addition, the fact that membership is compulsory, by imposing a pooling solution, avoids the worst problems of adverse selection; in consequence, premiums based on income rather than individual risk need cause no major inefficiency. These efficiency arguments for compulsion and public provision, taken together, suggest that using publicly-organized pensions for distributional purposes does not necessarily cause substantial efficiency losses.

Policy example 6.2

Alternatives in pension schemes

The implications of PAYG schemes *vis-à-vis* funded schemes, comprehensively documented in Barr (1998, pp.208–9) are briefly reviewed here.

PAYG schemes can be looked at in several ways. An individual A's claim to a pension is based on a promise from the state that if A pays contributions now A will be given a pension in the future. The terms of the promise are fairly precise. From an aggregate viewpoint, the state is simply raising taxes from one group of individuals and transferring the revenues thereby derived to another. State-run PAYG schemes, from this perspective, appear little different from explicit income transfers.

The major implication of the PAYG system is that it relaxes the constraint that the benefits received by any generation must be matched by its own contributions. With a PAYG scheme it is possible in principle for every generation to receive more in pensions than it paid in contributions, provided that real income rises steadily; this is likely when there is technological progress and/or steady population growth. As a result, full pension rights can be built up quickly, since pensions are paid not by one's own previous contributions, but by those of the current workforce.

PAYG schemes have several advantages: they are generally able to protect pensions in payment against inflation, and they can generally increase the real value of pensions in line with economic growth. The table below, adapted from Barr (1998, p.208) illustrates these advantages under assumptions of doubling the price index and doubling real growth, respectively.

Table 6.3 Real value of pensions

		Period 1	Period 2 (price index doubled)	Period 2 (real growth doubled)
1	Total income of workforce	£1000	£2000	£2000
2	Price index	100	200	100
3	Pension contribution rate	10%	10%	10%
4	Available for pensions	£100	£200	£200
5	Real value of pensions [= (row (4)/row (2)) × 100]	£100	£100	£200

In period 1 the total income of the workforce is £1000, so that a contribution rate of 10 per cent yields £100. If the price index is raised by 100 per cent, a contribution of 10 per cent will yield £200 in nominal terms and a maintained real value of pensions at £100. Alternatively, suppose that economic growth raises earnings to £2000, while prices stay at their original level of £100.

In this case the 10 per cent contribution rate has a real yield of £200, and so it is possible to double the real value of pensions.

Against the above advantages there is the risk that the pension levels can be endangered by an increasing dependency ratio, P/W, where P is the number of pensioners and W the number of workers. Increased longevity raises the number of pensioners, and longer education reduces the size of the workforce. Lowering the retirement age simultaneously reduces the workforce and increases the number of pensioners. Finally, any large 'bulge' in the birth rate can cause serious difficulties.

Funded schemes of whatever sort have two major implications: they always have sufficient reserves to pay all outstanding financial liabilities (since an individual's entitlement is simply his past contributions plus the interest earned on them); and a representative individual, or a generation as a whole, gets out of a funded scheme no more than they have put in, i.e. with funding, a generation is constrained by its own past savings.

The claimed disadvantage of PAYG finance, that it makes pensioners dependent on the future workforce, applies also to funded schemes. In both cases pensioners are dependent on future generations, since both schemes build pensions around claims on future production rather than by storing current production.

In general, the disadvantages of funded schemes tend to mirror the advantages of PAYG. Starting with inflation, it is important to distinguish (a) pensions in build-up, when contributions are still being paid, and (b) pensions in payment. Funded schemes can generally cope with inflation during the build-up of pension rights, and with a given rate of anticipated inflation once the pension is in payment. But they do not cope well with unanticipated post-retirement inflation. Where post retirement inflation is higher than expected, a pure funded scheme is generally unable to index benefits.

Questions for discussion and further research

1 Review your understanding of the following terms: semi-public goods, conversion of merit into public goods, personalized prices, exaggerated demand, transformation of public goods into marketable goods, QALY, human capital versus job competition, pay as you go versus funded schemes.

2 Select a specific country. For each of the following areas – (a) education, (b) utilities, (c) transport, (d) credit markets, (e) insurance, (f) housing – give examples of how the government in that country operates as (i) producer, (ii) regulator, (iii) purchaser of final goods and services, (iv) subsidizer.

3 The QALYs in health policy (Figure 6.3) is equivalent to educational earnings function in educational policy (Figure 6.4). State your position in regard to differences and similarities. Discuss limitations of *each* for policy making.

4 Give five conditions which should be met to allow the creation of a private insurance market. Use these conditions to demonstrate why there is a failure for an emergence of a private market for unemployment insurance.

Further reading

Public spending and taxation are key topics in public economics. Chapter 6 looks at these as far as microeconomic policy is concerned. For further reading on these topics see Brown, C.V. and Jackson, P.M. (1990): *Public Sector Economics*, Blackwell, Oxford; Cullies, J. and Jones, P. (1998): *Public Finance and Public Choice*, OUP, Oxford.

For public spending on physical infrastructure and related policy making see *Oxford Review of Economic Policy* (1997), Vol. 132, No. 4, special issue on public investment.

Policy making in case of semi-public goods such as health, education and other social services are treated in some detail in Barr, N. (1998): *The Economics of the Welfare State*, OUP, Oxford. For applicable policy making methods to social services, see Culyer, A.J. (1980): *The Political Economy of Social Policy*, Martin Robertson, Oxford.

Policy-making issues and analysis in case of various types of social insurance are surveyed in Barr, N. (1992): 'Economic Theory and the Welfare State, a survey and interpretation', in *Journal of Economic Literature*, Vol. XXX.2, pp.741–803. A theoretical treatment of social security is in Myles, G.D. (1995): *Public Economics*, CUP, Cambridge.

Chapter 7

Distribution: income policies and endowment strategies

···

7.1   Introduction

Welfare economics postulates that for a given income distribution, the market mechanism will result in an economically efficient outcome; that is, costs will be minimized while satisfaction will be maximized. However, the mechanism can provide as many technically efficient outcomes as there are possible distributions of income and wealth. An implicit assumption is required that the existing or some other distribution of income and wealth is 'fair' or 'equitable'. It has been suggested that a fundamental weakness of welfare economics is its apparent inability to choose between these possible outcomes so as to come to an agreement about what 'fair' distribution is.

The normative problem of what constitutes a 'fair' distribution rests upon what is meant by 'fairness'. Is there such a thing as an objectively fair or equitable distribution of income and wealth? The next section deals with these issues. Other sections deal with the positive explanation of income distribution and with

policies which bridge the gap between the normative and the positive.

7.2   Normative approaches

What is fair? For a very long time this question has been at the heart of political and moral philosophy, and has prompted economists and non-economists to formulate alternative social welfare functions (SWF). It would be highly presumptuous to think that any general agreement has been found on an answer to this question. This does not mean, however, that deliberations have not brought a better understanding of the question. Much has been learned and economists are now in a position to choose between workable approaches.

Normative theories of distributive justice represent sets of principles against which the economist can test whether a particular distribution of economic well-being is fair. Table 7.1 depicts four broad classes of theories of distributive justice: outcome or end-state theories

Table 7.1 Classification of normative theories to distributive justice

	process theories	*outcome theories*
Exogenous theories	Nozick Sen	Utilitarianism Egalitarianism Rawls
Endogenous theories	Blame-freeness	Envy-freeness

versus process theories, and exogenous theories versus endogenous theories; each of which ends up with a different view of what constitutes a fair distribution.

What is the difference between exogenous and endogenous justice theories? Exogenous justice theories define concepts of justice by relying on principles formulated without taking into account the individual ethical preferences of the population under discussion. These theories impose those principles from above upon the population. Exogenous concepts of justice developed in one society would not be accepted by a society with a significantly different culture, because the people here would reject the right of any external authority to impose its view of justice on their society. Endogenous justice theories will be more applicable here.

Take the following example of a society of people who actually believed in the free market axioms, i.e. individual rationality, economic competition, etc.; what notions of economic justice would they subscribe to? The individuals in this society would advocate what can be called endogenous justice theories. Individualists would rather use the preferences of the individuals in the society under consideration in judging whether a given social state is fair. A unanimous agreement among individuals in that society is required for declaring a particular state as fair. A social outcome is declared fair if *all* people think it is, and no external authority has the right to make that decision for them. Justice is thus a relative

concept that can be totally operationalized to the society's context. The opinion of outsiders, including analysts, is exogenous and hence irrelevant for determining what is fair in a particular society.

To begin with, we shall elaborate on the exogenous theories. Therein is often the distinction made between end-state and process-oriented theories. Social welfare functions (SWF) which emphasize the end-state work with *outcome theories of distributive justice* focus on the justice or fairness of the outcomes or ends of economic activity. On the other hand, *process theories of distributive justice* focus on the justice or fairness of the *mechanisms* or *means* whereby the ends are achieved. For example, the belief that everyone should have exactly the same income and wealth is an outcome theory. The belief that everyone should have the same *opportunity* to earn and accumulate wealth is a process theory.

Social welfare functions which emphasize *outcome* are either utilitarian, egalitarian or Rawlsian. All three are formulated in terms of the utility of individuals. First, there is the utilitarian view which is due to Bentham. It is argued here that society's welfare, W, is equal to the simple sum of the utilities, U, of different individuals, the poor, P, and the rich, R, thus $W = U_R + U_P$. In order for changes in the sum of utilities to make sense, cardinal measurability and full (or at least partial) comparability are assumed. The social welfare indifference curves are negatively-sloped straight lines, as is illustrated in Figure 7.1(a). That is, society is willing to give up one utility unit of the household U_R for a gain in the utility of the other household U_P, and vica versa. This holds regardless of the level of utility of either of the two households; the society is completely indifferent to the degree of inequality in the society.

Second, there is the egalitarian view where social welfare indifference curves are (strictly) convex or curved, corresponding with the Bernoulli-Nash social welfare functions, as in Figure 7.1(b). A simple example of a social welfare function able to produce such indifference curves is the following: $W = r \cdot U_R + p \cdot U_P$, where p and r are welfare weights that depend on the level of utility attained. Presumably, p is larger the poorer household P is, reflecting that society cares about the poor. If an action leads to a reduction in R's utility which is less than the weighted gain in P's utility, then society is better off. Redistribution of resource x should take place until the marginal utility of the additional resource x for each individual is the same.

Note that we are talking in both the utilitarian and egalitarian views about inequality in terms of units of *utility*. This does not indicate indifference to inequality of incomes, because the marginal utility derived from an additional dollar may vary between individuals. It is, for instance, well established that the utility of the last dollar spent is higher for the poor than for the rich. As a result, the utilitarian and egalitarian views will have similar implications for redistribution, even though the egalitarian will be more progressive than the utilitarian.

Third, an even stronger egalitarian premise in an absolute sense underlies the Rawls social welfare function (Rawls 1972). This argues that the welfare of society only depends on the utility of the poorest or worst-off household. If individual R has a utility of 200 and P has a utility of 100 then social welfare is equal to the

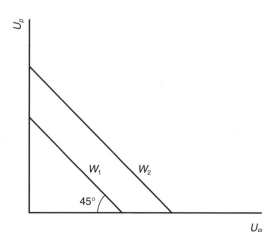

Figure 7.1(a)

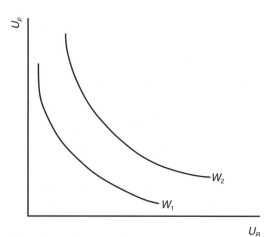

Figure 7.1(b)

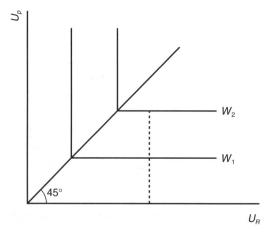

Figure 7.1(c)

utility of the worst-off, i.e. 100. More generally, $W = min\ (U_R,\ U_P)$. As illustrated by Figure 7.1(c), only vertical movement upwards along the dotted vertical line will improve social welfare. Society is better off if the welfare of the poorest household, household P in the figure, is improved. Starting from the dotted line and moving horizontally to the right, society gains nothing from improving the welfare of the 'richer' household R. Note that by implication a policy change that makes the worst-off household a little better off and the best-off household much better off turns out to be desirable since social welfare, so defined, is increased.

Rawlsian fairness is based on the following premises. Suppose that none of the individuals in a group knew ahead of time what their individual chances for economic success or failure would be, but that they could collectively determine the rules that would distribute economic rewards in the economy in which they would live. What rules of division would a group of equally-ignorant people develop? Would the group focus on the procedures by which the economic game was played? Or, would the group focus on the outcome of the economic game? They could, of course, focus on both. If the group focused on outcomes, what outcomes would be acceptable?

To make these questions more specific, suppose that there are 100 people in the group. No one knows whether he or she will receive substantially more or less than 1/100 of the income in the economy. If A, B or any other person among the 100 people had to determine how income *ought* to be shared *without any knowledge of what their shares would be*, how would they vote: 1/100 for everyone including oneself; everything for the lucky person and nothing for the remaining 99; or some other unequal division with random winners and losers?

Rawls argued, first, that if we determine the rules or outcomes *before* we know how income will be distributed, then the rules and outcomes acceptable to everyone would be fair. He then suggested that, without knowing what would happen to them, individuals would be risk averse and hence would vote for *neutral rules and for a more equal distribution of outcomes than actually occurs in the economy*. Indeed, Rawls argued that an individual would agree to an inequality in outcomes only if the inequality increased the income of the least advantaged person for some reason. Rawls' argument suggests that the fairest distribution gives the least well-off member of society the largest income possible.

In actual situations, many do not want a more equal distribution of economic rewards. The Rawlsian analysis suggests an explanation. Those who object know that they have advantages in the economic game. That is, in terms of a race, some people know that they start ahead of many others. Consequently, the necessary social, economic, and political arrangements that might lead to more equality are unlikely to emerge because many of the actors know, expect or hope that they have a high chance of being winners and a low chance of being losers. Moreover, when everyone knows that starting positions are unequal, they find equality of opportunity less attractive because fair outcomes require both fair rules and fair starting positions.

It is worth mentioning here that the Bergson-Samuelson social welfare function $W = W(u_1, u_2, \ldots, u_n)$ is the most general form of all three approaches discussed above: the utilitarian, egalitarian and Rawlsian. They all focus on individual utility.

Social welfare functions which emphasize *process*, such as Nozick (1976), argues that no outcome theory of justice can be valid and that a theory of justice must be based on the justice of the mechanisms through which the distribution of income and wealth arises. Nozick does not consider individual utility an appropriate yardstick for appraising justice, he instead emphasizes the process and argues for defining the justice of a system in terms of well-defined property rights, where private property can be acquired and transferred only through voluntary exchange.

A broader conception of justice which shares the process characteristics is that of Sen (1982). Goods have characteristics that people use to perform certain functionings, and it is the achievement of these functionings (being well-nourished, healthy, mobile, respected, etc.) that indicates welfare. Moreover, it is not only the effective performance of these functionings that is important, but also the entitlement and capability to perform them.

People accept that there will have to be a winner and a loser in any sports game, match or race, and no one seems to boycott all forms of tournaments. People accept this, however, only because they share a belief that the rules of the race are fair and that these rules have been equitably enforced. If the rules are unfair, then an unequal outcome would probably be judged to be an unfair outcome. For example, a race in which one person is allowed to start before the others or in which one person runs a shorter distance would probably be thought to be unfair, whatever the outcome. Put differently, starting at the same time and running the same distance are generally thought to be fair rules. With fair rules, unequal outcomes are fair; with unfair rules, unequal and even equal outcomes are unfair. The conclusion is that an economic outcome cannot be judged to be fair or unfair without considering how it came about.

The idea that fairness is characterized by fair rules pushes the inquiry one step back: it should be determined what fair rules are. Generally, it is argued that *neutrality of the rules or procedures* is an important element of fairness. Thus, rules that treat everyone equally are generally considered fair whereas rules that are different for different individuals are considered unfair. Even when the rules are neutral, however, the standard of 'fairness is fair rules' encounters another difficulty. As the race example illustrates, allowing someone to start early might make the outcome of the race unfair, despite the rules. Clearly, the starting position is particularly important. That is, fairness cannot depend simply on the rules that determine how individuals compete, but must also depend upon the position from which individuals start to compete. For example, a competitive free market society which values self-interest and profitable exchange highly would come out with its own normative view of fairness, as different from a tribal society where senior opinion is highly respected.

We may turn now to the *endogenous theories* about distributive justice. The standpoint here is that being a normative view of the fair distribution, it is only the sovereign group of people who, deducing from their own norms, can define what is fair. According to this standpoint, regimes of fairness which are exogenously proposed are not relevant. For instance, egalitarianism and utilitarianism are obviously outcome-oriented, but they belong to the exogenous theories of distributive justice, as is Rawlsian justice. Nozick's theory, on the other hand, is obviously process-oriented, but exogenous, since it starts with the presumption that a fair outcome is one generated by a fair process and then imposes this belief on all economies or societies studied. Clearly, however, such a belief is not shared by all societies and hence is not endogenous.

Endogenous theories are restricted to those of Varian and Schotter. First, Varian (1974) presents a notion of justice in which an allocation of goods is fair if it is *envy-free* in the sense that no individual in society envies the bundles of any other agent. Here, each individual evaluates all other individuals' bundles in terms of his or her own preferences. If all individuals prefer their own bundles to those of all others, the allocation is deemed envy-free and fair. Clearly, Varian's notion is endogenous and can be classified as outcome-oriented, since only individual preferences are consulted and the criterion is unanimity.

Second, the *blame-freeness* which is put forward by Schotter (1990) is defined

as a notion of justice that looks at the process defining a particular social outcome, evaluates the behavior that each person displayed during this process, and then declares the outcome just or not depending on whether the behavior defining it was reasonable. However, since blame-freeness is an endogenous theory, when we judge any individual's behavior we must do so strictly in terms of the preferences and ethical codes of the individuals in the society we are investigating and they must all agree that their behavior was reasonable. The most straightforward way to evaluate a person's behavior is to put oneself in his position and ask if you would have acted as he did under the circumstances. If the answer is yes, then you cannot blame him for his actions and in that sense his actions are justifiable. Furthermore, if no one can blame anyone else for his actions in determining a particular social outcome, then that outcome will be called 'blame-free' and is just in that sense. Blame-free outcomes can thus be defined as follows: An outcome v in society Z with institutional structure I is justifiable if no social agent in Z can blame any other agent for the actions he took in defining outcome v.

Source: Schotter (1990, p.124)

The following two examples illustrate the kind of questions to be dealt with. First, an entrepreneur, and all agree that he should maximize his profit, has the opportunity to exploit the exclusive rights for the use of a valuable resource that other firms need in order to exist. The entrepreneur, aiming at maximum profit, buys the resource, excludes all other firms from its use,

and establishes himself as a monopolist. Can such an act be justified by the entrepreneur under consideration? How can such an unavoidable but undesirable act be hindered? The government intervenes with regulations because the market fails. The second example is that of a recession which brings about factory closures. Workers who are heads of four-person households are laid off. With no income whatsoever, the laid-off worker steals to maintain his family. Can he be blamed under the circumstances? How can such a crime be avoided? The government intervenes with welfare transfers because of a market failure.

According to blame-free justice, a person who needs to answer these questions begins by asking himself what he would have done if placed in the situation described. He must check his own personal ethical system and decide upon an action. He would then compare his action to the one chosen by the person under consideration. If the two actions are identical, then the original act is a blame-free act. If this is true for all agents in society, then the action and the resulting outcome are universally 'blame-free' and justifiable. Along these lines, it is noted that because blame-freeness looks only at the personal ethics of the actors in society for its justification, these societies are likely to fall victim to their own personal ethical standards. For instance, if, in the above example of the monopolist, society consisted of a group of profit-maximizing oligopolists, the monopoly created there would have to be justifiable despite the intuitive feeling that the act is unfair. Similarly, one can expect stealing and other sorts of crime if an involuntarily-unemployed person has no income to live from.

Actions that are blame-free may define social states that are not Pareto-superior to the state existing before the act was taken. Clearly, in the monopoly case, competitive firms are made worse off as well as the fact that consumer surplus and society as a whole suffers. Yet, no firm blames the monopolist for his action. They would have done the same thing if they had been in his place. In the crime case, negative external effects are incurred on the victimized persons and yet these persons would have done the same if they had no other avenue for survival.

As a result, it can be seen that free markets are capable of determining outcomes in which people have incentives to violate the property rights of others in a blame-free way. Hence, a set of rational economic agents who believe in the market and in the endogenous, process-oriented theories of justice supporting it may very well be able to justify social outcomes that violate people's property rights. A rationality-based justice theory may not respect people's rights to keep what the market gives them.

The implication of blame-freeness for abiding with the law system is a critical issue. According to Schotter, the law is still the law and obeying it may have a rule-utilitarian justification that dominates the blame-freeness of a particular act. However, if certain laws are repeatedly violated by people in a blame-free way, then there is reason to believe that these laws are incomplete and there is a place for introducing other accommodations in the law.

The free market can result in such an unequal distribution of income (and possibly a corner solution) that lead displaced persons into crime activities which are nevertheless judged as blame-free. The state faces a dilemma. The choice is between more real resources going into combating crimes, or entitling and guaranteeing to all individuals a blame-free income (and limiting anti-crime allocations to individuals who commit blameworthy thefts).

The operationalization of the concept of blame-freeness by Schotter has much in common with that of entitlements by Sen.

According to Schotter, blame-freeness should have a unanimity requirement. All people in a relevant population should agree on what they call blame-free actions. The requirement can be weakened by considering solely the judgement of representative, average, wise, judicial, or reasonable persons. Note that in this sense the concepts of blame-freeness and entitlements are closely related.

The institutional structure of the economy under consideration forms the basis for judgements on the blame-freeness of any agent's acts and his/her entitlements. This is necessary because the entitlements that need to be judged do not exist in a vacuum.

7.3 Positive approaches

7.3.1 The normal distribution following a competitive economic choice regime

There is a wide range of concentration measures which describe the actual income distribution among the population in a region. The most commonly-used concentration measure is the Gini coefficient which can be derived from the Lorenz curve, obtained by plotting the percentage of total income (national income) earned by the various income groups within the population. The Gini coefficient gives the area between the observed Lorenz curve and the diagonal line of absolute equality as a proportion of the total area under the diagonal line in Figure 7.3. With complete equality, the poorest quarter would have a quarter of the national income, and the poorest half would have half of the national income, etc. The equality would move along the diagonal. With a great deal of inequality, as depicted by curve 1, the poorest 25 per cent can have 2 or 3 per cent of national income. More generally, as curve 2 lies more northwest of curve 1, the distribution of income in curve 2 is more equal than in curve 1. Note

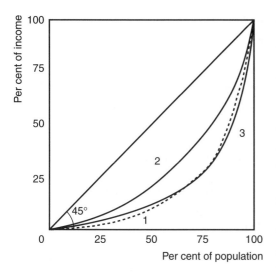

Figure 7.2

that when one curve crosses another, like curves 1 and 3 in the figure, it cannot be optically determined which distribution is more equal.

It can be shown, that for a quite broad class of social welfare functions, including the utilitarian form as a special case, moving from an income distribution such as 1 to one such as 2 in Figure 7.2 will increase social welfare. Intuitively, with diminishing marginal utility of income and equal capacities to enjoy income, a reallocation from a higher-income person to a lower-income person yields a utility gain to the lower-income person that exceeds the loss to the higher. Thus, social welfare must increase when we move from the more unequal income distribution to the more equal one.

The distribution of income as described in Figure 7.2 is generated not only by economic forces like differences in wage rates, but also by differences in the endowments or abilities of individuals. Let us now consider these differences.

Distribution of ability

Although persons are endowed with equal amounts of time, they are not endowed with equal abilities. Physical and mental differences (some inherited, some learned) are such an obvious feature of human life that they hardly need mentioning. But these differences produce differences in earnings and, therefore, differences in income and wealth.

It is impossible to know for sure how such an intangible thing as 'earnings potential based on ability' is distributed among the population. There are, however, many measurable characteristics of people that probably influence their earnings. For example, physical attributes such as height, weight, strength, endurance, as well as intelligence can all be measured objectively. All of these measurable attributes appear to have what is called a normal distribution in the population. For example, if the horizontal axis in Figure 7.3(a) measures intelligence levels and the vertical axis measures the number of persons at each intelligence level, the curve in the figure would trace the percentage of persons at each height. The distribution is symmetric. That is, for each person above the average score of ability there is another person who is below the average by the same amount so that the two are like a mirror image of each other.

Distribution of income

The range of individual ability is a major source of differences in income and wealth. But it is not the only source. If it were, the distributions of income and wealth would have a normal distribution curve that describes the distribution of ability and a large number of other human characteristics as in Figure 7.3(a). In real life, the distribution of income looks like Figure 7.3(b). There are many more people

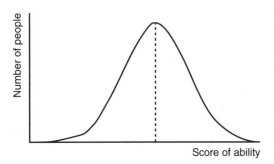

Figure 7.3(a) A normal distribution

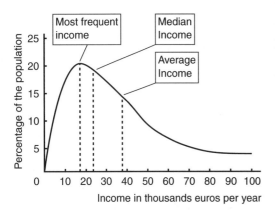

Figure 7.3(b) The actual distribution of income

below the average than above it and a relatively small number of people receive extremely high incomes. The asymmetric shape of the distribution of income and wealth has to be explained by something more than the distribution of individual abilities.

7.3.2   Features and determinants of the normal distribution

Choices and the distribution of income and wealth

A person's income and wealth depend in part on the choices that he or she makes. Households get paid for supplying factors of production – labour services, capital, and natural resources. The income received depends partly

on the price of those factors of production and partly on the quantities that the household chooses to supply. In most cases, people are not able to influence the prices of the factors of production. People, as suppliers of factors of production, are price takers.

In contrast, people can and do choose how much of each factor to supply. They also choose whether to get skilled or not, and whether to put their savings in the bank or not. Each individual chooses how much of each factor to supply. So the distribution of income depends not only on factor prices but also on people's choices about supplying factors.

Positive analysis shows that the choices that people make exaggerate the differences among individuals. Their choices make the distribution of income more unequal than the distribution of abilities and also make the distribution of income skewed. A skewed distribution is one in which there are many more people on one side of the average than on the other. In the case of income distribution, there are more people below the average than above the average. Insight can now be gained into how people's choices lead to an unequal and skewed income distribution.

An example of the distribution of weekly income in a hypothetical context is in Figure 7.4(a). The distribution is symmetric around an average rate of five euros an hour. But, since people who earn a higher hourly wage tend also to work longer hours, their weekly income becomes disproportionately larger than that of people with low hourly wages who work shorter hours, as shown in Figure 7.4(b). Choices, therefore, make the distribution of income skewed. Figure 7.4(b) shows a larger proportion of the population has an income below the average than above the average. The wage rate of the highest paid is only $9/5 = 1.8$ times that of the average wage in Figure 7.4(a); in contrast, the ratio of income of the highest to

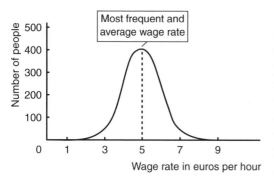

Figure 7.4(a) Distribution of wage rates

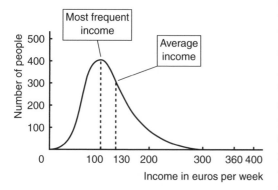

Figure 7.4(b) Distribution of weekly incomes

distribution of hours of work, labour earnings and other income sources in the determination of the distribution of income. The poorest 20 per cent of the population has 5 per cent of the income but does only 2 per cent of the hours of work. The richest 20 per cent receives 43 per cent of the income but does only 35 per cent of the work. It is the middle groups who do a larger percentage of the work than the percentage of income that they receive. There is a direct relationship between the percentage of the work performed and the percentage of income received by each of the five groups. But the poorest and the richest groups each obtain a bigger fraction of the income than the fraction of the work that they perform, while the middle groups perform a bigger fraction of the work than the fraction of the income that they receive. This paradoxical feature of the distribution of income and work reflects the fact that the poorest families receive a large amount of their income directly from the government while the richest receive a large amount of their income in the form of dividends and interest.

There are more causes for unequal incomes. A complete list of causes is reviewed below.

the average is 300/130 = 2.3 times in Figure 7.4(b).

The above example is, of course, artificial. But the point that it illustrates applies in the real world. Other things being equal, the higher the wage rate, the more labour a person will supply; therefore the distribution of income is more unequal than the underlying distribution of abilities. Even if the distribution of abilities is symmetric, the distribution of income will be skewed. More people will have incomes below the average than above the average.

How important is this source of income inequality? It is impossible to give a firm and precise answer to this question, but one can get some idea of its importance by considering the

1 *Differences in ability*. It is universally accepted that people have different capabilities. Some can work harder, learn faster, write better, bargain better, and so on. Hence it should not be surprising that some people are more adept at earning income. Precisely what sort of ability is relevant to earning is a matter of intense debate among economists, sociologists, and psychologists. The talents that make for success in school seem to have some effect, but hardly an overwhelming one. The same is true of innate intelligence. It is clear that some types of inventiveness are richly rewarded by the market, as is that elusive characteristic called 'entrepreneurial

ability'. Also, it is obvious that poor health often impairs earning ability.

2 *Differences in intensity of work.* Some people work longer hours than others, or labour more intensely when they are on the job. This results in certain income differences that are largely voluntary.

3 *Compensating wage differentials.* Some jobs are more arduous than others, or more dangerous, or more unpleasant for other reasons. To induce people to take these jobs, some sort of financial incentive must normally be offered.

4 *Schooling.* Potential workers can sacrifice *current* income in order to improve their skills so that their future incomes will be higher. It is now established that differences in human capital formation are an important cause of income differentials. This particular cause has both voluntary and involuntary aspects. Young men or women who choose not to go to college have made voluntary decisions that affect their incomes. But many never get the choice; their parents simply cannot afford to send them. For them, the resulting income differential is not voluntary.

5 *Work experience.* More experienced workers earn higher wages.

6 *Risk taking and good luck.* Those who gamble and succeed become wealthy. Those who try and fail go broke. Most others prefer not to take such chances and wind up somewhere in between. This is another way in which income differences arise voluntarily. Furthermore, some of the rich got there by good luck. A farmer digging for water discovers oil instead. An investor strikes it rich on the stock market.

7 *Bad luck or corner solutions.* Some of the poor got there largely by bad fortune. A worker trains himself for a highly demanded, well-paid technical occupation only to find that the opportunity has disap-

peared by the time that he can practise the occupation. A construction worker is unemployed for a whole year because of a recession that he had no part in creating. The list could go on and on.

8 *Distortive starting positions.* Gender matters. Those with higher incomes tend to be males, not females. And race matters. Those with higher incomes tend to be white, not black. Neither race nor gender are matters of individual choice; therefore, do the income differences associated with these two characteristics imply unfair starting positions and unfair social rules? Once again, should policies be designed that attempt to change the distribution of income so that gender or race do not matter when outcomes are determined, or should better opportunities be provided for women and minorities and, thus, allow the outcome to determine itself? If education should matter, does everyone have equal access to educational opportunities? If not, should the distribution of income change so that education matters less, or should better opportunities be provided for the disadvantaged to obtain an education?

9 *Inherited wealth.* Not all income is derived from work. The vast majority of people inherit nothing or a very small amount from the previous generation. A tiny number of people inherit enormous fortunes. As a result of bequests, the distribution of income and wealth is not only more unequal than the distribution of ability and job skills but also more persistent. A family that is poor in one generation is more likely to be poor in the next. A family that is enormously wealthy in one generation is more likely to be enormously wealthy in the next. But there is a tendency for income and wealth to converge, across the generations, to the average. Though there can be long

runs of good luck or bad luck, or good judgement or bad judgement, across the generations, such long runs are uncommon.

10 *Assortative mating.* Assortative mating means that people tend to marry within their own socioeconomic class. Marriage partners tend to have similar socioeconomic characteristics. Wealthy individuals seek wealthy partners. The consequence of assortative mating is that inherited wealth becomes more unequally distributed.

In concluding the positive analysis of inequality in the distribution of income and wealth, it can be stated that differences in individual characteristics are closely associated with differences in incomes. As long as the scarce skills and abilities cannot be obtained easily by everyone, an economy based on markets will create an unequal distribution of earnings. Some people with skills or abilities that are in great demand, but are very scarce, will end up enormously rich. Other individuals with skills or abilities that are in abundant supply or not demanded at all will end up poor. Thus, there may be a lack of mobility because:

(a) individuals have *innate* abilities that differ (as for example, someone with special talents);

(b) individuals *choose* not to make changes in order to increase their earnings; or

(c) because individuals are *not allowed* to make changes in order to increase their earnings (for example, by discrimination).

The relationships between earnings and individual characteristics, some of which can be chosen, some of which are innate, and some of which represent imposed bias which is due to informational imperfections, discrimination and other barriers, are important if policy makers are to identify the sort of needed and feasible action. Policy makers are inclined to focus on case (c). This represents an imposed bias and is, as such, a market failure. It is also the most reachable by appropriate policies.

7.4   Income policies

7.4.1   General

Identifying imposed bias

Abilities and the ownership of resources are not shared out equally and this generates the problems of inequality, affluence and poverty. Several imperfections in the market system, in combination with the legal system, lead to the same distributional problems. Blame-freeness occurs for many who cannot earn a living due to non-voluntary factors. Economic discrimination occurs as equivalent factors of production earn different incomes for equal contributions to output. Such discrimination exists in terms of sex, colour and social background. Discrimination is not simply related to employment opportunities but also to educational opportunities which, in turn, influence ultimate employment.

Inherited wealth and good and bad luck play also a role. The majority of the very rich acquired their initial wealth as a result of the activities of others. Some achieved their wealth through good luck, e.g. the farmer who finds oil on his land. And some can blame bad luck for their present situation, e.g. the worker who trains to be a skilled craftsman only to find that a fall in demand results in no job opportunities.

Ironically, the labour market can do its job too well and market clearance can end up with a 'corner solution', in which some workers are employed and reasonably remunerated and the incomes of other workers may be practically zero or at least below the poverty level. Especially in some developing countries, the number of unskilled workers is so high that efficiency would dictate paying unskilled workers a zero or near-zero wage. In economic jargon, their 'shadow wage' is zero. Hence, if there are no other means of maintenance, those workers would face starvation, all reasoned from grounds of economic efficiency.

The existence of corner solutions creates additional problems when 'cornered' agents respond antisocially, though rationally, to their elimination from the labour market. Since workers behave very much like business firms by entering those industries that seem most profitable and leaving those industries least profitable, rational workers are faced with the decision to allocate their time to a variety of activities such as remunerated employment, vocational training, house work and crime. For a rational worker, the problem is a maximization problem, whose solution would give time allocations to the alternative activities, in correspondence with relative prices.

A person who is facing a below-poverty wage – a corner solution – may rationally decide to allocate some of his time to illegal activities, such as stealing and drug trafficking. Such persons who are less averse to risk may allocate more of their time to criminal activity. The crime industry is specially attractive for the structurally unemployed as it is an industry with very low educational entry barriers.

The existence of such corner solutions and the crime associated with them is obviously an important factor to consider when discussing in a positive way the distribution bias and the proper role of government intervention in free labour markets. Obviously, if it can be shown that a segment of the population is paid an extremely low wage or none, and they cannot choose otherwise, then this would be all the proof needed.

The following examples, based on Schotter (1990, pp.73–7), illustrate the problem. S_1 in Figure 7.5 depicts what the labour supply curve

would look like if all low-skilled labourers offered their services to the market in order to employ all of them no matter what wage they received. Since there is no sensitivity to the wage the labour supply is depicted as a vertical curve. Under these assumptions, the intersection of D and S_1 depicts what the equilibrium wage for low-skilled labour would be if workers were insensitive to the wage they received from work – say about 1.50 euros or dollars an hour.

This wage for a family of four living in Western Europe or North America with two full-time, low-wage workers working 40 hours a week, 50 weeks a year would not be able to lift themselves out of poverty, especially when it is considered that taxes are with-held from their wages as well. As a consequence, such low wage rates do not exist in the labour market today because many workers refuse to work for them and, as a result, leave the labour market. Because of this, the supply curve shifts upwards to the elastic form S_2 which results in a somewhat higher wage, say 2.0 euros or dollars, but already too high to absorb all the discouraged workers. Note that S_2 is the conventional elastic supply curve observed in

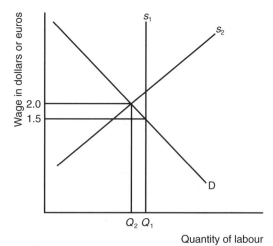

Figure 7.5

labour markets. It is elastic and downwards to the right because some potential workers withdraw from the labour force.

The implications of the above for microeconomic policy making are obvious. Policy makers cannot evaluate the market for low-skilled workers in the same way as the market for wheat. If the equilibrium price of wheat is low, little of it will be produced and the discouraged wheat producers will take their resources and employ them *productively* in their next best opportunity. Displaced workers, however, may allocate some of their labour time to socially destructive ends. Hence, there is a social cost (crime) which goes with low-equilibrium wages. The market fails by not capturing the social cost. The market solution in the form of a too-low or zero wage generates a negative external effect that may be a *rational* response to the set of market wages. This type of negative externality was encountered earlier in the chapter on externalities.

Policies to combat imposed bias

State intervention to redistribute income and wealth can be done in two ways. The first approach – market interventions – involves the manipulation of prices so that some earn more, while others earn less, than they would have done. Where governments impose minimum wage rates on employers or maximum rent charges on landlords, they are indulging in this type of behaviour. The working of the price mechanism is thus being distorted.

The second approach – transfer measures – involves taking from some people in order to give to others. Clearly this would involve taxation and government expenditure decisions. This approach alters the relative incentives that the market mechanism would provide. If a person is deprived of part of what he earns, his incentive to earn, so the argument goes, will

decrease. Although doubts have been expressed about the extent of this effect, such an outcome will distort the incentives thrown up by the market system.

Next to a discussion of these two approaches of income policies which are of particular validity in the short- and medium-terms, in this chapter we shall treat trade-offs between growth and redistribution and the role of re-endowment strategies in the long-term.

7.4.2   Earnings policies

Economic effects of a *fixation of minimum wages* for unskilled workers are demonstrated in Figure 7.6. In the absence of government intervention the equilibrium wage would be W_0 with Q_0 workers being employed. If this wage is considered 'unacceptably low', the government may set a minimum wage of W_1. Unfortunately, this increase in real income may occur at the expense of the number of workers employed, which falls to Q_1, with perhaps as many as Q_1Q_2 unemployed. Q_2 is the number of workers attracted to the market at the higher wage rate.

An alternative policy is the combination of a minimum wage and a wage subsidy to the

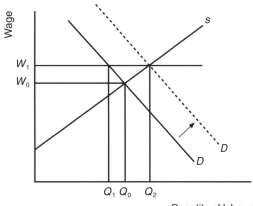

Figure 7.6

perspective employer. This is a more attractive policy. The demand curve will shift upwards, as shown in the figure, and absorbs more employment. The wage subsidy can be partly or wholly financed from the unemployment benefits which would otherwise have been paid to the unemployed.

7.4.3 Transfer policies

In most industrial countries, *targeted welfare policy* means that relief is given – in cash or in kind – to persons who have themselves contacted the authorities and who have been able to demonstrate a specific kind of need accepted as valid ground for government support. Normally, these 'acceptable' forms of need refer to certain kinds of unemployment, illness, absence of a family head, etc. Targeted welfare policy thus implies a screening of applicants so that people with certain kinds of need are 'rewarded' while others are not.

An alternative is a *generalized welfare policy system* which consists of negative income taxes (NIT) that are made to shift gradually to positive income taxes, this next to accentuating progressiveness in income and wealth taxes. Such a system would meet a given distribution goal more efficiently.

In popular discussions the NIT is largely thought of as an antipoverty programme, not as a tool for general income equalization. A negative income tax means that an income earner (with possible exceptions) will receive payments if his income falls short of a certain level. His disposable income may then develop as shown in Figure 7.7. Without any income earnings at all he will receive a maximum amount – a guaranteed minimum income – of, say, 1000 euros or dollars per year. If he earns an income of 1000, he will receive an amount of, say, 500, and so on up to a break-even level of income earned of, say, 2000 at which no payments

(negative taxes) are received, nor are any ordinary positive taxes paid. The marginal negative income tax rate here is 50 per cent. Above the before-tax income level of 2000, taxes are paid as usual. The personal income tax is thought to be a means of promoting equality. Indeed, it is probably given more credit for this than it actually deserves. The reason is that the personal income tax is widely known to be progressive, meaning that incomes after tax are distributed more equally than incomes before tax because the rich turn over a larger share of their incomes to the tax collector. Research suggests that the degree of equalization attributable to the tax is, however, rather modest.

Taxes on inheritances and estates levied by both the state and the federal governments are another equalizing feature of the generalized welfare policy system. These are aimed at limiting the incomes of the rich, or at least at limiting their ability to transfer this largesse from one generation to the next. Usually the amount of transfers involved is too small to make much difference to the overall distribution of income. Normally speaking, total receipts from estate and gift taxes by all levels of government are

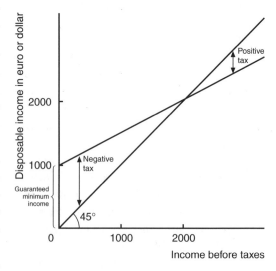

Figure 7.7

well under 1 per cent of total tax revenues in any country.

Targeted and generalized welfare benefits policies may overlap as in the case of in-work tax benefits which, in practice, concentrate on specific groups without intentionally excluding the larger labour force.

Policy example 7.1

Alternatives in transfer policies

In choosing between the *targeted* and *generalized welfare policy systems*, the following four sub-targets for welfare policy can function as criteria of social efficiency. They are objective criteria and, in principle, are completely separable from political values for determining which groups to support and with how much.

1 support those who are eligible for support;
2 avoid giving relief to those not eligible for support;
3 maintain individual incentives for earning a living, that is, to maintain work incentives;
4 keep administrative costs for welfare policy at a low level.

Targeted welfare policies

If the value premises on which distribution policy is based imply that only people with specific kinds of need should be eligible for support, the targeted policy measures may appear to be efficient in at least one respect: those who are not eligible for support are not given any help (aside from pure cases of fraud).

On the other hand, the targeted welfare system may be *inefficient* in two other respects. Firstly, not everybody who is eligible for support receive assistance within the framework of existing welfare programmes. Secondly, criteria for assistance are so crude that small changes in work income have sometimes led to larger changes in welfare payments in the opposite direction.

Generalized welfare policies

These make primary use of negative income taxes, next to a secondary use of other progressive income and wealth taxes. The appraisal of negative income taxes in terms of the above mentioned four criteria of social efficiency have been reviewed in many sources. The following summary is based on Bohm (1987, pp.97–8).

1 As a system of negative income taxes implies that 'welfare payments' are tied to earnings, these payments can be arranged to be made more or less automatically, for example by a system of 'preliminary payments', a kind of negative with-holding tax. By contrast, as it was pointed out, traditional policy requires information and initiative on the part of the poor. Moreover, the means tests of traditional policy might be regarded as a humiliating process and might thus deter those who are entitled to support from actually trying to get it. This implies that the traditional welfare system will actually reach a smaller proportion of the target population than a system of negative taxes and hence be less efficient in this respect.

2 The risk of making welfare payments to those who are *not* eligible for support exists in a system of negative taxes in the sense that fraudulent income tax returns can now also be made by those who have small earnings. This system, then, may turn out to be less efficient as far as unwanted welfare payments are concerned, even though there are also possibilities of fraud in the traditional welfare system.

3 It is sometimes suggested that incentives to work will be lower, or even disappear in some cases, under a system of negative taxes. Whether or not this is reasonable to assume would to some extent depend on the level of negative taxes. But even if quite substantial amounts were involved, full-time work could still be relied upon to provide a significantly-higher level of disposable income, thus maintaining at least some work incentives. Furthermore, since work is not only a way to make a living but also an opportunity to do something, voluntary unemployment may be expected to stay at low levels. In fact, it seems quite possible to design a system of negative taxes so that work incentives would not be lower than in the traditional system. In the example treated earlier in connection with Figure 7.8, low-income earners always retained 50 per cent of their earnings. Thus, the frustrating situation of a complete withdrawal of welfare payments in the presence of small changes in earnings, which was seen to happen under traditional welfare policy, need not arise here.

4 The evidence from a set of negative income tax experiments in the United States suggests that there is a small negative effect on labour supply. But, in addition, there are indications that those who succeed in being hired under a system of negative income taxes actually tend to stay employed for a longer period of time (as compared with people in control groups without any such system). This may be interpreted as follows: a negative income tax system provides income security to the individual, enabling him to spend more time searching for a job (among other things) and it is more likely that he ends up finding one that suits him better.

7.5 Trade-offs and re-endowment strategies in the long run

So far, our discussion may be summarized as follows. An economy, which is capable of adjusting quickly to equilibrium positions and in which the actual income distribution is the desired one, does not need economic policy other than the reallocation policy implied by welfare theory; that is, policy measures aimed at making the allocation Pareto-optimal in equilibrium positions. However, as we indicated earlier, market adjustments to equilibrium positions are, in reality, often quite slow; sticky wages and unemployment, general or local, are perhaps the most common example. Hence, the government intervenes directly in the market mechanism, and thereby the welfare postulates lose their relevance. Besides, use of the tax system, which is unavoidable, is found to be no less distorting than direct intervention in the market.

Departure from the welfare postulates becomes necessary when it is furthermore recognized that there are long-term interactions between efficiency and equity. Specifically, this section discusses the trade-off between growth and distribution, and how this trade-off is mitigated by intergenerational mobility.

The big trade-off

The term relates to the 'big trade-off' between equality and growth, and is due to Okun (1975). The idea behind it is that, to achieve greater equality, taxes have to be imposed on more productive activities and transferred to less productive activities. Taxing people lowers their income and makes them work and save less. A reduction in factor supplies results in a smaller output and less consumption not only for the rich but also, possibly, for the poor. Furthermore, any redistribution must be administered by tax-collecting and -transferring agencies which costs resources. If all these effects are considered, the poor person may receive only a small proportion of the dollar tax collected from the rich person.

When the reallocative, disincentive and administrative aspects of redistribution are taken into account, it is not obvious that taking a dollar from a rich person to give to a poor person increases the welfare of the poor person. The wealth available for redistribution could be reduced to the point where everyone is worse off. Taking account of the disincentive effects of redistribution and the resource costs of administering the redistribution is what produces the 'big trade-off'. A more equally-shared pie results in a smaller pie.

As a result, for a growing economy, the optimal distribution of income should always involve *some* inequality, because the total amount of income in society is not independent of how it is distributed. Figure 7.8 illustrates

this. The curve *abcde* represents possible combinations of GDP and income equality that are obtainable. If, for example, point *c* is the current position of the economy, raising taxes on the rich to finance more transfers to the poor might move the economy downward to the right, towards point *d*. Equality increases, but GDP falls as the rich react to higher marginal tax rates by producing less. Similarly, reducing both taxes and social welfare programmes might move the economy upward to the left, towards point *b*. Notice that, to the left of point *b*, GDP falls as inequality rises. Here there is no trade-off – perhaps because very poorly-paid workers are less productive due to inadequate investment in human capital, poor nutrition, or just a general sense of disaffection.

The curve *ABCDE* represents possible combinations of GDP and equality under some new, more efficient, redistributive policy. It is more efficient in the sense that, for any desired level of equality, we can get more GDP with the policy represented by *ABCDE* than with the policy represented by *abcde*.

Intergenerational mobility and re-endowment strategies

Are there policies for achieving higher growth and more equity in the longer term, and thus avoiding a trade-off as described above? If the time horizon is expanded to consider intergenerational mobility and endowment strategies to enrich the productive levels of those child segments of future generations which are currently denoted as poor, the outcome can be the creation of new long-term mechanisms of growth with equity which escape the trade-off. Chapter 8 will touch again on these long-term mechanisms of growth with equity.

Incomes increase with age and they do so fairly uniformly across the income distribution. This means that some, but not all, of those at

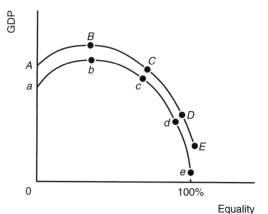

Figure 7.8

the bottom of the income distribution are there because they are young. These individuals can expect to move upward with age. Unfortunately, there is far less data on other aspects of economic mobility.

Mobility and equality are substitutes, in an important sense. That is, if no one changed position in the income distribution, then narrowing the distribution would create more equality. If the distribution remained the same but a substantial fraction of the population changed position each year, however, then there would be more equality as well. This makes the development of public policies a delicate matter because policies that narrow the inequality in the distribution but make mobility more difficult may very well *increase* rather than decrease truly-experienced inequality at the individual career level. Conversely, policies that enhance mobility may very well *increase* measured annual inequality while decreasing truly-experienced inequality. Public policies may or may not have this effect, so evaluating those policies by the distribution of annual incomes alone requires cautious judgement.

Education is often thought of as one of the principal ways to escape from poverty and to promote economic growth in the long-term.

Policy example 7.2

Redistribution dynamics

One example of the redistribution of endowments over time, their effect on intergenerational mobility and the relative income positions of the current generation is available from the Panel of Income Dynamics studies.

Results for the USA in the table below show that about 36 per cent of the children with parents in the highest fifth of the income distribution also found themselves in that position in 1981, whereas 44 per cent of the children of those in the bottom fifth of the income distribution found themselves in the same position as their parents in 1981. This does indicate that the children of the very rich and very poor were somewhat more likely to be rich or poor, but it also indicates that the chances were less than 50–50 that a child would do as well as his or her parents. One caution – these children were young entrants in the labour force while, obviously, their parents were older. Age-related differences in income account for part of these differences between the incomes of the old and the young. The endowment mechanisms behind these mobility trends lie primarily in the expansion of educational opportunities to families with limited access.

Table 7.2 Intergenerational changes in income positions

Parent's income position, 1969, by quintile	Young adult's income position, 1981 by quintile				
	Highest	Second	Third	Fourth	Lowest
Highest	36	23	19	13	9
Second	25	26	22	17	10
Third	17	26	23	23	11
Fourth	15	19	19	24	23
Lowest	2	9	18	27	44

Sources: Ulla (1984, pp.62–76) and Duncan et al. (1984)

There is no doubt that many children have used this route successfully, and still do. The educational effects meant here are those of the long-term as they take a generation or more to be realized. By contrast, a variety of educational programmes collectively known as public assistance are specifically designed to alleviate poverty, are mainly meant to help adults, and are intended to have quick but not necessarily long-term foundational effects.

Questions for discussion and further research

1 Review your understanding of the following terms: outcome and process theories of normative income distribution, Rawls' theory of justice, Sen's entitlements, Varian's envy-free, Schotter's blame-freeness, Pareto's alpha, assortative mating, NIT, Okun's big trade-off, re-endowment strategies and intergenerational mobility.

2 Study the following statements and comment on their implications for policy making:
(i) People who earn more per hour tend to work more hours. Show graphically how the distribution of income is affected. (ii) An intergenerational measure of the degree of equal probabilities of moving upwards or downwards in the income distribution is superior to static measures of equality.

3 What is the position of the three utility-oriented normative theories of distributive justice with respect to introduction of (i) minimum wages, and (ii) progressive taxes?

4 Demonstrate graphically that a wage subsidy in combination with a minimum wage is superior to a minimum wage.

Further reading

On inequality and measurement aspects of income distribution see Sen, A.K. (1992): *Inequality re-examined*, Harvard University Press, Cambridge, Mass. See also an extensive review of Sen's in Sugden, R. (1993): 'Welfare, Resources, and Capabilities', in *Journal of Economic Literature*, Vol. XXXI.4, pp.1947–62.

On normative approaches to income distribution, see Rawls, J. (1972): *A Theory of Justice*, Clarendon Press, Oxford. See also Schotter, A. (1990): *Free Market Economics*, Blackwell, Cambridge, Ma.

On positive analysis of income distribution the following four references review recent evidence in different country contexts: Levy, F. and Murnane, R.J. (1992): 'U.S. Earnings Levels and Earnings Inequality, a review of recent trends and proposed explanations', in *Journal of Economic Literature*, Vol. XXX.3, pp.1333–81; Oxley, H., Burnlaux, J.M., Dang, T.T., D'Ercole, M.M. (1997): 'Income Distribution and Poverty in 13 OECD Countries', in *OECD Economic Studies*, Vol. 29, pp.55–91; Brainerd, E. (1998): 'Winners and Losers in Russia's Economic Transition', in *American Economic Review*, Vol. 88.5, pp.1094–116.

The literature on microeconomic policies of income distribution via wage interventions, income transfers, and resource re-endowment of the less privileged is vast. To facilitate focus in further reading, a selection of comparative regional policy reviews can be found in the following selection of three references: Dolado, J. et al. (1996): 'The Economic Impact of Minimum Wages in Europe', in *Economic Policy*, 1996 Issue; Haveman, R. (1996): 'Reducing Poverty while Increasing Employment, a primer of alternative strategies, and a blueprint', in *OECD Economic Studies*, Vol. 26, pp.7–41; Macfarlan, M. and Oxley, H. (1996): 'Social Transfers: Spending Patterns, Institutional Arrangements and Policy Responses', in *OECD Economic Studies*, Vol. 27, pp.147–94.

Chapter 7 ended with a consideration of the trade-off between growth and equality. This topic is highlighted again in Chapter 8, in the context of an increasing role for the state in mitigating the trade-off in the long-term. For a review of theory and empirical evidence on the trade-off in the long-term, see Aghion, P., Caroli, E. and Garcia-Penalosa, C. (1999): 'Inequality and Economic Growth: The Perspective of the New Growth Theories', in *Journal of Economic Literature*, Vol. XXXVII.4, pp.1615–60.

State intervention: review of mechanisms, limitations and reforms

8.1 Introduction

In general, market failures call for government actions. Government actions can belong to the sphere of regulations, control and stimulation, as in the case of policies for competition; or to the sphere of the state budget, which includes use of taxes, subsidies and public spending. The latter is the main resort in policies of technology, industry, public goods and social welfare.

But the government also has public failures. In the sphere of regulations it may favour one or the other party in economically-inefficient ways. In the sphere of state budget, the actions may lead to static inefficiency in the sense of an overproduction of public goods and resource misallocation. The overexpansion of the public share in the whole economy can also lead to dynamic inefficiency in the sense of a lower growth in the long-term.

Public failure is the focus of this chapter and the causes behind the failure will be discussed under four headings:

1 Subjection of state to influence from electorate and pressure groups
2 Bureaucratic bias
3 Motivational problems
4 Price distortions.

It will be also seen that the above factors can lead to the relative overproduction of public goods *vis-à-vis* private goods, and to an excessive share of the public sector in the national income. This may in turn result in static and dynamic inefficiencies. There are other factors than state failure which lead to a higher share of the public sector. These factors will be dealt with briefly in section 6. The need for monitoring state performance and introduction of state reform is dealt with in two illustrations at the end of this chapter.

8.2 The electorate and pressure groups

8.2.1 The political market place

Taking the standard case of a parliamentary democracy, it can be stated that government response to market failures is only partly determined by the economics of the failure. Popular vote and pressure groups play prominent roles in shaping government policy. In seeing how the electorate influences government behaviour, it is helpful to apply standard microeconomics to the political market place, see for example Hartley and Tisdell (1981). Just like any other market, the political market place consists of buyers and sellers who undertake mutually-beneficial exchange within constitutional borders. The voters are the buyers: they demand goods and services as well as policies from the governing party. In exchange they supply production factors like labour for public-sector employment and taxation. The buyers are assumed to maximize their utility, which is derived from alternative policies, taking into account different prices and taxation schemes that are related to these policies.

The elected politicians can be considered as business shareholders, or potential suppliers. It is assumed that political parties maximize votes. Individual politicians do not necessarily do this. In reality, some or many can be egotistic, self-interested, and trying to maximize rewards and satisfactions of office rather than seeking office to implement their beliefs. The winning political party in an election becomes the actual supplier. The winning political party of course wants to stay in office after the next election and therefore is assumed to seek re-election, whereas the opposition will be striving for office.

The winning party's plans are implemented by government bureaucracies who can be compared to business executives. Bureaucracies are responsible for public goods like defence, roads

and education. As we will see, bureaucracies play an important role in government failures, resulting in misallocation of resources, by unnecessarily increasing the public share. The behaviour of bureaucracies has largely to do with asymmetric information: bureaucracies are experts in their field of research whereas their superiors only have a general idea of what is going on in the departments. Because it is too costly for any individual minister to monitor bureaucracies, they have an opportunity to biasly influence the quantity and efficiency of public-sector output. There are several models that describe bureaucratic behaviour. A crucial assumption in these models is that bureaucrats maximize their budgets.

Another actor in the political market place is the interest or pressure group. There are several types of these groups, such as employers, trade unions, farming, high unemployment areas and so on. These groups have one thing in common: they influence policies to meet their objectives. In this way public expenditures may rise to an unnecessarily high level. Just like the bureaucracies, this is due to information problems.

We started with the voters, to be compared with consumers. Voters are also subject to information constraints, and searching information costs money. Also, their knowledge is limited. This provides an opportunity for politicians, bureaucracies and interest groups, which do dispose of specialist information, to influence opinion, voting and policy.

8.2.2 Political market failures

Just like a normal market, the political market may lead to suboptimal outcomes. Perfect competition, in the context of political markets, exists if parties would compete and thereby eliminate abnormal 'profits' that might arise due to discretionary behaviour on the supply side. So with a large number of voters and political parties and with no significant entry barriers, a Pareto-optimal solution would result, in which parties respond to demands of voters. However, in reality a lot of these conditions are not satisfied, just like in normal markets. Various imperfections exist, which lead to Pareto-suboptimality. Examples of imperfections are:

- Indivisibilities whereby competition is of the all-or-nothing type; the winning party gets the whole market.
- Uncertainty and imperfect information faced by voters.
- Interdependent behaviour (externalities) from the side of interest groups who influence voters and policy makers (and thereby policies).
- Voters cannot commit politicians to do as they have promised, so there is room for discretionary behaviour on the side of politicians.
- The electoral system influences the preference revelation of voters: usually one votes for a package instead of specific issues. This means that indivisibilities are present: voter preferences are not genuinely revealed.

Now that the political market place has been described, the question can be answered as to how exactly the electorate influences public policy, and in particular, the size of the public share in the whole economy.

8.2.3   The median voter and the public share

We assume that there is a democracy, in which the majority voting rule applies. This rule says that in the choice between two alternatives, the alternative that receives the majority of votes wins. As voters maximize utility, they will choose that political party that gives them the highest utility. Voters will consider the past

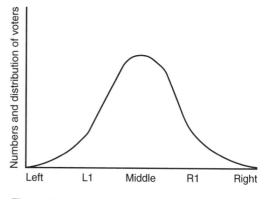

Figure 8.1

record of political parties, related to what they had promised to do initially, as a basis for future performance and based on this they make their final decision on which party to elect.

Vote-maximizing political parties want to find out the preferences of citizens. Assume that a decision on one issue has to be made. The opinion on this decision can be represented from left (socialist) to right (conservative) on the x-axis in Figure 8.1. Each voter is assumed to have single-peaked preferences so that he/she chooses the party closest to his/her preferred position. The political votes are normally distributed along the x-axis as shown in the figure below. The peak of a normal distribution lies above the middle of the x-axis (the median).

Assuming that two parties strive for office, the optimal strategy for both parties is to adopt the policy favoured by the median voter. Thus, the majority-voting equilibrium is the policy preferred by the median voter. If a party chooses R1 or L1 it can gain votes by moving towards the middle of the figure. The problem for each party is to find the exact location at the middle of the distribution.

Three important implications can be drawn from this result.

1 Consensus politics is likely to emerge. Both parties agree on any policy issue favoured by a majority of voting. Of course, parties will try to differentiate their policies. Otherwise, both parties will look the same. The limits to differentiation are given by the voters: moving to either of the political extremes will, beyond a certain point, lead to net losses of votes.

2 Policies of democratic governments tend to favour producers more than consumers. Voters whose income is directly influenced by a policy are likely to be well informed (producers), whereas voters whose income is not directly influenced (consumers) will be less informed. Therefore, policies of democratic governments tend to favour producers more than consumers. Examples are: tariffs and import control that favour domestic firms and create domestic jobs, while consumers pay in the form of higher prices; or policies that support higher prices in agriculture so as to protect farmers, and the price incidence is shifted to consumers.

3 Redistribution will be towards the median voter. As policies tend to focus on the median voter, the median voter, and thus all voters that favour the same policies as the median voter, automatically become a powerful interest group: any policy which negatively influences their income will be rejected. This means that either the policy has to be revised or redistribution of income towards the median voter has to take place. Both measures are, of course, to prevent loss of votes. If the median voter belongs to the middle class, redistribution will be towards this middle class, whereas if the median voter is relatively poor, redistribution will be directed towards the poor. Downs (1957) calls this the coercion-via-the-ballot-box argument whereby many poor outvote the fewer rich to impose redistributive tax and benefit regimes. Apart from their electoral power (when forming a majority), the middle class and the poor could influence policy by acting as a 'real' interest groups, e.g. poverty lobbies.

What happens to the public share as a consequence of redistribution of income towards the median voter, crucially depends on the median voter's income. This can be shown by Figures 8.2(a) and 8.2(b), based on Stiglitz (1988), below. Figure 8.2(a) shows what happens with uniform taxation, Figure 8.2(b) shows the result of progressive taxation (rich people are taxed relatively more than poor people). The preferred level of public expenditures is given by the maximum utility of a certain level of public expenditures (public goods). At this point, the marginal cost in utility terms, or the foregone utility of consumption of private goods due to taxation, is equal to the marginal benefit (utility) of increased public expenditure. In other words, the net marginal benefit (utility) from additional government expenditures is equal to zero. Poor individuals are less willing to give up consumption of private goods for an increase in public goods compared to rich people. They also gain from additional public goods, but this gain is normally less than the foregone utility of consuming private goods due to higher tax payments. Therefore, rich individuals prefer higher levels of expenditures on public goods. This is shown in Figure 8.2(a). Now poor individuals have to pay relatively less taxes as expenditures on public goods increase. As a result, poor individuals prefer a higher level of public expenditures. This is shown in Figure 8.2(b), where the preferred quantity of public goods by poor individuals actually exceeds that of rich individuals.

Some qualifying notes on this theory of voting are justified. First of all, alternative distributions

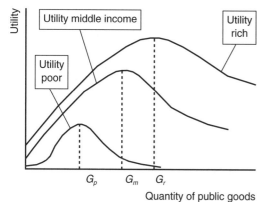

Figure 8.2(a) Public share under uniform taxation

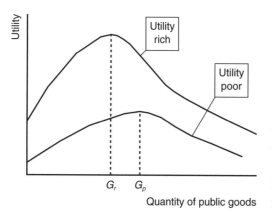

Figure 8.2(b) Public share under progressive taxation

next to the normal distribution are possible. For example, the distribution might be uniform: the voters are evenly distributed across the whole political spectrum. This results in a multi-party system. Also, the voters might be equally distributed between the political extremes.

Secondly, alternative voting rules are possible, for example, the unanimity rule or proportional representation instead of the majority voting rule. From the Pareto-efficiency point of view the unanimity rule is simple and direct, because everybody has to agree with a certain policy change. If at least one person is worse off, he/she will vote against the change so that

the change is prevented. However, this leads to an enforcement of the status quo: policy is unlikely to change. In contrast, the majority voting rule is more complex since it allows for potential Pareto-improvements which have to be appraised. If, with a majority supporting the policy change, potential gainers are able to compensate losers, the policy change is a potential Pareto-improvement. Besides, in practice, potential gainers are not always able to compensate losers so that the situation after the change (even if compensation takes place) is not Pareto-optimal anymore. Furthermore, the inability of potential gainers to compensate potential losers might induce these losers to bribe the gainers to vote against the policy change.

Thirdly, up to now, public goods were considered as homogenous goods. In practice public goods differ in quality, which makes them heterogeneous. Therefore, public goods that differ in quality are normally considered as two different products. This implicates that if the median voter demands a higher quality (a more expensive good), public expenditure will rise.

A fourth point to consider is that a majority-voting equilibrium might not exist. This is known as the paradox of the voting: the outcome of the voting is dependent on the way the alternatives are presented. If, in Figure 8.1, preferences are not single-peaked but have multiple peaks (the utility derived from a certain policy goes up, then down, and then goes up again) a majority-voting equilibrium might not exist.

Finally, whether the high preference of poor people for more public goods, and thus a bigger government, will also mean that the poor people will realize the highest benefits from the public goods, is not certain. In some countries there is evidence that tertiary redistribution benefits the rich more than the poor as far as health and education facilities are concerned. Housing, public parks, etc. are more utilized by the poor, so that it is more likely that poor people mostly benefit from it.

8.2.4 Pressure groups and the public share

Pressure groups are groups that try to influence policy in their own favour. For example when several firms strive for a monopoly position each of them might try to 'buy' these rights by lobbying for protection against competition. The firm who bids the most is likely to get the monopoly position. Each firm's maximum bid will be equal to the expected profit that will be made in the monopoly position.

The foregoing example shows that lobbying for favourable policies can be regarded as an auction: the governments supply favourable legislation to groups which outbid their rivals. A group is willing to pay a price equal to the expected profit of protective legislation. Payments in general may take the form of bribes, votes, cash contributions to the governing party, supply of persuasive information, provision of campaign speakers, and so on.

Note that these payments are not necessarily socially wasteful: e.g. in our example the payments are not more than transfers from the (potential) monopolist to the government. The government, however, spends the received payments. First of all it supplies favourable regulations to the one that outbids his/her rivals, which mostly lead to social distortions (deadweight loss). Furthermore, the rest of the money is likely to be used in a non-optimal way by politicians and bureaucracies. For a recent overview of the modelling of government as a rent-seeker, see Nitzan (1994).

The most influential type of interest group is the one that arises from the income-earning side of the voters. In the market, substantial information and transaction costs are present.

In such an environment, people are likely to be best informed in the area of their speciality, which is their income-earning (production) activity. So producer groups, like firms and unions, are important sources of information which have to be taken into account by the government.

An additional advantage that adds to their strength is that they dispose of substantial amounts of money which can be used to influence government policy. In order to influence politics, producer groups have to show that they are more knowledgeable than the best-informed voters. This is very easy because voters are usually generalists, whereas producer groups are specialists. To become a specialist in a certain area a lot of information has to be acquired, while producer groups already dispose of most of the information. If new information is required it is easy for them to acquire it, not least because of scale economies in the collection and distribution of data. Also, producer groups like trade unions can charge the costs to the enterprise.

Producer groups not only acquire information just because they have to, but also because they find it worthwhile to: the potential returns from purchasing information to influence policy are high enough to make the initial investments worthwhile. Of course, income earners will gain directly from any policy that is in their favour. And because this money is spent in a lot of areas, the area of earning is much more vital to them than their spending or consuming activities.

This all sounds reasonable, except for one thing: it seems unlikely that vote-sensitive governments ignore large numbers of consumers and focus only on a small group of producers. Vote-maximizing governments will only be concerned about the income of voters if this affects votes. If this is not the case, or if the voter does not realize that his/her income is affected, the government does not need to look after the effects on income of voters and can behave discretionary.

The argument above still does not explain why consumers do not organize themselves in an interest group, to protect themselves against producers, and so influence policy in their favour instead of the favour of producers. The reason is given by the fact that it is costly to form such groups: consumers have to be located, and negotiations have to take place about how much each individual has to contribute to the group and about how the benefits are divided up. For an individual consumer it is too costly to acquire all relevant information and the benefits to this consumer are likely to be (relatively) small because others can free-ride. So overall the government will tend to oversupply policies favouring producer groups.

There are organizational limits to the number and size of interest groups as formulated by Olson (1971). Large groups have higher costs of communication, identifying potential group members, bargaining, higher cost of staffing, and so on. If the group is small, these costs are much lower. As a result, more groups will be formed.

On the benefit side there is a problem of free-riding: the benefits of government policies, partly brought about by lobbying of interest groups, are available to *all* so that no individual has an incentive to join a specific group. In that case, no group would exist, but reality shows otherwise. Olson concluded that groups only exist if they are small (low costs of forming and maintaining the group), or if there is coercion or some incentive to make individuals act in their common interest.

Olson explains the existence of large groups in terms of their linkage with private organizations. These groups come into being either through coercion (people working in a certain branch are obligated to become a member of a certain group) or by offering private (non-collective) benefits to individual members. Examples of groups that result from coercion are professional bodies consisting of accountants, doctors or lawyers, who govern themselves by specifying rules of conduct and minimum standards and qualifications for practitioners. These bodies have the power to discipline members who fail to maintain the required standards. Examples of benefits that can be acquired by membership of a professional body, are favourable access to insurance, access to recognition, exchanges in conferences and journals, and professional support. So both negative (coercion) and positive (incentives) stimuli are used to maintain large organizations, which can then act as powerful interest groups.

8.3 Bureaucratic bias

Bureaucracies are governmental departments. They advise governments (local, regional, national) on present microeconomic policies, and on opportunities for new initiatives. In practice this ranges from the provision of public goods, like defence, to purchasing goods and services from the private sector. They also take care of collecting taxes, regulation of firms and industries, and of redistribution policies.

In the context of the political market place, bureaucracies are the suppliers of goods, services and information to the governing party and the community. Because of their protected position (entry is restricted, and all property rights are allocated towards the existing bureaucracies) they are the sole suppliers in their specialist area.

Because each bureaucracy specializes in a certain area, there is usually no competition within the public sector. The lack of competition leads to opportunities for discretionary behaviour. The special position of bureaucracies is similar to that of the interest groups: they are also extremely well informed in their specialist area, and in the absence of alternative information resources the government is not sufficiently well informed to question a bureau's behaviour.

To increase their departments, bureaucracies often want parts of the public sector to be centralized. In this way, a bilateral monopoly will come into being: the bureau is the sole supplier, whereas the government is the monopsonist who purchases goods, services and information in return for an agreed budget.

How does the opportunity for discretionary behaviour arise? Discretionary behaviour is typical for large organizations operating in non-competitive markets with ill-defined objectives. The larger an organization, the bigger the control loss which gives rise to opportunities for discretionary behaviour. In such an environment, top executives will find it difficult and costly to ensure that their orders are carried out. With more levels in a hierarchy the chance that the original order will be changed (accidentally or not) increases. In such an environment bureaucrats have an incentive to deliberately distort or hoard information for the furthering of their own objectives. This is reinforced by the fact that the employment contract of a bureaucrat is often incomplete and lacking in efficiency incentives. In private markets such things could also exist, but consumers, competitors and such institutions as the stock exchange serve as 'policing' mechanisms. They provide incentives to improve efficiency. Unfortunately, such controls are absent in the political market place so that another solution has to be found. Measures to reduce distortions are the appointment of external advisors or independent audits. Also, incentives might be created by awarding the release of new, valuable information.

Various models of bureaucracies' behaviour will be discussed below based on presentations by Hartley and Tisdell (1981), and Cullis and Jones (1998). These are known as those of maximizing bureaucracies, information misrepresentation and paperwork models.

Maximizing bureaucracies model

Niskanen (1971) assumes that bureaucrats maximize their budgets. By increasing their budgets they can satisfy personal needs like perquisites of office, job opportunities, higher salaries, and so on. The government, the sole purchaser of goods and services from bureaucracies, has to pay for these large budgets. The political market place thus is characterized by a bilateral monopoly with bureaucracies acting as monopolists and the government acting as monopsonist. Niskanen assumes that bureaucracies are perfect price-discriminating monopolists as they take away all consumer surplus from the purchasing government. This is shown in Figure 8.3 below.

The government will demand a certain amount of goods and services from the bureaucrats. This demand is determined by the median voter (remember: a vote-maximizing govern-

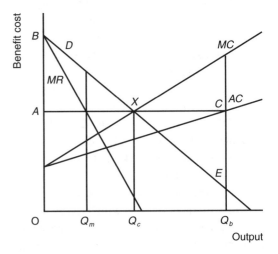

Figure 8.3

ment will adopt the policy that is favoured by the median voter). So *D* represents the demand function of the median voter. *MR* is the marginal revenue and *MC* and *AC* are the marginal cost and average cost, respectively. A bureaucracy maximizes its budget, but of course, under the constraint that total cost is covered (by total revenue). The maximum output level at which the budget is maximized, subject to the cost coverage constraint is *Qb*. The total cost is equal to *OACQb*. The budget (revenue for the bureaucracy) is represented by *OBEQb*. Because *OACQb* equals *OBEQb*, all costs are covered.

As expected the solution is not socially optimal: *Qc*, the socially optimal output level (found by equalizing the demand curve and the *MC*) is less than *Qb*. The consumer surplus at *Qc* (*ABX*) is fully captured by the bureaucracy. The bureaucracy uses *ABX* to increase total output to *Qb*. Going from *Qc* to *Qb*, extra cost equal to *QcQbCX* arises, which is not fully covered by the increase in the budget of *QcQbEX*. *ABX* is then used to cover this 'extra' cost (*XCE*).

The figure can also be used for analysing the difference between a public and private monopoly. The solution under a private monopoly would be *Qm*, which is less than *Qb*, the solution in case of a public monopoly. *Qm* is socially preferable to *Qb* because at *Qm* the consumer surplus is still positive, while at *Qb* it is zero.

Information misrepresentation model

Figure 8.3 has shown that bureaucracies by maximizing their budgets, tend to 'overproduce' compared with the socially optimal output level. Additional misallocations are caused by the distortion of information from agent (bureaucracy) to principal (the government, or the minister in charge): bureaucracies

have an incentive to misrepresent information on costs and benefits, because by doing so bureaucrats can increase their budgets to an even greater extent.

First of all, departments have an incentive to exaggerate or overestimate the demand for policies or projects that they have to carry out. They are likely to stress (exaggerate) benefits of projects in the form of creation of employment, technology push and an improvement of the balance of payments.

Bureaucracies often make use of expert knowledge of interest groups, particularly producer groups, who are willing to help because they benefit from the project (or policy). Also, departments can hire independent consultants to provide further expertise supporting their case. Governments are likely to listen to the advice of producer groups because they are vote maximizers: the median voter is usually uncertain about costs and benefits: voters with median voter preferences are usually wary of the costs but positive about the potential benefits. In such circumstances the government is likely to listen to those people who are best informed.

At the same time, the costs of projects and policies are usually underestimated so as to make them look more attractive in terms of costs and benefits (including external effects). Projects that seem to be relatively cheap are more likely to be accepted by the government. In this way 'too low' cost estimates can lead to the purchase or spending of 'too much'. This also implies that, in the implementation, the project will cost more than the biased low figure of the (average) cost in the budget. But any recognition of this will in general be too late because, once the implementation has started, the process is usually not reversible.

Again, a lot of producer groups like architects, engineers, scientists, surveyors, unions, are involved and have an interest in the continuation of the project. Using the support of these interest groups bureaucrats can easily show vote-conscious politicians that the project is in the 'national interest' and will produce substantial social benefits (in the form of jobs, and so on).

One might say that cost escalation also occurs in the private market, and therefore is not necessarily a typical public failure. But private firms are less likely to underestimate costs in the first place, or to continue a project with unnecessarily high costs in the second place, simply because their profitability and thus competitiveness in the market will suffer from both.

Figure 8.4 shows what happens when bureaucracies misrepresent information on costs and benefits. Bureaucracies will create an impression of allocative efficiency by overestimating demand, so that the original (true) demand curve D_0 shifts to the right to D_1. At the same time costs are underestimated, which shifts downwards the original marginal cost curve MC_0 to MC_1 and respectively AC_0 to AC_1. Compared to the original situation, output increases substantially from Q_0 to Q_1.

In general one may conclude that the system creates incentives to spend and to overproduce. Obviously, the tax payer is the one that ultimately bears the full cost.

Several modifications to the Niskanen model have been introduced. One of the shortcomings is that the prediction that the public sector will be too large is difficult to test. Also, the model is not so realistic in assuming that the public sector itself is technically efficient. We have seen that the opportunity for discretionary behaviour of bureaucrats leads to technical and allocative inefficiencies. By modifying the utility function of bureaucracies (they maximize a utility function containing both output goals as well as preferences for discretionary expenditures, i.e. pursuit of goals like on-the-job leisure) these facts can be accounted for.

Paperwork model

This model incorporates the presence of X-inefficiency (slack) in the public sector. The model distinguishes *general* public costs (administration costs), as different from *specific* public good costs. Specific public good costs were mentioned in the foregoing discussion. It was argued there that costs of a specific public good will be *underestimated*, whereas now it is argued that bureaucracies will *overestimate* general administration costs, the so-called paperwork. Therefore, the distinction between general and specific costs is an important one.

Costs of administration, a typical characteristic of bureaucracies in dealing with the private sector, has been introduced to model X-inefficiency: it can be used as an output indicator to inflate costs. The government cannot easily check this, so that a higher budget to cover these 'costs' is easily obtained. Once a bureaucracy has obtained such a budget it can try to shift some of the costs of paperwork onto private firms. The bureaucrats can use the 'cost savings' for

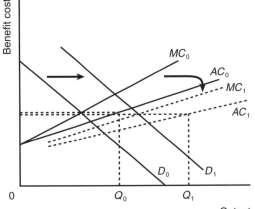

Figure 8.4

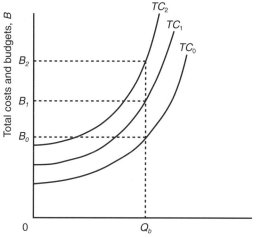

Figure 8.5

their own purposes (e.g. office perquisites). Figure 8.5 shows how this works.

The government requires an output of Qb from the bureaucracy, and in return the government will pay the total cost for it. The true cost of the bureaucracy of producing Qb is represented by $TC1$. The budget at these true costs is equal to $0B1$. The bureaucracy will try to get a higher budget by misrepresenting information on costs: the department will claim that its true cost is represented by the $TC2$ curve. In that way it will obtain a budget of $0B2$. Now, by hiving off some of the cost of paperwork to the private sector, the bureaucracy can increase its discretionary expenditures even more. As a result the bureau's new total cost curve is equal to $TC0$, so that the total amount of discretionary expenditure amounts to $B2B0$.

There are limits to the opportunity of this kind of discretionary behaviour: firms will respond by lobbying politicians, arguing for less bureaucracy, and for the work to be 'hived off' to the more efficient private sector.

The above paperwork model, combined with the misrepresentation of information, leads to the following conclusions:

Bureaucracies, in maximizing their budgets, have an incentive to misrepresent information on costs and benefits. In particular, when a *specific* project or public good is under consideration, bureaucracies will *underestimate* costs (overestimate benefits), while costs of *general* public administration will be *overestimated*.

8.4   *Motivational effects*

Motivational problems are present in publicly-owned and planned enterprises. These problems concern the ratchet effect, and the soft budget constraint. See Berliner (1952) and Kornai (1979), respectively.

The ratchet effect arises in a situation where the central planners fix a future output target for the public enterprise Q_{t+1} at a higher level than the achieved current output Q_t. Calculative managers of the public enterprises will deliberately produce low Q_t or pass to the central planners underestimates of their real production to avoid compelling targets. The ratcheting of targets by the central planners creates an X-inefficiency. The problem can be solved by persuading public enterprises to disclose their true estimate of maximum enterprise output, given input authorizations.

The soft budget constraint problem applies in situations when the state guarantees that the operations of loss-making public enterprises will be continued nevertheless. As a result there is no incentive for the public enterprise to economize in the use of capital and to minimize on other costs.

Both effects are incentive problems which are best analysed in the framework of principal-agency theory. The two effects are also linked to each other in the context of cross-subsidization, as when the ratcheting of output targets for the better performing enterprises is used to finance the soft budget constraints of the loss-making enterprises. Responding rationally to this cross-subsidization, both firms will not maximize their effort and will end up in lower efficiencies.

8.5 Allocative effects

While the supplementation of market forces by allocation policies may, in certain cases, improve resource allocation, it may also in other cases create a distorted mix of output and input. Allocation policies necessarily require the collection and use of taxes. This section demonstrates allocative effects of levying taxes. There are five reasons for collecting taxes, these correspond roughly with the five market failures treated earlier. Taxes are collected and used for the purposes of:

(a) maintaining a legislative, executive and judiciary system capable of guarding fair and competitive market practices;
(b) stabilization of prices and activities as a reaction to uncertainties and excessive market fluctuations;
(c) discouraging negative externalities such as environmental pollution, as well as enhancing positive externalities such as industrial development;
(d) provision of collective goods and services; and
(e) redistributing income.

Taxes collected for spending on strengthening market institutions, stabilization in the face of uncertainties, and correcting externalities are designed to make allocation of resources more efficient in the sense of Pareto-optimality. In principle, tax collection and use for meeting collective needs and income redistribution may distort the allocation of resources if the ensuing effects run contrary to consumer preferences. In practice, it is difficult to prove such distortions empirically. Apart from the spending avenues, there is the incidence effect of levying the tax and this depends on the type of tax levied.

The simplest case is that of an excise tax on good j, t_j. The tax will result in a consumer price p_j which differs from the producer price, that is $p_j - t_j$. For goods i and j the consumers are faced with $MRS_{ij} = p_j/p_i$. Producers are faced with $MRT_{ij} = (p_j - t_j)/p_i$. With $MRS_{ij} \neq MRT_{ij}$ the conditions for Pareto-optimality are violated and both consumers and producers will have to adjust their utilities downwards as a result of the relative price distortions. Sales taxes give a distortive effect similar to the excise tax but are biased against consumption and in favour of savings. An income tax has a substitution effect (makes work less remunerative and encourages leisure) and a negative income effect (implying less leisure to maintain same income level). The distorted outcome is a mixture of both effects. A lump-sum tax is not related to the individual's economic activity and does not have a substitution effect. This neutral character of the tax makes it highly recommendable for economic policy.

Policy example 8.1

State intervention in developing economies: problems and reforms

The effectiveness of state intervention in developing economies is hampered sometimes by failure to deliver fundamental public goods and services such as basic needs and property rights, adequate taxes, and noncorrupt practices. Until the last century, many of these problems were also present in Western Europe, North America and Japan. But reforms took place and these countries turned into modern states with judiciary systems. The experience of the industrial countries is relevant for developing countries. The following paragraphs review state reforms and policies relevant and applicable for the developing world.

The World Bank Development Report (1997) recommends a two-point strategy:

1 Take appropriate steps to match tasks run by the state to the capability of that state
2 reinvigorate public institutions so as to raise state capability and address more challenging tasks.

As regards the first point, the key to an effective implementation of any state policy is a good fit between the policy measures in question and the institutional capability of the state. It is not desirable for the state to assume responsibilities and actions when results are sub-optimal to the situation without these actions. An excessive defence sector, extensive state enterprises and strict bureaucratic regimes are actions which go far beyond state capability in many developing countries.

As regards the second point, institutional capability can and should be enhanced by upgrading the performance of state institutions and improving pay and incentives. Four basic mechanisms need to be applied in achieving higher performance. Effective rules and restraints via separation of power, building accountability, fighting corruption, and the group of economic instruments consisting of lowering controls on business activity, removing entry barriers, and privatizing state firms.

The World Bank Development Report (1997) also puts emphasis on:

• Subjecting the state to greater competition pressure by supporting a staff-recruitment system based on merit and not favouritism, introducing efficiency-based internal promotions, working towards adequately compensating the civil service, and promoting more competition in the provision of public goods.
• Bringing the state closer to the people by giving them a voice, broadening participation and devolving power carefully.

The above reforms imply decentralization which may have negative effects such as rising inequality and the risk to local governments of local capture. To remedy these negative effects social adjustment strategies need to be adequately formulated and implemented.

8.6 State intervention and social efficiency in the longer term

8.6.1 Four developmental factors

The previous discussion of public failure has shown how an oversized public share in the GDP combined with resource misallocation can occur in the medium-term. How does this trend affect the two welfare criteria of growth and equity? There is empirical evidence for the medium-term of a negative relationship between public share and economic growth. There is also empirical evidence on a positive relationship between the public share and indices of income inequality (cf. World Bank 1997). The underlying causes are many and complex as the discussion below will show.

In the longer term, developmental factors will significantly shape the form and size of state intervention. The resulting national performance regarding growth and equity is often mixed and depends on the developmental factor in question. There are very significant developmental factors, different from public failure in the narrow sense, which contribute to the same tendency of a greater state intervention over time. In this section four main factors will be discussed. These are:

1 Long-term productivity characteristics of public services
2 Pressure of demographic changes on public transfers
3 Growth and redistribution stages and policies
4 Intermittent social upheavals.

Even then, given the low score on economic efficiency of a higher public share, there may be a function for the state to take long-term measures to reduce the significance of the four factors so that the pressure for a higher public share is moderated.

8.6.2 Productivity characteristics of public services

In general, public expenditures can be divided into two categories: exhaustive public expenditures and transfer expenditures. Exhaustive public expenditures consist of purchases of current goods and services (e.g. consumption goods, labour) and capital goods and services (e.g. investments in roads and education). Exhaustive expenditures can therefore be considered as the purchases of inputs by the government, for which an (input) price has to be paid. These inputs are then used to produce public sector outputs. This means that, unlike many people claim, an increase in public sector expenditure does not necessarily imply an increase in public sector output. The second category (transfer expenditures) is more important in the context of demographic changes and therefore will be discussed in relation to demographic changes.

One of the main causes of an increase in exhaustive public expenditures is the inability to keep up with private sector productivity. As a result, increases in costs are not fully compensated by productivity increases which are caused by economies of scale and technological change. This leads to an increase in the price of the inputs used in the public sector production resulting in higher public (exhaustive) expenditures.

Baumol (1967) analysed this problem formally. In his analysis he distinguishes two types of sectors: progressive (private) and non-progressive (public) sectors. A progressive sector is characterized by economies of scale and technological change, which lead to increases in productivity per unit of labour. In the non-progressive sector labour productivity grows at a much lower rate. He recognizes that this difference in productivity is caused by differences in the nature of the product that is produced.

Most of the public sector is, in fact, a service sector. This implies that the product (service) which is produced (delivered) is labour-intensive, and, more importantly, that 'labour' itself is the end product. Substituting capital for labour is, then, simply impossible without changing the nature of the product. This is because one tries to replace something (labour) that is part of the product itself. In the progressive sector, labour can easily be substituted by capital without changing the nature of the product, because labour is just an input (an instrument) to the production process from which the end product results. So here, substitution of capital for labour does not change the nature of the product at all, while doing this in the public sector would change the product completely.

This does not mean, however, that productivity increases are impossible in these services. They do in fact occur, but only occasionally or at a very slow rate. The problem of introducing technological change in the non-progressive public sector is that consumers expect a certain degree of labour content in the production of non-progressive sector goods. As a result the scope for improving technology is very limited.

What happens over time with labour costs crucially depends on the productivity differential. In the progressive sector increases in labour productivity are followed by equal increases in wage rates. As a result, unit costs remain constant over time. In the non-progressive sector, the growth in productivity stays behind, relatively to the progressive sector (this gives rise to the productivity differential). But, in order to prevent labour moving from the non-progressive to the progressive sector, wages in the non-progressive sector have to match those in the progressive sector. Given that the productivity growth is less in the non-progressive sector, this implies that unit costs will rise. With an income elasticity of demand that exceeds the

price elasticity of demand, the output of the non-progressive sector will not fall. Rising input costs will then lead to higher total costs of the non-progressive sector and thus to higher exhaustive expenditures.

This theory of exhaustive public expenditure growth is summarized formally by the following model. X_1 is the output of the non-progressive sector, X_2 the output of the progressive sector. The production functions of each sector are then as follows:

(8.1) $X_{1t} = a_1 L_{1t}$

(8.2) $X_{2t} = (a_2 e^{rt}) L_{2t}$

with L_1 and L_2 being the labour force in the non-progressive and the progressive sector respectively, t is the time index and a_1 and a_2 are constants. The production in the progressive sector is assumed to grow at an exponential rate of r.

Equations 8.1 and 8.2 are used to derive the ratio of government output to total output, as shown in equation 8.3 below.

(8.3) $X_{1t}/(X_{1t} + X_{2t}) = a_1 L_{1t}/(a_1 L_{1t} + (a_2 e^{rt}) L_{2t})$

It is assumed that wage rates are equal between both sectors and that they follow increases in productivity in the private sector.

(8.4) $w_t = w_0 e^{rt}$

w_0 is a constant, and w_t is the wage in period t.

From the equations above, unit costs can be derived for the public sector in Equation 8.5 and for the private sector in Equation 8.6.

(8.5) $C_{1t} = [(w_0 e^{rt}) L_{1t}]/[a_1 L_{1t}] = w_0 e^{rt}/a_1$

(8.6) $C_{2t} = [(w_0 e^{rt}) L_{2t}]/[(a_2 e^{rt}) L_{2t} = w_0/a_2$

From Equations 8.5 and 8.6 it follows that unit costs in the public sector will rise steadily, while private sector costs remain constant. This is the main conclusion of the model. An implication is that if the ratio of public sector

157

output to private sector output is to remain constant, then it must be that labour is transferred from the private to the public sector. This is indeed observed in reality. Also, public exhaustive expenditures will rise faster than private sector expenditure on inputs.

8.6.3 Pressure of demographic changes on public transfers

Demographic changes primarily influence transfer expenditures. Transfer expenditures consist of public expenditures on pensions, subsidies, unemployment benefits, and so on. It is important to notice that these expenditures do not represent a claim on resources of society (in contrast with exhaustive expenditures!). Rather, transfer expenditures are flows of income from individuals in society to other individuals in society passing the government sector as an intermediary. These flows can be compared with reimbursements made by an insurance company for which premiums have already been paid in the past.

When, over time, the demographic composition of the population changes, this influences the amount of transfer payments. Clear examples of this are an increase (decrease) in the percentage of elderly or unemployed persons in society, which lead to a higher (lower) public share. Obviously, the factors leading to an increase in the public share are outside the scope of the government sector, and therefore cannot be seen as a government failure.

A demographic change like population growth is often seen as a factor that increases public expenditures. The larger population demands more goods and services from the public sector. To meet this demand more inputs are needed, i.e. the derived demand for inputs increases and thus public (exhaustive!) expenditures.

This intuitive result needs closer examination: the ultimate effect of population growth

on public expenditure is dependent on the nature of the public good or service. If the good is a pure public good, then, by definition, the marginal cost of an extra unit of the good is zero. In that case there is no reason to expect public expenditure to rise. Of course, not all public goods are pure public goods: different goods have a different 'degree of publicness'. In general it can be said that the higher the degree of publicness, the less the increase in public expenditure will be.

If public expenditures increase to a lesser degree than the change in the population (as is the case with near public goods), it is likely that the demand for the service will change: as total public expenditure has to be allocated over a much larger group, the share of each member in expenditure will fall. This is equivalent to a price change which causes the demand for the level of the service to rise.

8.6.4 Growth and redistribution: stages and policies

This section reviews work on the long-term interactions between growth and redistribution. The works of Musgrave (1969) and Rostow (1971) are primarily descriptive: they look at the time pattern of public expenditure in view of the development process of a country. There are, in general, three phases in the development process: the start-up phase, the middle stages of growth, and the stages of maturity.

In the start-up phase, public sector investment as a share of total investment is relatively high. This is necessary to start up the economy for economic growth. Government investments in the early stages, therefore, consist primarily of investments in physical and social infrastructure: roads, education, health, law, etc.

Once the start-up phase has passed, the government continues to invest in the same types of sectors, but now these investments are complementary to private sector investments. Market failures can arise which frustrate the push towards maturity. It is the government's task to deal with these market failures. Whenever this happens, government expenditure rises.

As for arriving at the stages of maturity, Musgrave argues that, as total investment as a proportion of GNP rises, the relative share of public sector investment falls. Rostow argues that, once the maturity stage is reached, the mix of public expenditures will shift from expenditure on infrastructure to expenditure on education, health and welfare services, like income maintenance programmes. Redistribution policies also become more important. Several works of Perotti reviewed in Perotti (1996) are more explanatory compared to the stages of growth theory of Musgrave and Rostow. He tries to explain growth from income distribution and finds four mechanisms through which distribution influences growth. They are called the *fiscal policy* approach, the *sociopolitical instability* approach, the *borrowing constraints/ investment in education* approach and the *endogenous fertility* approach. Table 8.1, based on Perotti (1996), summarizes these four mechanisms.

As one can see, the mechanisms have in common that equality positively influences growth. But the ways through which this occurs

(step 2) differ significantly. For the last two mechanisms, a higher growth is brought about by more investment in human capital (which implies a productivity increase), and by lowering fertility and increasing investment in human capital simultaneously. The first two mechanisms are important in the context of the influence on the public share, and are therefore discussed below.

The fiscal policy approach uses the median voter theorem to explain the effect of equality on growth. In general the preferred level of public expenditure and thus the preferred level of taxation is negatively related to the income of an individual. Since this is also true for the median voter, the median voter's income and the level of expenditure and taxation are negatively related. At the same time, the level of expenditure and thus taxation negatively influences growth through their disincentive effects. In sum, this means that more equality, implying less need of redistributive expenditure and less distortionary taxation, leads to higher growth.

The sociopolitical instability approach emphasizes the phenomenon of when income distribution is highly unequal in a state, people who have relatively little income will ask for redistribution policies. They organize themselves into a group (when it is easy to form such a group) and put pressure on the government.

Table 8.1 Four mechanisms of redistribution and growth

Mechanism	Step 1	Step 2	Step 3
Fiscal policy	Equality↑	$E\downarrow$, $T\downarrow$*	Growth↑
Sociopolitical instability	Equality↑	Sociopolitical instability↓	Investment↑ and growth↑
Borrowing constraints/ investment in education	Equality↑	Investment in human capital↑	Growth↑
Endogenous fertility	Equality↑	Fertility↓ and investment in human capital↑	Growth↑

*E stands for redistributive government expenditure, T for taxation.

This can be done by using political channels, engaging in rent-seeking activities, or by using ways outside the political market place, engaging in protests, coups, assassinations and so on. The point is that inequality will lead to sociopolitical instability. At the same time, sociopolitical instability discourages investment and thus growth because of uncertainty and productivity decreases caused by market disruptions. In sum, equality ensures sociopolitical stability and therefore leads to higher growth.

As is clear from the sociopolitical instability approach, the best the government can do is to anticipate (as far as this is possible) by redistributing income beforehand, so that a situation of socio political instability is less likely to occur. The government therefore has to increase the public share by an amount that is reserved for redistribution purposes. By doing so, the government equalizes income distribution and thereby solves the original source of the problem.

Additional advantages are that there is less need for future redistributive expenditures and distortionary taxes (fiscal policy approach), and that higher growth is ensured (as predicted by all four mechanisms). This implies that a country in general is doing better and (important for the government) that citizens (the median voter) are content so that re-election is more likely to occur.

8.6.5 Social upheaval

Periods of social upheaval can often be recognized by sudden changes in the time pattern of public expenditures. For example, during war, public sector expenditures rise at a higher rate in order to finance military necessities. Peacock and Wiseman (1961) have made a profound study of the time pattern of public expenditures that accounts for the influence of periods of social unrest on public expenditures. The advantage of their analysis is that it fully incorporates the influence of politics on public expenditures: the (median) voter likes the benefits of public goods, but dislikes paying taxes for it. Political parties are vote-maximizers and therefore have to focus on the median voter, and so on.

As an economy grows, tax revenue (tax rates are constant) increases proportionally, thereby enabling public sector expenditures to grow at the same rate, in line with GNP. In normal times, therefore, public sector expenditure shows a gradual increase.

During periods of social upheaval this gradual pattern will be disturbed. Public expenditure will suddenly rise disproportionally, whatever the cause of the unrest. Examples are periods of war and famine. To finance the increase in expenditure, it is necessary to raise taxes. This is largely accepted in times of social unrest, because people recognize that necessity. Peacock and Wiseman call this a *displacement effect*: during crises, public expenditures, financed by an increase in tax levels, displace private expenditures. After the period of the crisis expenditures do not fall to their original level. This is because it is not possible for a country to finance all costs by taxation.

A second effect that Peacock and Wiseman observed is the *inspection effect*: in difficult times people are more aware of social problems. The government therefore increases the provision of services, which are financed by higher tax levels. This is accepted by the electorate for the reason mentioned before.

Peacock and Wiseman's theory has not gone without criticism. There is especially disagreement on what happens after the period of social upheaval. Peacock and Wiseman have argued that there is a permanent displacement of private civilian expenditures by public expenditures. Others, including Musgrave, have argued that this is not the case: in the long-term there is no displacement effect, because after the period civilian public expenditure returns to its old level.

Policy example 8.2

Correlations between government institutional capability, government policy distortions and economic growth performance

The World Bank Development Report (1997, p.13) reports on correlations which show that countries with higher institutional capability have low policy distortions, which eventually result in high economic growth. These relations have been brought together by the World Bank (1997) in Figure 8.6, which demonstrates that countries with good economic policies and stronger institutional capability grow faster.

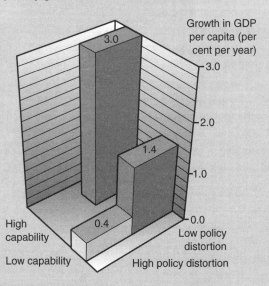

Figure 8.6

The obtained results behind Figure 8.6 are based on a regression using panel data from 94 industrial and developing countries for the period 1964–93. Each growth rate is the average for a group of countries, controlling for education, income and other variables. The institutional capability index is a composite index of measures of the quality of government put together from responses of foreign investors that focus on red tape, regulatory environment, corruption bias and the like. The policy distortion index is a composite index of indicators of the country's openness to foreign trade, the country's currency overvaluation, and the gap between local and international prices.

Questions for discussion and further research

1 Review your understanding of the following terms: bureaucratic bias, public share, absence of a majority-voting equilibrium, information misrepresentation model, ratchet effect, soft budget, progressive and non-progressive sectors, displacement effect.

2 The majority voting model is useful in explaining the growth of government

expenditures. Show understanding of this by answering the following questions from Stiglitz (1998):

(i) Should changes in median or average income better explain increases in the demand for government services?

(ii) What should be the effect of an increase in the costs of producing public good caused by government inefficiency? Would it make a difference if the increase in cost is a result of government paying above-market wages (wages higher than those paid comparable workers in the private sector)?

(iii) Does your answer to the last question depend on whether the median voter is a government employee?

(iv) Why might you expect that, if income per capita remains the same but the number of individuals in the economy increases, the demand for public goods would increase?

3 It has been stated that there is a political market which is explainable in terms of the economic market. Outline the composition and mechanisms of this political market and list its correspondences and differences with the economic market.

4 Discuss the general possibilities of downsizing of government budgets, and in particular the reduction of state expenditure from the points of view of: (i) politicians (ii) bureaucracies, (iii) users of public services, and (iv) producers of public services. End the discussion with specifying factors of special relevance which can modify the results in the (v) richer developed countries, and (vi) poorer developing countries.

Further reading

Application of economic theory to political behaviour is treated at length by various authors in Auerbach, A.J. and Feldstein, M. (eds) (1987): *Handbook of Public Economics*, Vols. 1 and 2, North-Holland Publishing Co., Amsterdam.

Successful state intervention is limited not only by failure aspects in issues of public choice but also by failures in governmental behaviour.

For further reading on the first type of failures, see Buchanan, J.M. and Tullock, G. (1962): *The Calculus of Consent*, University of Michigan Press, Ann Arbor; Mueller, D. (1989): *Public Choice II*, CUP, Cambridge.

On the second type of failure, the following four references are relevant: Stigler, G.J. (1971): 'The Theory of Economic Regulation', in *Bell Journal of Economics and Management Science*, Spring issue, pp.3–21; Inman, R.P. (1987): 'Markets, Governments and the New Political Economy', in Auerbach A.J. and Feldstein, M. (eds) (1987): *Handbook of Public Economics*, Vol. 2, North-Holland Publishing Co.; Eggertsson, T. (1990): *Economic Behaviour and Institutions*, CUP, Cambridge. See also Rees, R. (1993): *The Economics of Regulation and Public Enterprises*, Harvester Wheatsheaf, Oxford.

Our approach towards decomposing causes behind the increasing share of the public economy is complemented by reading a comparable exposition in Brown, C.V. and Jackson, P.M. (1990): *Public Sector Economics*, Blackwell, Oxford. The topic is also discussed by Perotti in the context of growth and distribution in Perotti, R. (1993): 'Political Equilibrium, Income Distribution and Growth', in *Review of Economic Studies*, pp.755–76.

Chapter 9

The social order: review of mechanisms, outcomes and prospects

9.1   Interdependent behaviour and economic performance

Good or bad performance of the market and state in a specific country depends on the behavioural rules which guide interactions among members of the population of that country and determine its social order. The performance of markets and states are dominated by the social orders in which they both function. A fuller understanding of the performances, failures and prospects of markets and states requires relating them to the social order in which both the market and state are embedded.

Behavioural rules, also known as social institutions, or more generally the social order, are formed in the processes of *interdependent behaviour* between individuals in many behavioural settings, including homes, schools, businesses, governments, and the like. If the behavioural rules are of the cooperative type, the likelihood of market imperfections and failures, and public interventions and failures, are

reduced. Non-cooperative behaviour places heavy burdens on the market and the state in achieving social efficiency.

Insight into how interdependent behaviour is generated and how it affects economic life is crucial. Interdependent behaviour interacts with the previously elaborated themes of indivisibilities, externalities, collectivities and uncertainties, and conditions the economic outcomes underlying all four themes. This is also the reason why we chose to postpone treatment of the role and implications of interdependent behaviour until the last chapter of this book.

Externalities that have been discussed so far have a primarily technical nature. The good itself incorporates non-excludability features. Clear examples of this are the interactions between bees and nectar and the example of the flower garden in a shopping centre, both examples represent positive externalities. In a similar way, two examples of negative externalities can be recalled: environmental pollution and smoking. However, major externalities are caused by the behaviour of a certain actor who influences the behaviour of other actors. Usually this takes place in groups. In those environments the behaviour of one actor is dependent on the behaviour of another actor. As a very general example of this interdependent behaviour, consider herd behaviour. This is the phenomenon that describes how people in groups tend to think and behave in the same way. They imitate the actions of others who belong to the same group. The first mover in the group acts in a way that he or she thinks is right, using his or her information set. The followers use this action as a signal and copy the behaviour of the first mover, while they ignore their own information set. Ultimately it is possible that the whole group ends up in a 'bad' equilibrium due to a 'bad' action of the first mover. Similarly, a 'good' action of the first mover can bring the whole group in a 'good' equilibrium. The spilling over of behaviour of the first mover to the others, or the interdependence of behaviour within the group, indicates an externality: a herd externality

Interdependent behaviour and collectivity are intimately related. If interdependence of behaviour is present, actors influence each other in the decision-making process, which leads to interdependence of the resulting outcomes. Interdependent behaviour ultimately leads to a shift downwards in Pareto-optimality or, in case of positive spill-over effects, to a shift upwards in Pareto-optimality. If cooperative behaviour is rightly conceived by the population at large as a merit good this makes it a public asset which would make it fall in the category of collective needs.

Interdependent behaviour and uncertainty are intimately related, as well. When proponents of cooperative and non-cooperative behaviour would be identified separately, adverse selection occurs less, risk and uncertainty are reduced and more exchange takes place. In the case of cooperative behaviour, moral hazard is absent, transaction costs are reduced and more complete markets are realized.

9.2 Mechanisms of interdependent behaviour

9.2.1 Four common themes

The economic literature on mechanisms of interdependent behaviour is diversified and expanding. The common themes underlying these mechanisms can be regrouped into the following four categories.

1 Non-conscious behaviour in the sense of innate behaviour.
2 Semi-conscious behaviour in the sense of imitative and adaptive behaviour.
3 Conscious economic behaviour in the sense of rational self interest.
4 Conscious extra-economic behaviour in the sense of rational self-denial and adherence to ethical values.

Mechanisms belonging to the first category explain interdependent behaviour of human beings by comparing it with animal behaviour. Animals have innate instincts, which control their actions. These instincts are carried over by birth and do not change significantly over time. When a certain situation prevails animals act unconsciously, upon their instinct. Instinct is the driving force behind each activity, no reasoning takes place. Thus, animal behaviour has the following characteristics: it is inborn, instinctive, inert and unconscious, and takes place in groups. Group behaviour among human beings also manifests a significant degree of unconscious behaviour driven by instinct. This type of behavioural externalities is dealt with in section 9.2.1.

Mechanisms belonging to the second category manifest semi-conscious experiences of first observing and later adapting, which is common in non-human and human group behaviour. Examples are herd behaviour and imitative behaviour. Adapting behaviour to observation and learning can also be classified here. This is treated in section 9.2.2.

The third category, treated in section 9.2.3, consists of theories that explain behaviour from a (neoclassical) economic point of view. The Homo economicus is the benchmark. The Homo economicus acts in his own self interest subject to budget and time restrictions and along neoclassical behavioural assumption, even though the neoclassical behavioural assumption can give room for an interpretation along non-egotistic motives of behaviour, but not intentionally so. The point is that even if there is room for altruistic behaviour, this kind of behaviour still can be explained within the neo-classical model in terms of egotism and selfishness: it is in the individuals' own self-interest to behave altruistically because this enlarges his/her utility. In this way altruistic behaviour has not a non-selfish but a selfish motive. Overall, behaviour in this category is *fully conscious* and follows a purely *economic rationale*.

The fourth category, treated in section 9.2.4, adds something more to the explanation of behaviour. Next to pure economic rational behaviour, people also exhibit *moralistic behaviour*. This is where ethical values appear. People may not only act according to their own self-interest, they may also show concern for other people's well-being. Emotions play a prominent role: emotions commit people to certain persons or activities. For example, if one feels that one should help people who are in need one will offer one's services to a person who, at a certain time, is in destitution. This commitment has in essence a moral character. Keywords of this category are: moralistic

behaviour, feelings, emotions, commitment, character, ethic, norms and values.

Altruistic manifestations in the individual's behaviour can be interpreted in terms of all four categories. Because of its overlapping character we treat this in more depth, and particularly in relation to its sustainability, in section 9.2.5; and end with a discussion of implications for policy in section 9.2.6.

9.2.2   Non-conscious behaviour

Theories of genetic inheritance are the only theories belonging to this category. Genetic inheritance deals with inborn, innate characteristics that are carried over from birth. As such genetic inheritance has to do with instinct rather than the consciousness mind. Theories that are discussed hereafter already contain some consciousness, although the presence of consciousness is minimal in the beginning.

9.2.3   Semi-conscious behaviour

Under the heading of semi-conscious behaviour we bring together herd behaviour, bounded rationality and imitative behaviour.

Herd behaviour

This constitutes perhaps the first theory of semi-conscious behaviour. People who often see each other think and behave in the same way. They adopt the same actions, speak the same language and gestures, and understand each other quite well. The approach to understanding the formation of convergent actions in herd behaviour is informational cascade models. These are reviewed in among others. Banerjee (1992), Bikhchandani, Hirschleifer and Welch (1998).

Here, group members acquire information by observing the actions of the first mover in the group. So the first mover is imitated by its followers, in a sequence, which lead to an equilibrium of actions in the same direction. Information cascades are based on the following optimal decision rule by individuals. Each individual starts with his own private information, observes how his predecessor's actions add to the public information, and then decides on a particular action x. Let d be the difference between the numbers of predecessors who adopted and who rejected action x. The decision rule is to adopt regardless of private signal, if $d > 1$, and to follow the private signal if $d = 0$. In a situation of $d = 1$ the rule is to adopt if the private signal is positive and toss a coin if the private signal is negative. An early preponderance towards adaptation causes people to ignore negative private signals, and sooner or later an UP cascade is triggered, ending with all persons concerned doing the same thing. Similarly, a DOWN cascade is triggered in case of $d < -1$, etc. The equilibrium of actions which results can be interpreted in terms of externalities as being positive if it is gainful for the group's welfare, or negative if it is harmful for the group's welfare, or it can also be externality-neutral.

Bounded rationality

In economics it is assumed that there is perfect, logical, deductive rationality. However, in reality, rationality is bounded: beyond a certain level of complexity human logical capacity cannot cope. Moreover, in complicated situations we cannot rely upon other agents to behave under perfect rationality. That is why we can only guess their behaviour. What we do then is to look for patterns: when a certain problem prevails we construct simple models by using the patterns we observe. Arthur (1994) calls these models, hypotheses or schemata. From these models we deduct implications and

act on them. If, in practice, these implications are not right or, if our actions did not perform well, we discard our current hypotheses and replace them with new ones.

This process of pattern recognition, hypotheses formation, deduction using currently held hypotheses, and replacement of hypotheses as needed is called *rationally-bounded inductive reasoning*.

What is the relationship with interdependent behaviour? Assume that, for a certain problem, several agents form mental models, hypotheses or, subjective beliefs. Each agent holds one in mind at a certain time, or a combination of several. Note that these beliefs are subjective so that each agent might have another hypothesis or combination of several hypotheses in mind. When one or more hypotheses cease to perform, an agent discards them to the back of his/her mind and replaces them by one or more new ones. So each agent keeps track of the performance of his/her collection of belief-models; once actions are taken, the whole picture is updated including the record of performance of agents' hypotheses, this kind of behaviour is interdependent because agents compete with each other (Arthur 1994):

> Just as species, to survive and reproduce, must prove themselves by competing and being adapted within an environment created by other species, in this world hypotheses, to be accurate and therefore acted upon, must prove themselves by competing and being adapted within an environment created by other agent's hypotheses. The set of ideas or hypotheses that are acted upon at any stage therefore coevolves.
>
> Source: Arthur (1994, p.408)

Rationally-bounded inductive reasoning belongs to the category of bounded rationality because behaviour is semi-conscious: agents learn in time which of their hypotheses work and which do not. Those that do not work have to be replaced by new ideas. In this way learning and adaptation of behaviour to observation takes place.

Imitative behaviour

There are various models of imitative behaviour. Bergstrom and Stark (1993) have developed a first model of evolution based on imitation showing that there are four possible outcomes (regions): an equilibrium of only cooperators, only defectors, a polymorphic equilibrium and an area with two stable equilibria (one of cooperators and one of defectors).

The second model of imitation is also by Bergstrom and Stark (1993). In this model they try to derive the implications of provincialism for interdependent behaviour. In their example they assume that farmers live along a road around a lake. Each farmer plays a prisoner's dilemma with his two adjacent neighbours. The payoffs are observed by the son of the farmer and, depending on who has the highest payoff, this son either imitates his father or one of his neighbours. If specific assumptions are made, remarkable results emerge, like cycles. Cycles or, repeated patterns, come into being if it is assumed that sons ignore the payoffs of the fathers and instead only consider the payoffs of the neighbours.

9.2.4   Conscious economic behaviour

Self-interest resulting in nonco-operative behaviour and negative externalities

Two criminals have committed a serious crime. The prosecutor can only put them in jail for a minor offence which is equal to one year in prison (both remain silent). But if one confesses while the other one remains silent, the confessor will go free while the one who remains silent will get 20 years in prison. If both confess they will have to spend five year

Table 9.1 The prisoner's dilemma game I

Prisoner a \ Prisoner b	Confess	Remain silent
Confess	(−5, −5)	(0, −20)
Remain silent	(−20, 0)	(−1, −1)

each in prison. The prisoners are not allowed to communicate with each other.

The dominant strategy for *a* is to confess: by confessing *a* gets a lighter sentence, no matter what *b* does. The same is true for *b*: the dominant strategy for *b* is also to confess. Each gets a 'payoff' of −5, while each would have got −1 if both remained silent. This is the essence of the prisoner's dilemma game in Table 9.1: if both players act in a self-interested way they are actually worse off than if both had shown restraint.

Frank (1988) stresses the fact that this is a result, not of the impossibility of communicating with each other, but of a lack of trust. Even if the prisoners have agreed to remain silent, each of the prisoners has an incentive to break this promise: they do not feel committed to stick to the agreement.

There are, however, economic rationales through which the payoffs of (−1, −1) are reached and co-operative behaviour resulting in positive externalities is sustained. The introduction of extra-economic behaviour such as feelings and emotions can solve this problem too, see section 9.2.5.

Self-interest resulting in co-operative behaviour and positive externalities

The above-shown prisoner's dilemma game is a one shot game. However, the results change significantly if the players are confronted with *repeated instances* of the prisoner's dilemma game. Early studies of Rapoport and Chammah (1965) investigated the behaviour of people in

Table 9.2 The prisoner's dilemma game II

Player a \ Player b	Defect	Co-operate
Defect	(2, 2)	(6, 0)
Cooperate	(0, 6)	(4, 4)

repeated prisoner's dilemma games. The prisoner's dilemma as shown in Table 9.1 is slightly changed: both players can either play a strategy of cooperate, or defect. Furthermore, the payoffs are changed from years in prison to monetary payoffs.

Again the dominant strategy for both players in the above one-shot game is to defect, while both would be better of if they had cooperated.

Chammah and Rapoport show that both players of the prisoner's dilemma game have a strong tendency to cooperate if the game is repeated several times. When a cooperator finds out after a game that the other defects he/she can take retaliatory actions. Because defection invites retaliation both players usually agree to cooperate. Chammah and Rapoport called this strategy a 'tit-for-tat' strategy. Formally it is defined as 'cooperate on the first move, then on each successive move do whatever the other player did on the previous move'. So after a game in which one co-operated and one defected, the cooperator will also defect so that both players are worse off. That's why it is in both players' interest to cooperate and pursue a tit-for-tat strategy. Such a strategy leads to cooperation in every play of the game and renders the highest possible aggregate payoff.

Axelrod (1984) investigated the performance of a tit-for-tat strategy against numerous counterstrategies. He found out that the tit-for-tat strategy did extremely well under certain conditions. The emergence of cooperation requires that the set of players is reasonably stable. All players should be able to remember the actions of the other players in previous games. Further-more, each player should be able to influence the payoffs in the future because retaliation is the only effective way to prevent people from defecting. If all these conditions are met (which is often the case in reality) co-operators can identify each other and can discriminate against defectors. The emergence of cooperation ensures that the highest possible payoff is realized so that cooperators survive in evolution (survival is dependent on the payoffs that are generated).

Internalization rationales

Seemingly cooperative behaviour fits within the neo-classical model via internalization rationales (cf. Becker 1981). An altruist and his beneficiaries – assumed to be selfish – internalize all externalities affecting each other. Applied to the family, the two members of the family are better off by actions that raise the total family income and worse off by actions that lower it. The altruist (a father) would avoid actions that raise his own income if they lower the income of the beneficiary (the daughter) even more. Having in mind the total family income, the father may act to lower his own income if this raises the daughter's income even more. The daughter will also be careful in her actions towards the father. If raising her own income will lower his even more, she should expect a reduction in allowances from him, and it is likely that the reduction is higher than the rise in her own income, because family income goes down. The daughter, although she may be pursuing her own selfish interest, will abstain from actions that harmed the father and is altruistic in effect. For example, take d for daughter and f for father, I for income, E for expenditure and A for the allowance paid by f to d. Since d maximizes $Z_d = I_d + A$, she refrains from actions that raise I_d if A is lowered even more, and she takes actions that lower I_d if this results in A raised even more.

Becker calls the phenomenon, whereby sufficient caring by an altruist induces a selfish beneficiary to act as if she cares about her benefactor as much as she cares about herself, the Rotten Kid Theorem. Becker elaborates the theorem to explain efficiency inheritance and division of labour, among other aspects of family behaviour. The Rotten Kid Theorem states that each beneficiary, no matter how selfish, maximizes the family income of his/her benefactor, and thereby internalizes all effects of his/her actions on other beneficiaries.

A corollary of the theorem is that each beneficiary, no matter how envious of other beneficiaries or of his/her benefactor, maximizes the family income of the benefactor, and hence helps those envied.

Reciprocity

Yet another conscious economic behaviour which leads to cooperation is based on reciprocity. Sometimes people act benevolently toward other people purely for selfish motives: they 'do good' in the expectation of getting something in return (reciprocal altruism). Although the result looks cooperative, taking this as altruistic behaviour is unjust. That's why economists have made a distinction between hard-core and soft-core altruism. The kind of behaviour described above is an example of soft-core altruism. It is the kind of altruism where selfish motives do play an important role: people consciously pursue their own material interests.

The point about the tit-for-tat strategy or internalization rationales is that they are not genuinely altruistic behaviour. Just like reciprocal altruism (altruism for which you want something in return) selfish motives play an important role. In order to explain genuine (hardcore) altruism Frank introduces emotions. This is discussed in section 9.2.5.

9.2.5   Conscious extra-economic behaviour

Moral sentiments and commitment model

While it is generally accepted that sometimes non-egoistic behaviour can lead to material benefits, there is also grounds for arguing that there is room in societies for altruistic behaviour for its own sake.

In the previous section it was shown that rational people come to the 'equilibrium' represented by the strategies (defect, defect) while (cooperate, cooperate) gives a higher payoff to both players. This 'equilibrium' will never come into being because, even if both agree to cooperate, neither of the players feels committed to stick to this agreement (both have an incentive to cheat).

The other way of thinking is to identify other stable forces of an immaterial nature that govern behaviour next to material incentives. Frank (1988) argues that, while material incentives indirectly govern behaviour, behaviour is directly governed by a complex psychological reward mechanism. Frank takes food intake as an example. People eat not in response to a rational calculation about caloric needs. People eat because they feel hungry or like to enjoy taste. It is as if 'inborn neural circuits' tells them that food intake will relieve the unpleasant feeling of hunger or provide the pleasure of taste. These are the reasons why people eat.

Rational calculations are an input to the reward mechanism and it is in this sense that they play an indirect role. A overweight person finds it in his or her own self interest to lose weight and therefore refrains from eating. This decision does not follow directly from his or her rational calculation. At best, the rational calculation passes information to the reward mechanism that eating will have adverse effects. This gives the person an option which competes directly with the impulse to eat.

According to the reward mechanism theory, emotions or feelings compete with information derived from rational calculations. This offers a way out to the commitment problem because these feelings alter the payoffs. An example is aversion to guilt feelings. People who are capable of strong guilt feelings will not cheat even if it is in their material interest to do so. Note that this is not because of a chance of being caught but because people simply do not want to cheat. Guilt feelings thus serve as a commitment device which solves the commitment problem. In this way interdependent (extra-economic) behaviour comes into being (both parties commit themselves to a certain action). In the prisoner's dilemma problem guilt feelings ensure that, once player *a* and *b* have agreed to cooperate, neither of them cheats. Guilt feelings prevent both players from cheating.

Guilt feelings by themselves are not enough to solve the commitment problem: it is necessary to explain how moral sentiments might have evolved. For moral sentiments to survive they must have a material payoff. We know cooperation only pays off if a person is able to cooperate with other cooperators. This means that a non-cheater must be able to identify other non-cheaters, otherwise the commitment model as described above does not work. Frank suggests two ways of discerning emotions in people. In other words there are two ways along which moral sentiments might have emerged. These are *reputation* and *physical signs*.

By never cheating one will acquire a good reputation, the benefits of which will outweigh the gains from cheating: a reputation for being honest acts as a credible signal of trustworthiness. This attracts other honest cooperators. Both parties benefit from this because they get the highest payoffs. There is however a flaw in the reputation argument: the argument implicitly states that because there is always some possibility of being caught, it is never rational to cheat. This is false: in certain cases (golden opportunities), where the probability of being caught is low, it pays off to cheat. When somebody is confronted with such a golden opportunity we simply do not know if he/she will cheat (even if this person has a good reputation). If this person chooses not to cheat it tells us that he/she is prudent, not necessarily honest.

A way out of this flaw in the reputation argument is easily found, however: the reputation argument assumes that dishonest persons choose on the basis of rational calculations. As we have seen rational calculations only play an indirect role in motivation. This is also true for dishonest persons. The payoff from an opportunity to cheat, associated with the right feelings, stimulates a person to do so. Feelings could thus stimulate a person to cheat. Similarly, with a high probability of getting caught, feelings arise that counteract the feelings of wanting to cheat.

The introduction of feelings and emotions creates a link between reputation and the true character of a person. For dishonest persons, cheating does not only take place in golden opportunities: dishonest people often cheat in cases where there is a good chance of being caught. They give in to their temptation while it is not very rational to do so. Sooner or later the cheaters are likely to be caught and will get a bad reputation. Persons with a good reputation are then more likely to be honest. So by introducing feelings and emotions, reputation tells us much more about the true character of persons.

Moral sentiments can also emerge along with physical signs which serve as signals. Frank (1988) states

> moral sentiments are accompanied by observable physical signs that allow outsiders to discern their presence.
>
> Source: Frank (1988, p.92)

This signalling makes it easier for cooperators to find each other. Because cooperators get the highest payoffs (they cooperate with each other), they will survive in evolutionary competition.

Both ways suggested by Frank lead to genuinely altruistic behaviour: people do not cheat because of guilt feelings. Also both pathways predict a stable equilibrium of honest persons and opportunists. This is because, in a population consisting entirely of cooperators, it would not pay to scrutinize people for physical signs of honesty, and it would also not pay to gather information about people's reputation. For these reasons defectors would begin to prosper. So in either pathway the presence of opportunistic persons is inevitable.

Goodin (1993) elaborates on the work of Frank. He develops two models of moral sentiment, one is the moral character building, the other is morality keeping in practice. From these models implications for the welfare state are derived.

Moral character building and morally keeping in practice

The first model by Goodin bears similar characteristics to Frank's commitment model. One's character does not change rapidly: it is built up slowly and changes equally slowly. The core of moral character is the commitment to certain persons and projects. Preceding these commitments are reflections on all relevant aspects of engaging in such commitments. Thus all commitments are thought of profoundly and are not just simple decisions. As a consequence, these conscious commitments, which form the basis of one's moral character, are less in need of reinforcement than skills that are learned and get rusty if not practised for a long time. This means that it is useful to let people do things themselves but constant exercise is

not required. Furthermore, the state does no great harm in speaking morally to society. On the contrary, by preaching the moral character is built up. Also, other kinds of government interferences are not harmful. The link with the commitment model of Frank is easy to make. When people have committed themselves to a certain project guilt feelings arise if not holding on to this commitment. These guilt feelings prevent people from cheating; they prefer to co-operate (behave altruistically).

The second model due to Goodin states that moral skills get rusty where people cannot exercise them. The state is compared with an addictive drug (Goodin 1993):

> the more of it we have the more we 'need' and the more we come to 'depend' on it.
>
> Source: Goodin (1993, pp.63–78)

In this way public responsibility for social welfare undermines private altruism. The model of morally keeping in practice is based on the atrophy thesis. Atrophy refers to the tendency of bodily parts to weaken and wither away from lack of use, as in the case of a paralysed limb. Advocates of this thesis say that, in a similar way, our moral skills get rusty if they are not practised enough.

Evidence of moral atrophy can be subdivided into two categories:

(a) Dependency and responsibility: when an accident happens and a lot of people are present, each individual is less inclined to render assistance compared to a situation where this individual is alone. Examples: a car accident on a crowded street attracts little response and standing up for elderly in a bus when all places are occupied is seldom.

(b) Prior help: this increases the propensity to help somebody in the future. For example, a person who has helped somebody before is

171

more likely to render assistance (even more assistance) in the future. Also, when a person sees somebody helping another person who is in need, this increases the helping behaviour of this person in the future. Furthermore, a person who has been helped in the past is more likely to render assistance in the future.

The implications for the welfare state that follow from the model of morally keeping in practice stand in sharp contrast with the model of moral character building. Whereas the first model argues strongly against the welfare state, the latter is broadly consistent with substantial public interference. In the model of morally keeping in practice, the role of the government is limited so that people can frequently exercise their moral skills. Alternatively, in the model of moral character building occasional reminders of people's moral skills are enough to ensure some private altruism. In this model, private and public altruism can go hand in hand; public interference is not obstructing private altruism in any sense.

Other relevant models of human behaviour

Even though the above review of conscious extra-economic behaviour is a very brief one, and is at parts incomplete, it is important to supplement the coverage by a behavioural model which Gintis (1998) calls *Homo reciprocans*. Here the individual is motivated by both reason and emotion:

> he comes to strategic interactions with propensity to cooperate, responds to cooperative behaviour by maintaining or increasing his level of cooperation, and responds to free-riding on the part of others by retaliating against the offenders, even at a cost to himself, and even when he could not reasonably expect future personal gains to flow from such retaliation.... Homo reciprocans is

thus neither the selfless altruist of utopian theory, nor the selfish hedonist of neoclassical economics.

Source: Gintis (1998, p.7)

Note that reciprocity here is used in a different way than in the case of tit-for-tat strategies discussed in section 9.2.4. The implication of the *Homo reciprocans* behavioural model is that the promotion of pro-social behaviour may be better achieved by a combination of preference changes and incentive changes, rather than incentive changes alone. The preference changes can be stimulated by the enhanced practicising of the targeted preferences between and among the individuals concerned in a network of interactive behaviour. This way of conceiving group behaviour makes it possible that the contributions of Frank and Goodin on the importance of moral character building and of morally keeping in practice be incorporated into a broader analytical framework of endogenous social orders.

9.3 More on the dynamics and sustainability of altruistic behaviour

For altruism to survive it is necessary that a certain percentage of the population actually behaves that way. We shall see some dynamics in the theory of Bergstrom and Stark (1993). But the point is more clearly illustrated by using the model of Simon (1993), which shows that altruism will appear in populations which are confronted with bounded rationality and docility.

Bergstrom and Stark show that cooperative behaviour (altruism) can survive in evolutionary competition even in single-shot prisoner's dilemma models. This is a somewhat remarkable result because cooperation benefits the opponent at a cost to oneself. Bergstrom and Stark introduce two models, a model of *asexual*

Table 9.3 The prisoner's dilemma game III

	Player b	Cooperate	Defect
Player a			
Cooperate		(R, R)	(S, T)
Defect		(T, S)	(P, P)

reproduction and a model of *sexual reproduction* (the second one being an extension of the first). In both models they combine game theory with evolutionary economics by assuming that an individual's strategy is determined by genetic inheritance. For both models, the prisoner's dilemma displayed in Table 9.3 is used.

Note $S < P < R < T$ so that Defect is the dominant strategy for both players. (P, P) is the resulting payoff. Since $S + T < 2R$ total payoffs are maximized when both players co-operate.

In the *asexual reproduction* model each individual will automatically get two daughters when a certain age is passed. Each daughter inherits a genetically-programmed strategy from the mother (either cooperate or defect). The daughters use this strategy in a prisoner's dilemma game, which they play only once. The payoff determines the chance of survival and reproduction: the higher the payoff, the higher the chance of an individual to survive and reproduce. Two situations are possible.

First, consider a population consisting only of cooperators. The payoff of each sister is R. A mutant who decides to defect in a game with her cooperating sister would get a higher payoff, T. But, all descendants will also defect and hence will get a payoff of P, which is less than R. This means that in the long run the descendants will reproduce less rapidly than the cooperating part of the population and eventually will disappear.

Second, the other possibility is a population consisting entirely of defectors. The payoff for each individual is P. Imagine that a mutant invades this population, the mutant being a cooperator. This co-operator would get a payoff of S which is less than T. But the cooperator's descendants (all cooperators) would be better off: they all get a payoff of R, with $R > P$. The mutant's descendants would reproduce more rapidly and will eventually dominate the population: the defectors would disappear.

The above two possibilities show that, whatever the original situation is, the only dynamically-stable equilibrium is one in which every individual co-operates with her sister. Dynamically stable means stable in time; some constant combination of strategies that manages to survive in evolution.

The *sexual reproduction* model is an extension of the model of asexual production above: it changes somewhat, but the mechanics behind it mostly stay the same. There is now a sexually-reproducing population. Each individual (who survives) will have exactly three offspring, instead of two in the case of asexual reproduction. These three offspring play a prisoner's dilemma game with each other. Again the sum of the payoff determines the probability that an individual survives to reproduce. The strategy played by each individual depends now on two genes. There are C-genes (Cooperate), and D-genes (Defect). One of these genes is selected at random from one of the parents. This means that an individual will either have two C genes (cooperator), two D genes (defector) or a C gene and a D gene. If, in the last case, the D gene is dominant, then they always defect. Similarly, if the C gene is dominant, they always cooperate. Similar to asexual reproduction, two contextual groups are examined (i) a population consisting entirely of cooperators and (ii) a population of only defectors in which one gene mutates into either a C gene or a D gene. Which group, the cooperators or the defectors, will ultimately survive depends on the payoffs. Bergstrom and Stark particularly find that, just like in the case of asexual reproduction, co-operation (altruism) can survive in evolutionary competition. The cases in which altruism survives are determined by the values for the payoff variables P, R, T and S.

Bergstrom and Stark have shown that in some situations altruism, interpretable in the present context as cooperation, can survive in evolutionary competition. In this theory altruism is transmitted via the genes. Interdependence of behaviour arises because children inherit the behaviour of their parents. It can thus be characterized as non-conscious and inborn behaviour. Attention can be directed now to Simon (1993) who develops models of sustainable altruism and co-operation, based on the three other behavioural postulates: semiconscious behaviour, conscious economic behaviour and conscious extra-economic behaviour.

Simon has as central concepts *altruism*, *fitness*, *bounded rationality*, and *docility*. Altruistic behaviour reduces the actor's fitness, while it increases the fitness of others. If the net effect is positive, altruism will increase the prospects of a group's survival. Simon defines fitness as 'the number of progeny an individual produces or, for species, the average number of progeny of members of the species'.

Due to bounded rationality people are docile: they largely depend on suggestions of others because, in general, we trust the information given by people who surround them; they expect this information to be better than information obtained by themselves. Simon defines this as 'the tendency to depend on suggestions, recommendations, persuasion, and information obtained through social channels as a major basis for choice'.

On average, docile behaviour contributes to the fitness of the group, such that nondocility is

driven out in evolutionary competition. This result is obtained as follows: since docile persons depend a lot on advice of others, they often make choices that reduce their own fitness. This is ultimately due to the same bounded rationality that makes docility on average enhance their fitness. So society can 'tax' docile persons by advising them to behave altruistically such that the individual's fitness decreases. As long as the cost of altruism for this person is less than the gain obtained by others, it will increase the fitness of docile persons. It follows that societies that induce altruism in docile individuals will survive in competition with societies that do not.

A refinement to this model can be added. Docile altruistic persons can differ in their intelligence. Intelligent altruists are able to distinguish fitness-enhancing from fitness-reducing advice (altruism) and are therefore fitter than unintelligent altruists and selfish individuals. The conclusion that altruism survives does not change because even intelligent persons are bounded rational and therefore benefit from docility.

What is the relationship of the above theory with interdependent behaviour? Bounded rationality makes people docile. We learn from people who surround us what is good for us and what is not. This is interdependent behaviour. Being dependent on the people who surround us or, in other words, on the group we belong to, means that people in such a group are loyal to each other: they will strive for economic and political gains for the group. Also, people will be violent against outsiders (e.g. ethnic conflicts). In this way *group loyalty* comes into being. Group loyalty provides an important basis for altruism – do 'good' for the group at the cost of your own fitness – and so it governs the behaviour of group members.

According to the theories of Simon and Stark, interdependent group behaviour has several underlying motives. It can therefore be put in all four categories of interdependent behaviour. First of all it can be explained in terms of non-conscious behaviour, being innate and controlled by instincts: people behave unconsciously upon their instincts. Interdependent behaviour according to Simon can also be considered as being semi-conscious: people adapt their behaviour to what they observe in reality (learning by doing): they learn from their own mistakes and from other people's experiences (imitation). One could also argue that a rational economic motive plays a role: it is in people's own self interest to be loyal to the group because, on average, the whole group benefits from this. Extra-economic motives might also play a significant role: people are emotionally attached to the group they belong to and are prepared to sacrifice almost everything that is in the interest of the group's survival, whether this is rational or not.

Policy example 9.1

A model of altruism

We present here the modified version of the model of Simon (1993) in which the refinement of differentiated intelligence matters is incorporated.

Three types of people can be distinguished: selfish persons, intelligent and unintelligent altruists. The net fitnesses of these persons (fS, fI and fU respectively) are determined by the following three equations:

(9.1) $fS = fn + faI^*qI^*cI + faU^*qU^*cU$

(9.2) $fI = fn + fd^*dI + faI^*qI^*cI + faU^*qU^*cU - c^*cI$

(9.3) $fU = fn + fd^*dU + faI^*qI^*cI + faU^*qU^*cU - c^*cU$

The f's are fitness coefficients, which are defined as below:

- fn: normal fitness of an individual.
- fd^*dI and fd^*dU: increments in fitness for people who are able to benefit from docility (selfish people in this model do not benefit from docility).
- faI and faU: increments in fitness from other persons' altruism (selfish individuals also benefit from this).
- cI and cU: the extent to which I and U behave altruistically (selfish people do not behave altruistically).
- dI and dU: ability of I and U to benefit from docility (selfish persons do not benefit from docility).
- qI and qU: the percentages of I and U altruists in the population.
- c: the cost of altruism.

It is assumed that all persons benefit equally from altruistic behaviour of altruists. Furthermore $dI > dU$: intelligent altruists benefit more from docility than unintelligent ones. Also $cI < cU$: corresponding to the theory, intelligent persons behave less altruistic than unintelligent persons. Incorporation of these two inequalities in Equation 9.2 and 9.3 shows that the fitness of intelligent altruists (fI) will always be greater than the fitness of unintelligent altruists (fU).

The second assumption, which corresponds with the theory, is that $fd^*dI > c^*cI$ such that the fitness of intelligent altruists is greater than the fitness of selfish persons. Similarly, to ensure that the fitness of unintelligent altruists is greater than the fitness of selfish persons, it is assumed that $fd^*dU > c^*cU$.

Simon assigns the following values to the parameters of the model: $fn = 1.01$; $fd = 0.02$; $c = 0.005$; $fal = 0.01$; $faU = 0.005$; $q_0I = \frac{1}{3}$; $q_0S = \frac{1}{3}$; $q_0U = \frac{1}{3}$; $dI = 2$; $cI = 0.8$; $cU = 1$; $dU = 1$.

Using these parameters the net fitnesses of the altruists (intelligent and unintelligent) and selfish persons can be calculated. We get $fS = 1.0143$; $fI = 1.0503$ and $fU = 1.0293$. In general, fitness coefficients can be considered as the expected number of progeny of each type of individuals. In this model fS, fI and fU are the average number of offspring of each selfish person, intelligent or unintelligent altruist respectively.

How do the relative populations of (un)intelligent altruists and selfish persons change over time? Using equal numbers in the three groups, Simon shows that after 30 generations the intelligent altruists are in the majority ($qI = 0.53$; 53 per cent) and the selfish persons will disappear rapidly ($qS = 0.18$; 18 per cent). The unintelligent altruists also disappear, but more slowly than selfish persons: $qU = 0.29$ (29 per cent). These numbers can be obtained by using the fitness coefficients 1.0143, 1.0503 and 1.0293 of the first generation to calculate the population percentages of the second generation. These population percentages can then be used to calculate the fitness of people in the second generation. This process continues for a while; after 30 generations the above mentioned population percentages are obtained.

Of course the results are largely dependent on the base values of the parameters. In the table below, for different values of q_0I, q_0S and q_0U, the relative populations of selfish persons, intelligent and unintelligent altruists are calculated. To observe developments in time the relative populations are calculated for different time periods. Each time period stands for one generation. The table entries are the percentages of selfish persons, intelligent and unintelligent altruists respectively.

Table 9.4 Simulation results of a model of altruism

q_0S, q_0I, q_0U	$t = 30$	$t = 60$	$t = 90$	$t \to \infty$
$\frac{1}{3}, \frac{1}{3}, \frac{1}{3}$	18, 53, 29	9, 70, 21	4, 83, 13	0, 100, 0
$\frac{1}{2}, \frac{1}{4}, \frac{1}{4}$	31, 45, 24	16, 65, 19	7, 80, 13	0, 100, 0
$\frac{2}{3}, \frac{1}{6}, \frac{1}{6}$	48, 34, 18	27, 56, 17	13, 75, 12	0, 100, 0
$\frac{5}{6}, \frac{1}{12}, \frac{1}{12}$	69, 20, 11	49, 39, 12	27, 63, 10	0, 100, 0
1, 0, 0	100, 0, 0	100, 0, 0	100, 0, 0	100, 0, 0

As one can see in the table, the percentage of selfish people in the beginning is slowly increased at the cost of the percentage of intelligent and unintelligent people in society. The table shows that the more selfish persons are present (relatively) in the beginning, the more slowly they will disappear. Of course the end result (column of $t \to \infty$) stays the same: the parameter values are consistent with the model of Simon, who assumes that altruists are fitter than selfish persons so that altruism ultimately (for $t \to \infty$) will survive, while selfish individuals will disappear. Note that in the last row of the table some begin values for the relative population sizes are zero so that, in time, these percentages do not change (and stay zero).

Of course other factors, next to the number of altruists and selfish persons in society, also play a role in the altruists' survival. For example if co-operators are easily identified, co-operators can easily find each other. As a consequence they generate the highest payoffs and will survive in evolution. Frank (1988) calls this 'strength in numbers'. Co-operation, or altruistic behaviour, only pays off if a co-operator finds another co-operator. Only then 'economies of scale' are realized. Also, uncertainty and bounded rationality, as in the theory of Simon, make people benefit from docility. So, certain states of nature ensure that people don't only act in their own self interest. Furthermore, symptoms of emotions, showing that somebody is an altruist are partly biological and can partly be cultivated by cultural training. For the part that can be cultivated by training the government can play an important role.

9.4   Policy implications of interdependent behaviour: norm formation and social institutions

Interdependent behaviour leads to positive or negative externalities. The government should stimulate the positive externalities while it should reduce negative external effects. Classifying externalities that arise from interdependent behaviour into positive and negative externalities is not an easy task. This is caused by the fact that we talk about people and their behaviour, both subjective concepts. One person considers certain behaviour as positive because it has a positive effect on him or her, while somebody else regards it as negative because his or her situation is negatively influenced. For example, when more people go to Spain for their vacations and this behaviour spills over to other people, then for the Spanish tourist sector this is a positive externality, while for the Italian tourist sector this is a negative external effect. So, it should be kept in mind that the classification of behavioural externalities is a normative issue.

But still there is a role for the government, because in some cases consensus among people, whether certain behaviour is good or bad, exists. In general the government should stimulate that generally accepted good behaviour which leads to positive external effects, while it should limit bad behaviour which has negative spill-over effects. But the government has to keep in mind that state interference in the social field could extinguish people's willingness to organize things themselves. This is the 'moral atrophy' thesis of Goodin (1993). Therefore, to maximize morally desirable outcomes the government should leave a couple of good works undone. At the same time, by exploiting one's capacity for moral behaviour, the government saves on scarce resources that can be used in other productive ways. Of course the atrophy thesis does not apply to all social activities. For example, if the government doesn't take care of putting a halt to the Mafia, nobody will.

Assuming that the 'moral atrophy' thesis (and thus the model of 'morally keeping in practice') applies, how much should the government leave undone?

Cost–benefit calculations

Pure cost–benefit analysis will show that it is often socially optimal to leave some evil uncorrected. Namely, if interfering is more expensive than leaving the evil uncorrected. This is a case-by-case approach: each time costs and benefits have to be estimated and compared to come to the conclusion that, from a welfare point of view, the government should, or should not, interfere. This elaborate procedure can, however, give insight to the relationship between the cost of government interference and the cost of leaving the evil uncorrected, as can be seen from the attached illustration box.

Moral atrophy

The moral atrophy thesis goes a step further by saying that even if cost–benefit calculations have a favourable outcome governments still should not interfere. This is because, according to the moral atrophy thesis, not interfering has long-term benefits: by not undertaking any actions, people develop their moral skills and learn to behave altruistically in similar situations in the future. Goodin calls this induced altruism. The strategy of leaving evil as it is can be considered as a strategy of 'investment' in human moral capital. The question that arises is, of course, how much to invest.

How much social evil to leave as a means of inducing future good behaviour depends on three variables: *frequency*, *strength* and *persistence* of induced altruism.

Frequency of induced altruism

The cost of the investment depends upon the frequency with which people use opportunities for altruistic behaviour that the government leaves behind. The more they take up the opportunities, the less the cost of the investment. It is expected that the relationship between the number of opportunities taken up and the cost of the investment is a non-linear one: in the beginning the people do not use much of the opportunities, while later on (as more opportunities are given) they will take more of them. This means that substantial investments in the beginning are necessary before any returns from investments arise. Aspects of frequency of altruism have already

been discussed in the theory from Simon (docile behaviour and group loyalty). As shown, one crucial aspect of altruism to survive in evolution is that it should be practised by a substantial part of the population. If it is not practised by a large part of the population, it actually takes a long time for altruism to dominate again in society.

Strength of induced altruism

This effects the value of the investment. The value of investment is dependent on the strength of the sense of benevolence that is cultivated by the investment. Evidence shows that the sense of benevolence is, in reality, not very strong. Where the cost of helping is high, people in general do not want to take the responsibility of rendering assistance. Similarly, where the request for help is large, people also shun responsibility by saying 'I did my bit'. In this way people, if confronted with situations of great need, constantly look for ways to limit the amount of assistance they are obliged to render. In other words: as the size of evil increases the tendency to learn-by-doing drops off. So, while in theory the method of 'morally keeping in practice' seems to work, there are situations in which the method does not work and state intervention is required.

Persistence of induced altruism

This is the last factor which effects the value of the investment. If a single experience of rendering assistance induces a person to engage in helping behaviour for a long time, then the investment has high returns, or a high value. If the opposite seems to be true, e.g. this person helps only one other time and then not anymore, the investment has relatively low returns and is, therefore, less attractive.

As mentioned before, moral atrophy does not

always apply. Some works can simply not be left undone. Also, sometimes government action does not harm private altruism. In these situations the model of 'moral character building' seems useful. The government does no harm by telling people that smoking is bad for your health, or by saying that people should use the car less to save the environment. Such preaching by the government only builds up one's moral character. It ensures that norms and values of a society are conserved and enhanced. A convenient way to do this is by using means of communication like education, television, radio, papers, advertisement billboards, and so on.

The fact that both models of moral development ('morally keeping in practice' and 'moral character building') apply in reality suggests that they should be considered as complementary. This is based on the following propositions that seem to be true in reality:

(a) Government intervention is the best, most efficient response to relatively major evils. Minor evils are better left to individual action.

(b) Altruism that is created by dependency relationships or by having received prior help will be weak, so that people are only willing to bear a small part of the cost involved in rendering assistance.

(c) The development of a sense of morality seems more a matter of building character than keeping moral skills in practice.

These propositions (if true) imply the following: private altruism is the best solution to minor evils for which people are also willing to bear part of the (relatively small) costs. Furthermore, if moral character building is more important than practice, moral skills are most effectively sustained by occasional reinforcements.

Policy example 9.2

Four evil cases for state intervention

Goodin (1993, p.70) derives four possible relationships between cost of government interference to correct an evil and the cost of leaving the evil uncorrected. These are shown in the table below.

Table 9.5 Cases for state intervention

Case 1	Government ought never to act if, at every given magnitude of evil, it is always more costly, on net, for government to act to remedy that evil than it would be to leave the evil unremedied.
Case 2	Government ought always to act if, at every given magnitude of evil, it is always more costly, on net, to leave the evil unremedied than it would be for government to act to remedy it.
Case 3	Government ought to act only against large evils if: (a) below a certain magnitude of evil, it is more costly, on net, for the government to act to remedy the evil than it would be to leave the evil unremedied; but (b) above that magnitude, it is more costly on net to leave the evil unremedied than it would be for government to act to remedy it.
Case 4	Government ought to act only against small evils if: (a) below a certain magnitude of evil, it is more costly, on net, to leave the evil unremedied than it would be for the government to remedy it; but (b) above that magnitude, it is more costly on net to act to remedy that evil than it would be to leave the evil unremedied.

Case three is the most realistic one: for minor evils government interference is, in most cases, highly inefficient, while for large evils the opposite is true. This is because the costs of governments are mostly invariant to the size of the evil that is dealt with. Also, the cost of not acting to remedy evil are ever increasing. Beyond a certain point then, government action becomes almost obligatory: the cost for society is unsustainable and citizens, who are not willing to take action against evil themselves anymore, stipulate for government interference.

Questions for discussion and further research

1 Review your understanding of the following terms: information cascades, up- and down-cascades, internalization rationales, moral character building, morally keeping in practice, docility and fitness, induced altruism, relationship between market, state and norm failures.

2 Work out a general framework of analyses, and a numerical example, which integrates such motivations as self-interest, altruistic behaviour, internalization rationale and reciprocity.

3 What are the meanings of moral character building and morally keeping in practice as proposed by Goodin? Are these different than the options put forward by Frank? Can these two options be incorporated in the general framework referred to above, or not? Motivate your answer.

4 Discuss each of the following statements separately, relate them to each other, and draw conclusions on agent interactions.

hypotheses, to be accurate and therefore acted upon, must prove themselves by competing and being adapted within an environment created by other agent's hypotheses.
Arthur

moral sentiments are accompanied by observable physical signs that allow outsiders to discern their presence.
Frank

the more of it we have the more we need and the more we come to depend on it.
Goodin

Homo reciprocans is thus neither the selfless altruist of utopian theory, nor the selfish hedonist of neoclassical economics.
Gintis

Further reading

The chapter treated different models of inter-individual behavioural interactions, mostly resulting in the evolvement of broadly-accepted behavioural traits among the interacting people. Self-interest and group-interest motivations are treated at various lengths in the following four publications. See Axelrod, R. (1984): *The Evolution of Cooperation*, Basic Books, US;

Becker, G.S. (1981): *A Treatise on the Family*, Harvard University Press, Cambridge, Mass; Frank, R. (1988): *Passions within Reason*, Norton, New York; Goodin, R.E. (1993): 'Moral Atrophy in the Welfare State', in *Policy Sciences*, No. 26, pp.63–78.

The implications of inter-individual behavioural interactions have been studied for a number of themes of relevance for economics. Of special interest in the context of Chapter 9 are the endogenization of individual preferences and the formation of social capital.

For further reading on endogenization of preferences, see Bowles, S. (1998): 'Endogenous Preferences, the cultural consequences of markets and other economic institutions', in *Journal of Economic Literature*, Vol. XXXVI.1, pp.75–111; Ben-Ner, A. and Putterman, L. (1998): *Economics, Values and Organization*, CUP, Cambridge.

On the formation of social capital in the process of interdependent behaviour, and its significance for efficiency and equity see the following four publications: Platteau, J.P. (1994): 'Behind the Market Stage where Real Societies Exist', in *Journal of Development Studies*, Vol. XXX, pp.533–77 and pp.753–817; Knack, S. and Heefer, P. (1997): 'Does Social Capital have an Economic Payoff? A Cross-country Investigation', in *Quarterly Journal of Economics*, pp.1241–88; Woolcock, M. (1998): 'Social Capital and Economic Development, toward a theoretical synthesis and policy framework', in *Theory and Society*, Vol. 27, pp.151–208; articles by Beall, J.; Fox, J.; Putzel, J.; and Harriss, J. and Renzio, P. in *Journal of International Development*, 1997, Vol. 9, special issue on social capital, pp.919–71.

References

Aghion, P. and Blanchard, O. (1996): *On Insider Privatization*. Mimeo. Obtainable from Philippe A. Aghion at University College London and EBRD, London.

Akerlof, G. (1970): 'The Market for Lemons: Quality, Uncertainty and Market Mechanism', in *Quarterly Journal of Economics*, August 1970, pp.488–500.

Arrow, K.J. (1951): *Social Choice and Individual Values*, John Wiley & Sons, New York.

Arrow, K.J. (1973): 'Information and Economic Behaviour', lecture presented to the Federation of Swedish Industries, Stockholm, reprinted in Arrow, K.J. (1984) *Collected Papers of Kenneth J. Arrow: The Economics of Information*, Harvard University Press, Cambridge, Mass. pp.136–52.

Arthur, W.B. (1994): 'Complexity in Economic Theory, Inductive Reasoning and Bounded Rationality', in *American Economic Association Papers and Proceedings*, 84, pp.406–11.

Audretsch, D.B. (1993): 'Industrial Policy and International Competitiveness' in Nicolaides, P. (ed) (1993), *Industrial Policy in the European Community: a Necessary Response to Economic Integration?*, European Institute of Public Administration, Maastricht, The Netherlands.

Axelrod, R. (1984): *The Evolution of Co-operation*, Basic Books, New York.

Banerjee, A. (1992): 'A Simple Model of Herd Behaviour', in *Quarterly Journal of Economics*, 107, pp.797–818.

Barr, N. (1998): *The Economics of the Welfare State*, Oxford University Press, Oxford.

Barrett, S. (1998): 'Political Economy of the Kyoto Protocol', in *Oxford Review of Economic Policy*, Vol. 14, No. 4, pp.20–39.

Barzel Y. (1989): *Economic Analysis of Property Rights*, Cambridge University Press, Cambridge.

Baumol, W.J., Panzar, J.C. and Willig, R.D. (1982): *Contestable Markets and the Theory of Industry Structure*, Harcourt, New York.

Baumol, W.J. (1967): 'The Macro Economies of Unbalanced Growth', in *American Economic Review*, 57, pp.415–26.

Beason, R. and Weinstein, D.E. (1996): 'Growth, Economies of Scale, and Targeting in Japan', in *Review of Economics and Statistics*, 78, pp.286–95.

Becker, G. (1981): *A Treatise on the Family*, Harvard University Press, Cambridge, Mass.

Bergeijk, P.A.G. van, Gerbrands, P.W.L. and Roelandt, T.J.A. (1997): *Markets and Innovativeness: Does Structure Influence Performance?* Paper presented at the Conference on the Impact of Technological Change on Firm and Industry Performance, Tinbergen Institute, Rotterdam, August 1997.

Bergman, L. (1990): 'Energy and Environmental Constraints on Growth', in *Journal of Policy Modelling*, 12, pp.671–91.

Bergson, A. (1938): 'A Reformulation of Certain Aspects of Welfare Economics', in *Quarterly Journal of Economics*, 52, pp.310–34.

Bergstrom, T.C. and Stark, O. (1993): 'How Altruism Can Prevail in an Evolutionary Environment', in *American Economic Association Papers and Proceedings*, Vol. 83, No. 2, pp.151–3.

Berliner, J. (1952): 'The Informal Organization of the Soviet Firm', in *Quarterly Journal of Economics*, 66, pp.342–65.

Bhargava, S. (1994): 'Profit Sharing and the Financial Performance of Companies', in *Economic Journal*, 104, pp.1044–56.

Bikhchandani, S., Hirshleifer, D. and Welch, I. (1998): 'Learning from the Behaviour of Others:

Conformity, Fads and Informational Cascades', in *Journal of Economic Perspectives*, Vol. 12, No. 3, pp.151–70.

Bohm, P. (1987): *Social Efficiency*, Macmillan, London.

Bresnahan, T. (1989): 'Empirical Studies of Industries and Market Power', in Schmalensee, R. and Willig, R. (1989): *Handbook of Industrial Organization*, North-Holland, Amsterdam.

Chichilinsky, G. (1994): 'North–South Trade and the Global Environment', in *American Economic Review*, 84, 4, pp.851–74.

Clarke, H.E. (1971): 'Multipart Pricing of Public Goods', in *Public Choice*, 11, pp.17–33.

Coase, R.H. (1960): 'The Problem of Social Cost', in *Journal of Law and Economics*, 3, pp.1–44.

Cohen, S.I. (1994): *Human Resource Development and Utilization*, Avebury, Aldershot.

Cullis, J. and Jones, P. (1998): *Public Finance and Public Choice*, Oxford University Press, Oxford.

Culyer, A.J. (1980): *The Political Economy of Social Policy*, Martin Roberson, Oxford.

Diamond, P.A. and Mirrlees, J.A. (1971): 'Optimal Taxation and Public Production', in *American Economic Review*, March and June, pp.8–27 and pp.261–78.

Downs, A. (1957): *An Economic Theory of Democracy*, Harper and Row, New York.

Duncan, G.J. et al. (1984): *Years of Poverty, Years of Plenty: the Changing Fortunes of American Workers and Families*, University of Michigan Press, Ann Arbor.

Earle, J.S. and Estrin, S. (1996): 'Employee Ownership in Transition', in Frydman, R., Gray, C. and Rapaczynki, A. (eds) (1996): *Corporate Governance in Central Europe and Russia*, Central European University Press, Budapest.

El Agraa, A.M. (1997): 'UK Competitiveness Policy vs. Japanese Industrial Policy', in *The Economic Journal*, Vol. 107, September 1997, pp.1504–17.

Ergas, H. (1986): 'Does Technology Policy Matter?', in Guile, B. and Brooks, H. (eds) (1986): *Technology and Global Industry, Companies and Nations in the World Economy*, National Academy Press, Washington D.C.

Filattchev, I. et al. (1997): 'Corporate Governance in Central and Eastern Europe', in Keasey, K., Thompson, S. and Wright, M. (eds) (1997): *Corporate Governance*, Oxford University Press, Oxford.

Fitzpatrick, G.D. (1986): *Microeconomics*, Oxford University Press, Oxford.

Frank, R. (1988): *Passions Within Reason*, Norton, New York.

Friedman, L.S. (1985): *Microeconomic Policy Analysis*, McGraw-Hill, New York.

Gintis, H. (1998): *The Individual in Economic Theory: a Research Agenda*, in http://www.unix.oit.umass.edu/~gintis.

Good, D.H., Roller, L.H. and Sickles, R.C. (1993): 'Airline Deregulation: Implications for European Transport', in *Economic Journal*, vol. 103, No. 419, pp.1028–41.

Goodin, R.E. (1993): 'Moral Atrophy in the Welfare State' in *Policy Sciences*, 26, pp.63–78.

Groves, T. (1970): *The Allocation of Resources Under Uncertainty*, PhD dissertation, University of California, Berkeley.

Guerrieri, I.P. and Tylote, A. (1993): *National Competitive Advantages and Microeconomic Behaviour*, Sheffield University Management School, Sheffield.

Harrington, W. (1988): 'Enforcement Leverage when Penalties are Restricted', in *Journal of Public Economics*, 37 (1), pp.29–53.

Hart, O. (1995): 'Corporate Governance: Some Theory and Implications', in *Economic Journal*, pp.678–89.

Hartley, K. and Tisdell, C. (1981): *Microeconomic Policy*, Wiley, Chichester.

Henry, C. (1991): *Microeconomics for Public Policy*, Clarendon, Oxford.

Hicks, J.R. (1939): 'The Foundation of Welfare Economics', in *Economic Journal*, 49, pp.696–712.

Jensen, M. and Kervin, M. (1990): 'Performance Pay and Top Management Incentives', in *Journal of Political Economy*, 98, pp.225–64.

Johanson, P.O. (1991): *An Introduction to Modern Welfare Economics*, Cambridge University Press, Cambridge.

Jorgenson, D.W. and Wilcoxen, P.J. (1990): 'Intertemporal General Equilibrium Modelling of U.S. Environmental Regulation', in *Journal of Policy Modelling*, 12, pp.715–44.

Joskow, P.L. and Rose, N.L. (1989): 'The Effects of Economic Regulation', in Schmalensee, R. and Willig, R. (eds) (1989): *Handbook of Industrial Organization*. Vol. 2, North-Holland, Amsterdam.

Kaldor, N. (1939): 'Welfare Propositions of Economics and Interpersonal Comparisons of Utility', in *Economic Journal*, 49, pp.549–52.

Kaplan, S.N. (1989): 'The Effects of Management Buyouts on Operations and Value', in *Journal of Financial Economics*, 24, pp.217–54.

Kornai, J. (1979): 'Resource-Constrained Versus Demand-Constrained Systems', in *Econometrica*, 47, pp.801–19.

Krugman, P. (1992): 'Toward a Counter-Counterrevolution in Development Theory', in *Proceedings of the World Bank Annual Conference on Development Economics*, World Bank, Washington D.C.

Krugman, P. (1995): 'Technological Change in International Trade', in Stoneman, P. (ed) (1995): *Handbook of the Economics of Innovation and Technological Change*, Blackwell, Oxford.

Lindahl, E. (1919): 'Just Taxation: a Positive Solution', reprinted in Musgrave, R.A. and Peacock, A.T. (eds) (1958): *Classics in the Theory of Public Finance*, Macmillan, New York.

Metcalfe, S. (1995): 'The Economic Foundations of Technology Policy', in Stoneman, P. (ed) (1995): *Handbook of the Economics of Innovation and Technological Change*, Blackwell, Oxford.

Morrison, S. and Winston, C. (1986): *The Economic Effects of Airline Deregulation*. The Brookings Institution, Washington DC.

Montias, J.M., Ben Ner, A. and Neuberger, E. (1994): *Comparative Economics*, Harwood Academic Publishers, Chur, Switzerland.

Mowery, A. (1996): 'The Practice of Technology Policy', in Stoneman, P. (ed) (1996): *Handbook of the Economics of Innovation and Technological Change*, Blackwell, Oxford.

Mueller, D.C. (1989): *Public Choice 11*, Cambridge University Press, Cambridge.

Musgrave, R.A. (1969): *Fiscal Systems*, Yale University Press, Yale.

Nelson, R. (1994): *National Innovative Systems*, Oxford University Press, Oxford.

Neven, D. and Seabright, P. (1995): 'European Industrial Policy: the Airbus Case', in *Economic Policy*, October 1995, pp.315–58.

Ng, D.C. (1971): 'The Possibility of a Paretian Liberal: Impossibility Theorems and Cardinal Utility', in *Journal of Political Economy*, November/December issue, pp.1397–1402.

Niskanen, W.A. (1971): *Bureaucracy and Representative Government*, Aldine Atherton, Chicago.

Nitzan, S. (1994): 'Modelling Rent Seeking Contests', in *European Journal of Political Economy*, No. 1, pp.41–60.

Nooteboom, B. (1993): 'Een Aanzet tot Industriebeleid', in *Economische Statistische Berichten*, March 1993, pp.245–9.

Nozick, R. (1976): *Anarchy, State and Utopia*, Basic Books, New York.

Okun, A. (1975): *Equality and Efficiency: the Big Trade-Off*, Brookings Institution, Washington D.C.

Olson, M. (1971): *The Logic of Collective Action*, Harvard University Press, Cambridge, Mass.

Opler, T.C. (1992): 'Operating Performance', in Leveraged Buyouts in *Financial Management*, 21, pp.27–34.

Papendreou, A.A. (1998): *Externality and Institutions*, Clarendon, Oxford.

Peacock, A.T. and Wiseman, J. (1961): *The Growth of Public Expenditure in the United Kingdom*, Princeton University Press, Princeton.

Pearce, D. (1998): 'Cost–Benefit Analysis and Environmental Policy', in *Oxford Review of Economic Policy*, 14, pp.84–100.

Perotti, R. (1996): 'Growth, Income Distribution and Democracy', in *Journal of Economic Growth*, 1, pp.149–88.

Persson, A. and Munasinghe, M. (1995): 'Natural Resource Management and Economy-wide Policies in Costa Rica, a Computable General Equilibrium (CGE) Modelling Approach', in *The World Bank Economic Review*, 10, pp.259–85.

Pigou, A.C. (1924): *The Economics of Welfare*, Macmillan, London.

Radner, R. (1968): 'Competitive Equilibrium Under Uncertainty', in *Econometrica*, 36, pp.31–58.

Rapoport, A. and Chammah, A. (1965): *Prisoner's Dilemma*, University of Michigan Press, Ann Arbor.

Rawls, J. (1972): *A Theory of Justice*, Clarendon Press, Oxford.

Rosenstein-Rodan P.N. (1943): 'Problems of Industrialization of Eastern and South Eastern Europe', in *Economic Journal*, 53, pp.202–12.

Rostow, W.W. (1971): *Politics and the Stages of Growth*, Cambridge University Press, Cambridge.

Russel, R.R. and Wilkinson, M. (1979): *Microeconomics*, Wiley, New York.

Schotter, A. (1990): *Free Market Economics*, Blackwell, Cambridge, Mass.

Sen, A.K. (1970): 'The Impossibility of a Paretian Liberal', in *Journal of Political Economy*, January/February issue, pp.152–7.

Sen, A.K. (1982): *Choice, Welfare and Measurement*, MIT Press, Cambridge, Mass.

Shapiro C. and Varian, H.R. (1999): *Information Rules*, Harvard University Business Press, Cambridge, Mass.

Simon, H. (1993): 'Altruism and Economics', in *American Economic Association Papers and Proceedings*, 83, No. 2, pp.156–161.

Stiglitz, J.E. (1993): *Economics*, Norton, New York.

Stiglitz, J.E. (1998): *Economics of the Public Sector*, Norton, New York.

Thompson, S. and Wright, M. (1995): 'Corporate Governance: the Role of Restructuring Transactions', in *Economic Journal*, 105, pp.690–703.

Ulla, M. (1984): 'Why the Income Distribution is So Misleading', in *The Public Interest*, 88, pp.62–76.

Unemo, L. (1993): *Environmental Impact of Government Policies and External Shocks in Botswana; a CGE Model Approach*. Beijer Discussion Paper Series, Beijer Institute, Stockholm.

Varian, H.R. (1974): 'Equity, Envy and Efficiency', in *Journal of Economic Theory*, 9, pp.1–23.

Vulkan, N. (1999): 'Economic Implications of Agent Technology and E-commerce', in *The Economic Journal*, Vol. 109, No. 453, pp.F67–F90.

Williamson, O.E. (1989): 'Transaction Cost Economics', in Schmalensee, R. and Willig, R. (eds) *Handbook of Industrial Organisation*, North-Holland, Amsterdam.

Winston, C. (1993): 'Economic Deregulation: Days of Reckoning for Microeconomists', in *Journal of Economic Literature*, XXXI, pp.1263–89.

World Bank (1997): *The State in a Changing World, World Development Report 1997*. Oxford University Press, Oxford.

Wright, M., Thompson, S. and Robbie, K. (1992): 'Venture Capital and Management-Led Leveraged Buy-Outs: a European Perspective', in *Journal of Business Venturing*, 7, pp.47–71.

Yarrow, G. (1985): 'Privatization in Theory and Practice', in *Economic Policy*, 1985.

Index

187